LEAVE HER ALONE

LEAVE HER ALONE

Megan McKenna

ORBIS BOOKS

Maryknoll, New York 10545

The Catholic Foreign Mission Society of America (Maryknoll) recruits and trains people for overseas missionary service. Through Orbis Books, Maryknoll aims to foster the international dialogue that is essential to mission. The books published, however, reflect the opinions of their authors and are not meant to represent the official position of the society. To obtain more information about Maryknoll or Orbis Books, please visit our website at http://www.maryknoll.org.

Published by Orbis Books, Maryknoll, NY 10545-0308

Manufactured in the United States of America

Scripture quotations are from the Christian Community Bible, copyright © 1995 by Bernardo Hurault.

Library of Congress Cataloging-in-Publication Data

McKenna, Megan.
    Leave her alone / Megan McKenna.
        p.   cm.
    Includes bibliographical references.
    ISBN 1-57075-265-6 (pbk.)
    1. Women in the Bible Biography.   I.   Title.
    BS575 .M43 1999
    220.9′2′082 – dc21
    [B]   99–31689

"There's something about the women in my life . . . ,"
glorious women:
Lynn, Kate, Eileen, Marguerite,
Phyllis and Barbara, Maureen, Mary, Connie, Sandy,
Andrea,
Annemarie and Lillian,
Pat, Barb and Kathy, Annick,
Sue, Beth, Dianne, Colleen and Diane,
Maura and Rita,
Henrietta, Pat, Eva,
Rosemary, Priscella, Erlinda, Louise,
Pat, Celeste and Maria, and sisters,
my sisters: Norene, Francine, Mimi, Alice, Jane,
Mary and Leanne,
Katy, Christi, and Shannon,
Eilish, Eileen, Rose, De, Dot,
Carmelites in Liverpool, Ruth,
Patti, Sue, Melissa, and Bernadette,
Ely and Yoko, Mary, Vivian, Moira,
Juanella and Leanore,
and Nena

Contents

INTRODUCTION

Every letter of Torah has the power to revive the dead. Believe it. For one soul, ... one heart, ... I give up everything.
— Rabbi Shlomo Carlebach

How much does it take to cover up the sun? Put your finger over your eye — you can't see a thing.   — Baal Shem Tov

T HESE TWO STATEMENTS confront us with two ends of a spectrum of the way we can approach the scriptures: with a wide-open reverence for mysterious power that conceals as much as it reveals; or with suspicion born of individual and stunted vision. The reflections in this book begin with the first attitude, assuming that the text is inspired by God and that it holds a key that can unlock underground passages and loose unparalleled power into our lives. Thus this book rejects the second attitude — the individualistic interpretation — as limiting and distorting. Only when the text is seen and reverenced in a context, a community of believers that struggles with its meaning and their lives, can there be true sight. Between the text and the community there must be reciprocity.

There is need to know, on occasion, what a story meant at the time it was composed, but it is more important to know what the story can mean here and now. Scripture stories are not just about characters or history; they are more about what we are being inspired to do with our own lives as individuals and even more importantly as a community of believers. One of the operating rules of scripture study in many places outside the Western world is this: when there is more than one true interpretation of scripture (and there is always more than one true interpretation of every piece of scripture), the interpretation that is most true is the one that calls us to a more radical transformation and conversion. Akin to this is another principle: the text is

1

good news; therefore, the interpretation must be founded on hope and the possibility of a more graceful and liberating reality for those most in need.

We should read the texts through a veil, as it were, a veil that filters out selfish intent, personal agendas, or anything that validates dominant and oppressive arrangements. The veil is that of suffering and mercy, born of the memory of the suffering servant, the crucified one raised from the tomb by a God who is faithful to life. Just as the prophets heard and proclaimed the Word of God through the experience and eyes of those most in pain and without justice, so the texts must remind and challenge us to read them through the eyes of the masses of people who do not know life as good news or the presence of the God of justice, truth, and life in our midst. Such a reading will bring comfort and solace, encouragement and righteousness, but also crisis and conflict, confrontation and harsh reminders that we have sold our birthrights as the children of God and chosen instead our culture's power and promises.

All the texts must be read with the bright shadow of the resurrection bent over us. This reality must cast its terrifying and holy power on our lives, as once the glance of Yahweh struck terror into the forces of the oncoming army of the Egyptians, as we are told by Miriam, who raised her voice in the people's victory song. And so this introduction will look at a number of accounts of this cornerstone of our faith and lives, as found in the earliest gospel, that of Mark. We begin with the theme of this book: a charge that confronts us in our blindness, fear, hesitation, ignorance, lack of understanding, or weakness of faith. They are words of Jesus to his disciples:

> Later Jesus showed himself to the Eleven, while they were at table. He reproached them for their unbelief and stubbornness in refusing to believe those who had seen him after he had risen.
>
> (Mark 16:14)

This appearance is Jesus' last in Mark's gospel. It is preceded by three other recorded appearances. The first, the longest, is the announcement by an angel (a young man in a white robe?) to the three women who went to the tomb when the Sabbath was over: Mary of Magdala, Mary the mother of James, and Salome. The angel announces that Jesus is not in the tomb, but goes before them into Galilee. They are commanded to "go and tell his disciples and Peter:

Jesus is going ahead of you to Galilee; you will see him there just as he told you" (Mark 16:7). The account of the second appearance is much shorter, and it is specifically to Mary of Magdala. It is characterized as being the first appearance of Jesus himself, and the text records that Mary obeyed the summons to report what she had heard and seen, but "they" would not believe it (or her) (Mark 16:9–11). It is thought that this is a short version of the account given in John 20:11, when Mary is weeping outside the tomb and does not recognize Jesus as he approaches her, until he calls her by name. And then, in the shortest of the appearance texts, Jesus shows himself "in another form to two of them [no names], as they were walking in the country" (Mark 16:12). There is speculation that this allusion is to the appearance to the two men on the road to Emmaus, which is recorded in great detail in Luke's resurrection accounts.

In Luke's first account, those who return from the tomb and state that Jesus is alive are greeted just as they were in the Markan text. It reads:

> Among the women who brought the news were Mary Magdalene, Joanna, and Mary the mother of James. But however much they insisted, those who heard did not believe the seemingly nonsensical story. (Luke 24:9–10)

The accounts are confusing regarding names, events, and sequence. But it is clear that at least four women are named, the two that appear in both being Mary of Magdala and Mary the mother of James. This Mary of Magdala is *not* Mary of Bethany, the sister of Martha, and is not the woman who anoints Jesus in any of the gospels. Is Mary, the mother of James, the mother of one of the disciples, James the lesser (not the mother of James and John)?

And other persons are mentioned. Earlier, at the death of Jesus, we are told that the only witnesses to the crucifixion were women, though it is the captain of the guard detail that supervised the execution who proclaims at Jesus' death, "Truly, this man was the Son of God" (Mark 15:39). In the next verses we are told:

> There were also some women watching from a distance; among them were Mary Magdalene, Mary the mother of James the younger and Joset, and Salome, who had followed Jesus when

he was in Galilee and saw to his needs. There were also others
who had come up with him to Jerusalem. (Mark 15:40–41)

These are members of Jesus' community, disciples and friends.
These are the faithful ones in terrifying circumstances. They stood at a
distance because the soldiers cordoned off an area around the crosses,
keeping everyone at bay. The scene would have been one of horror,
eerie silence, screams of the victims, and taunts of bystanders. This
was a public denunciation of those executed and was meant to be an
unforgettable lesson for family, friends, and followers. The general
rule was that the soldiers guarded those writhing in agony until they
were dead, keeping anyone from them and then guarding them so that
relatives could not take the bodies down and bury them. The corpses
were to hang there until birds and animals ate them. Any display of
mourning was strictly forbidden: no weeping or lamentation, no words
of comfort or displays of concern. This is why the eleven disciples of
Jesus were in hiding. Known association with the one executed could
result in one's being executed as well.

And that is what is remarkable about the presence of all these
women, in the crowd, at a distance, silent witnesses to all that happens. And then they are still bold enough to risk going to the grave to
anoint the body. Even today around the world it is sometimes forbidden that relatives, friends, or those connected to any religious group
bury the bodies of those cut down in the struggle for justice and freedom. It is so in El Salvador, Guatemala, and was the case in South
Africa and many other countries.

These are the witnesses, cowed, dazed, full of fear, but intent on
anointing the body of Jesus, affording his body their final service, a
corporal work of mercy. They have no idea how they will accomplish
it. Their talk is of the huge stone that will block the entrance to the
tomb, because they had waited around until after the body had been
placed inside. Then came the Sabbath and its demands for laying aside
all other concerns.

The account of their bending down to enter the tomb and of en-
countering the young man who tries to calm their fears gives only
the announcement of what has happened. The messenger proclaims:
"Don't be alarmed; you are looking for Jesus of Nazareth who was
crucified; he has been raised and is not here" (Mark 16:6). And the
text says they don't obey. They are alarmed. They don't say anything

to anyone else at first. They probably fled and later regrouped and began talking excitedly, exclaiming all at once. Grief had turned to wild hope and terrible confusion: Where was he? Was he alive? And eventually they did go to the others, but were not believed.

The short inclusion of Mary's story is an early tradition. She was a formidable presence, at least as strong as Peter, who dominated the Twelve when Jesus was absent. In the first story, the women are told to go tell Jesus' disciples "and Peter" the good news. This has usually been interpreted as making Peter the leader from the very beginning. However, this singling out of Peter at this juncture may mean the exact opposite. Peter has vehemently betrayed Jesus three times in public, disavowing any connection with him. And even earlier, following the Last Supper, Jesus had told the disciples what is going to happen to him and to them:

> After singing psalms of praise, they went out to the Hill of Olives. And Jesus said to them, "All of you will be confused and fall away; for the Scripture says: I will strike the shepherd and the sheep will be scattered. But after I am raised up, I will go to Galilee ahead of you." (Mark 14:26–28)

Obviously there was no clear leader of the group. All of the disciples would be confused. But Mary of Magdala was not confused. She had been there from the beginning, in the service of Jesus, the kingdom, and the Word. She had been a leader who held the group together, attending to the needs of Jesus and the others. And, it seems, she holds the women together who are grieving and struggling to stay as close to Jesus as possible until the end, and after. She sees Jesus and goes to the disciples who are now "mourning and weeping," but they will not believe it. It is not in their imagining, their memory, or their faith.

Jesus reproaches the Eleven who are in hiding for their "unbelief and their stubbornness in refusing to believe those who had seen him after he had risen." The story is told, and told again, and still faith is blocked like the tomb with the huge millstone that fills its entrance. Three, four, five women tell the story, yet those who said they were Jesus' friends refuse to believe them. They stubbornly cling to their unbelief and refuse to admit that another has been given something they ran away from. The two walking in the country — one of whom is later named Cleophas and one of whom many believe was his wife — tell them the story, and they are steadfastly resistant to a word of hope. In some ways it does not matter who tells the story, just that it is told, over and over again, until it begins to seep in through cold stone hearts and warm them again. Though these stories appear to be about women, they are about human beings, about all those who need the story of resurrection, of life and truth, and who need people who believe in it and put it into practice.

The reading of the stories is not meant to be accusatory so much as conversional. They are meant not to divide but to draw into communion. The stories' powers are there for dialogue, between us and the text and among ourselves. Our duty is not to denigrate the text, the past, or another, or even to expect answers as we read the stories. We must begin the readings and the reflections with respect and honor the text, love it, and develop a relationship with it and with others, especially those who disagree with our thoughts about its meaning. Like the boy Samuel in his bed when he heard the voice of Yahweh but did not recognize it, we must say, "Here I am Lord," as we stand before the text. And if we are silent and "ponder all these things, cherishing them in our heart" like Mary, then perhaps we will give the text, the Spirit, a chance to talk back to us. This must be our attitude.

One of the processes used in this book is that of midrash. The word comes from the Jewish word *lidrosh,* which means to search out, ask, explain, draw out, enlarge upon. It is a technique that investigates the gaps, spaces, dreams, the unspoken and forgotten — these are the doorways into the text and into the domain of the Spirit. The text is often unbearably terse. But words are more than their definition or strict meaning. They are a sound in our mouth when spoken aloud. They carry the memory of those who have gone before us who relied on them and staked their lives on them, sometimes risked their lives for them.

The text is like dough that needs to be squeezed, floured, kneaded, unraveled, wrapped up, combined with other ingredients of prayer and life, ritual and justice, and baked before it can be eaten or shared. The text, in the technique of midrash, talks to those who listen. It is not a one-sided dialogue on our end. Rather, it's a bit like spirit-retrieval, a journey where we find our way back into the stories and texts, following a spiral on ancient shells and fossils, finding in the remnants left behind a trail that draws us back and down and in.

A friend of mine has an old woven rug that is a cherished possession, a gift from his grandmother. It hangs on his wall in his study, and he intends to be buried in it, as is his people's custom. It is over a hundred years old, frayed and worn in places, but the pattern is still strongly defined in its texture. You have to look closely, even know where to look, to find the Spirit line, a place where the pattern is unfinished and left open. It is both the way the Spirit is let out and the way one enters the rug. The text is like that — one has to know it intimately to find the entrance into it and the place where the Spirit seeps out, looking for us. Perhaps our attitude has to be the same — we have to intend to be buried in its mystery and believe that its full meaning lies beyond our own lives.

Eudora Welty, a contemporary writer, says: "I read everything. . . . Just to feel the word entering into your soul kindles something." The Word of God obviously wants to do the same: kindle something in us, stir up old hopes, and give dimming dreams more vital design. The Jewish community believes in almost unlimited meaning in the text, the Word of the Lord. It is written:

> Is not my word like . . . a hammer that breaketh the rock in pieces? (Jer. 23:29). As the hammer splits the rock into many splinters, so will a scriptural verse yield many meanings.[1]

For instance, at the end of Mark's gospel we read that Jesus "speaks to them and was taken up into heaven and took his place at the right hand of God." Then comes what is now the last line of the gospel: "The Eleven went forth and preached everywhere, while the Lord worked with them and confirmed the message by the signs which accompanied them" (Mark 16:20).

That's the last line in the book as we have it now, but it's apparent that there were originally other "last lines." It is widely accepted that the original ending came at Mark 16:8, which reads: "The women went out of the tomb and fled, beside themselves with fear. And they said nothing to anyone because they were afraid." Do both endings speak the truth? Does one say more truth than the other? Let's dig a little. We know the women did eventually get past their fear and tell the Eleven, who didn't believe them. They were told to go back to Galilee, which is about ninety miles from the site of the empty tomb in

---

1. *Sanhedrin* 34A, quoted in Nahum N. Geatzer, ed., *Hammer on the Rock: A Short Midrash Reader* (New York: Schocken Books, 1948), frontispiece.

Jerusalem. And the three women, all the others who had come up with Jesus to Jerusalem, and the Eleven did return to their homes. What did they talk about in those ninety miles? What stories did they tell? What memories were shared? Did they go back to the beginning, when they first met Jesus in Galilee, and confess their conversions, healings, forgiveness, doubts, and struggles to continue following him? Among the community, overshadowed by resurrection's reality and the presence of the Jesus' Spirit among them, did they wonder if they had heard or understood anything he said at all?

Does the text itself turn in a spiral, back to the beginning for us so that we can reread, re-ponder, reevaluate, and reinterpret what we once were so sure of in light of what happened to him: crucifixion, death, and resurrection? Does the text itself tell us that the meaning of all things for us is different now that we have experienced crucifixion, death, and resurrection in our baptisms and confession among his followers? What are we to do now? What's back in Galilee?

Let's go back to the beginning:

This is the beginning of the good news of Jesus Christ, the Son of God. It is written in the book of Isaiah, the prophet, "I am sending my messenger ahead of you to prepare your way. Let the people hear the voice calling in the desert: Prepare the way of the Lord, level his paths." (Mark 1:1–3)

Are we now the messengers, sent ahead to prepare the way for the good news of Jesus Christ, the son of God?

This last of the add-on endings says that the Eleven went forth after Jesus left — finally! The person of Jesus now seated at God's right hand gave them the courage to get beyond their fear — or was it the example of the women who had gone before them and had been validated in their words, by no less than Jesus of Nazareth, the crucified one who had been raised from the dead? Did they finally get into the act? Or to change metaphors, did they finally join in the dance? A well-known song called "The Lord of the Dance" describes Jesus dancing in the world, bowed down under the weight of the devil, but still leaping up high, never dying. All of us — men and women, young and old, slave and free, Jew and Gentile, unbeliever, half-hearted believer, sometimes believer, as well as the steadfast and sure believer — are invited over and over again to come and join the dancers throughout all times and places.

A few last thoughts can perhaps serve as a prelude to the reading of the texts discussed in this book. The first comes from an ancient Jewish story called "The Walking Book"; it throws together many images that appear in the following pages:

> Once there was a Hasid living in a small village. He had no books whatsoever except one tractate of the Talmud, Hagigah,[1] and all his days he studied that tractate with devotion. He lived a very long life, and at the end, prior to his death, that tractate assumed the form of a woman.[2] Then, following his death, she walked before him, showing him the way to Paradise.[3]

Only the second reference applies here. The comment on it reads:

> [2] The female personification of the tractate is appropriate as an object of the Hasid's love; it might also reflect the female gender of the Hebrew word torah.[2]

Another quote reminds us why we read, delve into the text, study, and seek to reform our lives and the world:

> There's an old Talmudic teaching which says that every child is born with a message to deliver to the human race — a few words, maybe a work of art, maybe a bench he'll build, maybe something she'll say that completes the explanation of why we're here.[3]

The last quote is from Thomas Merton, a man who loved words, loved the scriptures, and loved God in his way, his time, and ahead of our times. He was often censored, his articles banned and severely edited, and he was often told to be silent. Sometimes he did, and then again, sometimes he didn't. He wrote:

> The world and time are the dance of the Lord in emptiness. The silence of the spheres is the music of a wedding feast. . . . Indeed, we are in the midst of it, and it is in the midst of us, for it beats in our very blood, whether we want it to or not. Yet, the fact

---

2. From Aryeh Nineman, ed., *Beyond Appearances: Stories from the Kabbalistic Ethical Writings* (New York: Jewish Publication Society, 1998), 17.
3. Sam Levenson, quoted in *Children in China* (Maryknoll, N.Y.: Orbis Books, 1998), 20.

remains that we are invited to forget ourselves on purpose, cast our awful solemnity to the winds and join in the dance.[4]

Come, leave aside some of your ideas, fears, prejudices, broken recordings, agendas — and dance. Leave her alone, leave him alone, leave them alone. Let them dance. Just because we can't always hear the music doesn't mean that it isn't there!

---

4. Cited in *Maryknoll Magazine* (October 1998).

ONE

"LEAVE HER ALONE"

John's Message

> Respect for the vulnerability of human beings is a necessary
> part of telling the truth, because no truth will be wrested from a
> callous vision or callous handling. — ANAÏS NIN

L EAVE HER ALONE." Jesus says these three words in response to Judas's evaluation of Mary's anointing of Jesus' feet with costly perfume and then wiping them with her hair. They are a command from the Master to the disciple who is out of line, who is speaking out of malice, ignorance, or blindness. Even without the context of the story, the words are about freedom and noninterference. And they infer praise, infer allowance for Mary and for her behavior and intentions. These words announce that Mary has been recognized and accepted — and so, defended and protected.

I often use the phrase "in the hearing is the meaning," and particularly in the context of John's gospel, it reveals layers of meaning and insight. The line is a corrective. It can even be a chastisement for a self-righteousness that defends one's own agenda and so severs connections with and condemns another. The command to "leave her alone" stops that process sharply and has inherent in it a positive judgment in opposition. It is a demand to desist, pointed personally and yet also collectively at "you."

Leave her alone. Leave her be. Leave her to her work. Don't hinder or interfere. Don't ridicule or belittle. Leave her with me! She's bound to me, not you. Leave her alone. Like the doctor's adage "to do no harm," this is a moral imperative. It is a testament regarding who

11

really sees, who has insight, who senses truth, who acts righteously, and even who can learn from whom.

Even more so, it is a confession, a statement of whose side the Holy is on, who Jesus sides with, who is privileged in closeness, who knows and has caught a glimpse of holiness, of wholeness, and wants to draw closer to it — who is therefore in relation to, and closer to, God. But the words are also a confrontation with what is not true, what is evil, false, sinful.

Leave her *alone.* The tenor of the words is the pivot of the story, and the story is about reactions: to people, to relationships, to what Jesus has done by raising Lazarus from the dead. The sound of the words is utterly human, and they reveal communion with another, with one who, like Jesus, is an outcast. The words bind Jesus and Mary together. One of the definitions of religion is to relink, rebind, bind together at the root, and so this story is about religion at its root and questions us on who and what we bind ourselves to and why. This identification-with reveals our own identity, our self-knowledge.

We will look at this story of Mary anointing Jesus' feet while Martha, Mary's older sister, waits on them at table. We will examine what provokes Judas's judgment as well as Jesus' judgment in retaliation and his defense and affirmation of the one so meanly singled out. Jesus' words sound like a corrective, yet they also express his understanding that his presence and power have evoked distress, gratitude, and confusion in Mary, the sister of Lazarus, whom he had raised from the dead. This deed of his has shattered her identity, her vision of life and death. Jesus' presence and actions are an intrusion into her life, her soul — a welcome intrusion, but one that is awesome and even disconcerting, that unleashes emotions and reactions that seem abnormal, out-of-place, senseless, even tasteless.

This is not a woman relating to a man. This is a woman who is on the edge of discovery, the edge of belief and faith, the edge of transformation. She is on the edge of consciousness of what *is* and *is not,* of sinfulness, lack, and inability to express what is welling up inside her. It is the story of a woman who is sensing, beginning to believe that this man is more than man — he is holy, other, powerfully bound to life and death, and intimate with the defining moments of life in ways none of us has ever known. And that makes him singular, alone in the midst of his friends — Mary, Martha, Lazarus, and the disciples. Her action is a gesture of reaching to touch, to root herself again in reality. She is asking: Is this man human? Is this man my friend? Is this man of God? Is this man bound to me? Is this man going to die? Is this power, this person, dangerous, attractive, world-altering, shattering, freeing? If he raised my brother from death and decay, then what will he do with my life and the life of others?

We will begin with this story and will then work backward and forward in the Earlier Testament stories and in the stories of Jesus looking at others who needed to be defended and protected in word and deed. We will look at words and who ultimately is revealed as being defended and acceptable to God and why they merit such attentiveness by the Holy One. And lastly we will look at examples of how such merit is remembered and repeated today, or should be imitated today in our world. The underlying issue will be the same in all the stories — Leave her alone! — with the unspoken corollary: If you don't, you will have to reckon with me! And that "me" is the person and the Word of God and those who are the friends of God.

Let us read the story in John now and listen to the meaning, remembering that the meaning is in the hearing and that reading aloud reveals what cannot be heard or known in the mind alone:

Six days before the Passover, Jesus came to Bethany where he had raised Lazarus, the dead man, to life. Now they gave a dinner for him, and while Martha waited on them, Lazarus sat at the table with Jesus.

Then Mary took a pound of costly perfume made from genuine nard and anointed the feet of Jesus, wiping them with her hair. And the whole house was filled with the fragrance of the perfume.

Judas, son of Simon Iscariot — the disciple who was to betray Jesus — remarked, "This perfume could have been sold for three hundred silver coins and turned over to the poor." Judas, indeed, had no concern for the poor; he was a thief and as he held the common purse, he used to help himself to the funds.

But Jesus spoke up, "Leave her alone. Was she not keeping it for the day of my burial? (The poor you always have with you, but you will not always have me.)"

Many Jews heard that Jesus was there and they came not only because of Jesus, but also to see Lazarus whom he had raised from the dead. So the chief priests thought about killing Lazarus

as well, for many of the Jews were drifting away because of him
and believing in Jesus. (John 12:1–11)

The first and last paragraphs bracket the story, giving it a fore-
ground and putting it in a perspective of resurrection (life being given
back to Lazarus) and killing (the intention to kill not only Jesus but
Lazarus because, now raised from the dead, he is the cause of others
coming to believe in and follow Jesus more closely). We are told that it
is six days before Passover, which would mean that the city is swelling
with pilgrims and Jews from the diaspora, those scattered among the
nations returning to the temple in Jerusalem in expectation of freedom
and liberation once again. In John's gospel the Passover falls on a Fri-
day, so this is the Sabbath, Jesus' last Sabbath meal with his friends
and disciples before his death. In the previous chapter we are told that
the city and the religious officials are seething with hatred and intrigue, plotting how to arrest Jesus, just waiting for the right moment
in the confusion of crowds and activities that marked the feast day.
We are told, "Meanwhile the chief priests and the elders had given
orders that anyone who knew where he was should let them know so
that they could arrest him" (John 11:57). This incident — so personal
and intimate, in a household of friends — takes place while others are
conspiring to kill Jesus. Time is running out. Jesus has six days before the conspiracy closes in on him and he is betrayed and murdered.
The raising of Lazarus from the dead has complicated matters: now
it seems best to kill both of them. Association with this man Jesus is
becoming life-threatening, for the officials see Jesus as disturbing organized religion and acceptable practices of temple worship, sacrifice,
and prayer.

And in the midst of this we are told simply: "Now they gave a
dinner for him, and while Martha waited on them, Lazarus sat at the
table with Jesus" (12:2). This is the Sabbath meal, a ritual within every
Jewish household, a time of blessing, of prayer, and of shared dreams
and hopes for freedom and liberation. Because this is the last Sabbath
before the feast of Passover, the meal and the prayers have added significance and power. This community gathers around Jesus while the
powerful plan death. This community is thus a protest against killing,
hatred, and any religious practice that would condone destruction of
human beings. As the Sojourners Community in Washington, D.C.,
would say today: "Celebrating life when death is the norm is to be a

community of resistance." For Abraham Heschel, Sabbath is "a treasure in God's storehouse. Her name is Sabbath. It is a time for the
sake of life."

Ritually, the Sabbath is when the Shekhina — the Spirit of God that
waits in exile with the people of God until the coming of the Messiah — goes to visit, to dwell with the righteous Jews who gather to
celebrate Sabbath, to remember the promises, and to tell again the stories of God's compassion and justice. For the duration of the Sabbath,
the Shekhina — the daughter of light, the King's daughter, who is also
sometimes called the Torah, the Word of God, the truth in love —
abides with them at the table, in the prayers, and in their presence.

Jesus' small community of twelve disciples and his three close
friends would have sung the psalms, read the Torah portion, and
feasted on the promises of God, while they wined and dined at the
table. Lazarus, we are told, sat at table with Jesus, in a privileged
place, by his side, guest of honor, intimate with the one who raised
him from the dead. He was close to the presence that had summoned
him forth from the tomb, close to the voice that had broken the barrier
of death and decay and had commanded him to "Come forth!" into
life, into the light again. He knew that voice as the voice of his friend,
and he would have hung on every word that Jesus spoke. In a word, he
would have been adoring this man who had power over life and death,
his own life and death and those of all others. The dinner party would
have crackled with energy, with a trace of fear and wild expectations.
What would Jesus do next?

We are told clearly that "Martha waited on them." Martha, the head
of the household, the eldest of the three friends of Jesus, has obviously
sent her servants away and honors Jesus by waiting on him and his disciples. It is her way of expressing her gratitude, her joy at her brother's
return to life. She graciously shifts her relationship to Jesus — she
shifts from being the hostess to one who serves at table. She hum-
bles herself before Jesus and those he brings with him to her house,
not servilely but with genuine love and devotion. It is her way. She
would have been the one to light the candles, summon the presence of
the Shekhina, and begin the ritual celebration of the Sabbath meal. It
is now time out of time, time made holy and sacred unto God, time
for the visions and dreams of Israel to take their rightful place in the
minds and hearts of the community. It is Sabbath, and it is Jesus' last
Sabbath with his friends.

Many of the words of the Passover ritual would have been upper-most in their minds, and words from the Torah, the commentaries, and the Midrash would have echoed in their hearts. After the experi-ence of Lazarus's being raised from the dead, what would this night, this day of Sabbath, bring forth? A midrash on Isa. 2:4, though com-posed much later in the history of Israel, reveals and conceals hidden mysteries of hope and God's designs of liberation. It speaks of what the Sabbath is, of what Passover is, of what God's intent has always been for Israel and for all of us. It is background for this story in theological language that is shared by the Jewish community and by Christians now:

> Nation shall not lift up sword against nation.
> Neither shall they learn war any more.

> Ko amar Ha-Rachaman, thus says the Compassionate One: As I parted the Sea of Reeds that you might re-emerge from My womb, now it is you who must widen the narrow passages so that justice and mercy can be reborn. Do not be afraid My beloved. Go forth into the night and become the light and the outstretched arm. And on the day when all the world is set to the rhythm of My timbrel, dominion and violence will be banished from the land. And you will know Me, The One Who Makes Life Holy.[1]

And now Mary enters. She takes a pound of perfume, incredibly expensive, made from genuine nard, and goes to Jesus at the table and anoints his feet, then wipes his feet with her hair. "And the whole house was filled with the fragrance of the perfume" (12:3). Whenever guests entered a house, they removed their sandals before reclining at table on long couches or benches. They would lie on their sides, their heads facing inward toward the table, their feet out and away. Mary obviously had access to wealth. In other translations we are told that the perfume cost the equivalent of 365 days' wages. She is making herself poor for Jesus, as her sister is making herself a servant for his sake, in gratitude for what Jesus has done for their beloved brother Lazarus. The roles are shifting in response to the altering of life and death among them.

---

1. Gila Gevirtz, quoted on *Cross Currents* cover (winter 1997/98).

The word that is used is important: she *anoints* Jesus' feet with the perfume and then wipes the excess off with her hair. Her hair is unbound. In her own house she would not be expected to cover her hair with a veil or cloth. And, as was the custom, her hair would have been long, uncut for years, her "crowning glory," as it is often referred to in Mid-eastern cultures. She would have been bent over his feet, with her hair hanging down over her head. She is making an act of obeisance, of devotion, of respect, a passionate one, one that is founded on gratitude. Her response is born of what is inexpressible.

In Hebrew society, those who were anointed were priests, prophets, and kings. Mary is recognizing and ritually confessing that Jesus is prophet, king, and priest in Israel. The prophets Elijah and Elisha had brought people back from the dead. Kings had power over life and death. The priests mediated between God and the people. Jesus, for Mary, has become all of these and more. He graces her home with his presence and calls her, her sister Martha, and her brother Lazarus friends. She knows that he loves her, loves them all, having put his very life in jeopardy when he raised Lazarus. In giving Lazarus life, he has endangered his own. They lived less than two miles from the inner city of Jerusalem, and their household was visited by many, the curious and those truly concerned. She has heard the rumors and knows about the growing hostility in the city — all of it centered around Jesus and aggravated by the raising of Lazarus.

To unknowing and unseeing eyes, she is acting rashly, imprudently, even, as Judas will say, wasting perfume that could have been sold for a market value of three hundred silver pieces. Later, we know, he himself will sell Jesus out for a mere thirty silver pieces. He is indignant at such extravagant waste of resources. His rationale at first seems innocent, even righteous enough: it could have been sold, the money then turned over to the poor. The gloss on the gospel text informs us, however, that Judas could care less about the poor and that he is a common thief, taking from the common purse that was used to give alms to the poor — in essence, he steals from the community, from the poor, and from God, because almsgiving was part of Jewish rituals and atonement. This description of Judas illuminates his accusation about Mary's deed. It reveals greed and a mean-spiritedness that must publicly try to shame another's good deed.

At this point we are told "Jesus spoke up." There is the sense that Jesus will not allow such a statement to go unchallenged. He speaks up, loudly enough so that all in the room, no matter what they might be thinking, will know precisely what he thinks of the situation and Mary's actions. He is not just a guest of honor at a meal in Martha, Mary, and Lazarus's house — he is a teacher, the Master of the disciples, and Lord. His response vindicates Mary's intention, behavior, and her relationship to him, but it also sets a precedence and takes what seems to be a very personal and singular response to his person and adds a theological and sociological reality — Jesus is making a statement about future judgments about money, excess, and actions that are border-line worship and unusual in the community. His words are pivotal to his own person and how we are to love him, how we are to respond to his presence and absence among us.

> "Leave her alone. Was she not keeping it for the day of my burial? (The poor you always have with you, but you will not always have me.)" (John 12:7–8)

These are loaded lines, and they have been used in the most bizarre ways to self-righteously defend behaviors that Jesus would never have endorsed. They have been quoted to mean that the poor will always be with us so there is nothing we can do about it, revealing a lack of faith, revealing selfishness and noninvolvement with the needs of the poor. They have been used to validate spending enormous amounts of money on houses of worship and extravagant accessories while the poor go hungry. However, exegetes and scholars of the scriptures often view the line as John's rendering of Matthew's chapter 25, the parable of the sheep and the goats, with its famous lines: "Whatsoever you do to the least of your brothers and sisters, you do to me" and "Whatsoever you fail to do to the least of your brothers and sisters, you have failed to do it to me."

Much of what Jesus says in the gospels is found in seed form in the books of the Bible that are foundational to the covenant and Torah, the law of the Jewish community, such as Exodus, Leviticus, and Deuteronomy. The book of Deuteronomy gives the following commands to the Israelites for the Sabbath year, which occurred every seventh year:

> If there is anybody poor among your brothers, who lives in your cities in the land that Yahweh gives you, do not harden your

heart or close your hand, but be open-handed and lend him all that he needs.

Be careful that you do not harbor in your heart these perverse thoughts: "The seventh year, the year of pardon, is near," so you look coldly at your poor brother and lend him nothing. He may cry to Yahweh against you, and you will be guilty. When you give anything, give it willingly, and Yahweh, your God, will bless you for this in all your work and in all that you undertake.

The poor will not disappear from this land. Therefore I give you this commandment: you must be open-handed to your brother, to the needy and to the poor in your land.

(Deut. 15:7–11)

The emphasis is mine. In other translations the line often reads: "The poor you will always have with you," the very words of Jesus to Judas, his disciples, and friends present at the Sabbath meal before his own death. "But you will not always have me": he is trying to tell them, what Mary probably suspects, that his death is imminent, that his presence will be harshly and violently taken from them before the week is out, betrayed by one of his own followers and abandoned by all of them.

Jesus is acknowledging Mary's gift, her generous, openhanded, and open-hearted giving in anointing him for burial. The wealthy kept nard, aromatic spices, myrrh, and aloes for their own deaths and burial chambers. Mary takes what she has kept for death and honors him in life. She anoints him not only for death but also for priesthood, prophecy, and kingship in God's sight. The highest act of mercy, the most meritorious corporal act of mercy in the Jewish community, was anointing for burial because it made the ones who performed the ritual unclean themselves, for they had touched death and had become ritually impure. In turn they had to remain apart from the community while they performed the ritual of cleansing and purification. Mary has unknowingly or with partial knowledge aligned herself with one who is already condemned to death, a religious and politically dangerous criminal, one who is poorest of the poor in the eyes of the Jewish community.

Jesus is declaring for his followers, for his community, that anything we do for the poor, who are always with us, we do for Jesus, who is always with us now, by his incarnation, suffering, and death, in the poor in our midst. We will always have Jesus now, in the poor. Whatever we passionately desire to do for Jesus, for God, in worship, obedience, and devotion, we can passionately, devotedly do by obeying the needs of the poor and honoring them in their flesh.

It must have been an uncomfortable moment at the dinner party, a glitch in the ritual celebration of a Sabbath meal. A rift opened, between those who would stand with Jesus as he was arrested, condemned to death, and crucified and those who would refuse to believe that such a thing was happening, let alone those who would betray him in deed, in word, and in running away to save themselves in fear and confusion. The setting of murderous intent, conspiracy, and betrayal has moved into the household, among friends and disciples. The issue at hand has to do with worship, with sacrifice and the poor, with the new temple of God that is now the Body of Christ among us, the poor, all those who suffer and die, are killed and betrayed by those who profess outwardly to be concerned about the honor of God and worship. The description of the effect of Mary's act of reverence toward Jesus' person is telling: "And the whole house was filled with the fragrance of the perfume." It suggests incense filling a place of worship, smoke billowing up and the chant rising along with it: "May our prayers rise like incense in your sight, O God" (from Vespers, the evening prayer of the church).

Jesus spoke up: "Leave her alone." She's with him. He's with her. Now the option is put before us: Where are we? Whose side are we on? When we celebrate Sabbath, the day of the Son, what are we feeding on? What word do we take to heart? Who do we defend in public? What do we do with our wealth and excess? The questions of conscience are seemingly limitless. This story changes everything. This story is subversive. How do you respond to resurrection? How do you practice downward mobility, like Martha and Mary, becoming servants, and making yourself poor in gratitude, by using your wealth, your treasured possessions and savings, for those who are in need now?

There are even more fundamental questions about ritual, about worship on our Sabbaths, our Sundays. Jesus speaks up in the gospels, defending, chastising, and standing in the breach between groups within the community and telling us we must choose where we stand. In this story, do we stand with those under the shadow of death or with those who control the money and the institutions and are respectable in our community? What words are we listening to in our assemblies? A priest in a rather poor parish once quoted something I said in a workshop in his deanery meeting, and the statement was met with silence, a silence that was awkward and angry. I had said that if a wealthy parish with a large church building has thousands of dollars, let alone hundreds of thousands of dollars, in its bank account and does not use it for the poor only blocks or a few miles away, then that is sin and the worship of the church is in question. Our worship of God, of the Body of Christ, broken and given to the Father in the power of the Spirit, is worship only if the ritual offering is backed up with a life that honors the broken and dying Body of Christ in the world today. They cannot be split apart.

The ritual of the bread and wine of our liturgies is preceded by the ritual of the Word spoken up among us. A story from the Zohar, translated by Daniel Chaan Matt, reminds us of the word we listen to, the word we feed upon, and the word we are called to put into practice:

> The food that comes from higher above is finer food,
> coming from the sphere where Judgment is found.
> This is the food that Israel ate when they went out of Egypt.
> The food found by Israel that time in the desert,
> from the higher sphere called Heaven —
> it is an even finer food, entering deepest of all into the soul,
> detached from the body, called "angel bread."
> The highest food of all is the food of the Comrades,
> those who engage in Torah.
> For they eat food of the spirit and the soul-breath;
> they eat no food for the body at all.
> Rather, from a higher sphere, precious beyond all: Wisdom.

This is wisdom — when Jesus speaks up. This is wisdom — to worship God and express our passionate love for the Lord by taking a year's hard wages and reverencing the bodies of the poor who need the money now. This is wisdom — to defend and speak up on behalf of those who take risks on behalf of those under the sentence of death. This is Wisdom . . . to align ourselves with those who suffer, those who are betrayed by institution and friend alike. This is wisdom — to attempt to express the impossible, in thanksgiving for the life of resurrection and a seat at the table of the Lord. This is wisdom — to know that the true identity of the priest, prophet, and king is founded in a lifestyle of deeds and connections between God and human beings. This is wisdom — to listen to the Word of the Lord and to live mindful of being in that presence always, but most especially when we are among the poor of the earth.

This meal is the occasion of joyous celebration. Mary and Martha provide a feast for Jesus and his disciples because their household, their family, is whole once again. Jesus has returned Lazarus, their beloved brother, to them with new life. Liturgy is about how to acquire joy and to dwell in its house, where Wisdom, the Word, sits at the door, waiting to welcome those who enter. But how to acquire joy and possess it lightly? A story told in the Eastern tradition imitates Mary and Martha's response to what they have known of Jesus' prayer and gift of life to them:

> A man and woman once asked Mother Macrina how they could acquire joy. She responded: "You can't acquire it, as though you could purchase it or barter or deserve it by your works. There is only one way to know joy. . . . It is to find it!"
>
> They were quick with the next question: "Where do we find it? How can we find it?"
>
> "Oh," she smiled and looked straight at them, "That is really very simple. . . . There is only one way. You must lose your self. . . . You must give away yourself, your heart and all you possess."[2]

Mary and Martha have begun in earnest their giving away, their losing of themselves, their laying aside of their possessions, and their giving over of their hearts and lives to Jesus, to the service of Jesus' word and kingdom as disciples themselves. The phrase "while Martha waited on them" reveals that she has become, in her serving at table, a deacon: one who performed the duties of the liturgical table in John's community.

This story makes clear that the roles of liturgical practice in the community flow from the practice of their underlying meaning in the life of the community's poor. Jesus speaks up, defends, and stands with those (e.g., Mary) who publicly risk humiliation, censure, and harsh dismissal of their corporal works of mercy by those (e.g., Judas)

---

2. Irma Zaleski, *Stories of Mother Macrina,* a version of which is found in *Parabala* (summer 1998).

in the community who judge from the perspective of gain, stability, what is acceptable practice and propriety. This is the role of the church, the priest, the preacher, and the leader of prayer in the community's ritual and life. This speaking up was described eloquently by Oscar Romero, archbishop of El Salvador, who spoke up, as did Jesus, on behalf of the poor and was violently silenced, though in vain. He said:

> A church that doesn't provoke any crises,
> a gospel that doesn't unsettle, a word of God that doesn't
> get under anyone's skin,
> a word of God that doesn't touch the real sin of a society
> in which it is being proclaimed —
> what gospel is that?
>
> Very nice, pious considerations that don't bother anyone,
> that's the way many would like preaching to be.
>
> Those preachers who avoid every thorny matter
> so as not to be harassed,
> so as not to have conflicts and difficulties,
> do not light up the world they live in.
>
> They don't have Peter's courage, who told that crowd
> where the bloodstained hands still were
> that had killed Christ:
> "You killed him!"
>
> Even though the charge could cost him his life as well,
> he made it.
>
> The gospel is courageous;
> it's the good news of him who came
> to take away the world's sins.[3]

Mary knows when to be extravagant, knows that the bridegroom will not long be with them, and knows that the day will soon be upon them when they will not be able to express so personally their love for the Lord of life who dwells among them. All of us in the church, now two thousand years later, are summoned to the expression of our

---

3. Oscar Romero, *The Violence of Love,* ed. James R. Brockman (Farmington, Pa.: Plough Publishing House, 1998).

love of the Lord of life in the Body of Christ, the poor. Kabir, the poet, reminds us: "Who is a holy person? The one who is aware of others' suffering." Our capacity for awareness, for response and for sharing — that is what makes us human and holy.

On the level of economics, we must ask questions of our society in regards to welfare, food stamps, and gross inequalities between the rich and the poor, first on the immediate level of daily consistent care of basic necessities and then on the theoretical and institutional levels that change market, banking, and custodial systems within the economy. What would an economy look like that took seriously first and foremost the needs of people — especially children, the poor, women, the elderly, the weak, and the marginalized — and of the earth itself, that was based on sharing, on equality, and on the common good of the majority who are not wealthy?

Our ritual of bread and wine, of a meal shared with hospitality, of devotion to the suffering Body of Christ in our midst, demands that we become socially and economically knowledgeable and practice an economy of sustainable respect for people, for the common good, and for earth itself. Perhaps on an individual level, it's time to go back to fasting before receiving Eucharist; better yet, perhaps we should divest ourselves of our excess and what we've been saving for later before we sit at table with the crucified and risen one who feeds us wisdom and the bread of resurrection life.

In our story, Jesus' life is about to be taken. It was deliberate, calculated by those with power and the disciples and friends of Jesus were caught off-guard. Most ran. Most cowered in fear for their own lives. Most forgot his words and his friendship, presence, and power among them. Most reverted to their old ways of life. Most despaired. Most of us do the same to one degree or another. When confronted with global statistics, our eyes glaze over and our hearts become numb. The richest 1 percent of the world's population use 80 percent of the world's resources and wealth, and the poorest 15 percent of the population live on around 1 percent of the resources. But, as Ruben Alves says, "The overwhelming brutality of facts is not the last word." Indeed, for those of us who have known and met Jesus the Christ, who raised Lazarus from the dead and was raised by the Father and who dwells among us still in the power of the Spirit, the last word is: resurrection! The last word is: "Leave her alone! Leave those who share, those who risk, those who do the corporal works of mercy, those who are prophetic in their silence, their words and deeds . . . leave them alone!" For this is where hope lies. These are the ones who move in close and bend over Jesus' body to anoint him, before he has died, whose intimate relationship with the Lord of life will not allow them to sit and contemplate but drives them to move and reach out to touch with oil, with nard, with the balm of healing peace, with the sweet scent of compassion.

Anne Wilson Schaef writes:

> As a society, we are responding [to global dysfunction] not with action, but with a widespread malaise. The market for antidepressants has never been better. Apathy and depression have become synonymous with adjustment. Rather than looking for ways to change, to save ourselves, we are becoming more conservative, more complacent, more defensive of the status quo. . . . To say that the society is an addictive system is not to condemn the society, just as an intervention with an alcoholic does not condemn the alcoholic. The most caring thing to do is not to embrace the denial but to confront the disease.[4]

This is what Jesus does in this story. He intervenes. He confronts. He praises and defends those who resist, those who seek to do something different, to change, to transform themselves and their small household. In a book called *Tales of the Heart: Affective Approaches to Global Education,* Tom Hampson and Loretta Whalen list some of the characteristics that are addictive in our national life, both for individuals and for groups and institutions. The terms could be used to describe behavior and attitudes practiced by many in this story of John's gospel. They are: "self-centeredness, the illusion of control, fear, negativism, dishonesty, defensiveness, confusion, blaming, denial, tunnel vision, frozen feelings, forgetfulness, ethical deterioration."[5] The community of those who practice resurrection must resist and offer alternatives to these behaviors and attitudes, beginning with speaking up on behalf of those who are already trying to put into practice, however hesitantly and awkwardly, something new, something graceful, something human, and something redeemed.

---

4. Anne Wilson Schaef, *When Society Becomes an Addict* (San Francisco: Harper and Row, 1986).

5. Tom Hampson and Loretta Whalen, *Tales of the Heart: Affective Approaches to Global Education* (New York: Friendship Press, 1991), 33.

How do we do this? First, by remembering, by going back into our traditions and histories and putting back together again what was and what could be again, by honoring those who sought in the midst of suffering, persecution, and death to be human. Not long ago, a most remarkable book was published called *In Memory's Kitchen: A Legacy from the Women of Terezín,* edited by Cara De Silva. It was compiled from a hand-sewn copybook written by starving women in the Czechoslovakian concentration camp called Terezín, or Theresienstadt. The story of how it survived and came to be published is itself miraculous. One of the major authors of the cookbook was Mina Pachter, who was seventy when it was written. Just before she died of starvation on Yom Kippur in 1944, she gave the copybook to a friend in the camp and asked him if he survived to get it to her daughter, Anny, in Palestine. He carried the manuscript in its handwritten form around with him for twenty-five years. Anny had moved to New York, and one day, through a series of coincidences, it was delivered to her. Anny said:

> When I first opened the copybook and saw the handwriting of my mother, I had to close it. I put it away and only much later did I have to courage to look. My husband and I, we were afraid of it. It was something holy. After all those years, it was like her hand was reaching out to me from long ago. . . . By sharing these recipes, I am honoring the thoughts of my mother and the others that somewhere and somehow, there must be a better world to live in.[6]

Why does this story of a cookbook resonate so with us? Perhaps because we are all hungry. We all need to eat on a regular basis, and it is food that connects, links, and draws us together as human beings, bringing communication, joy, sharing, and sustenance together at the table. Michael Berenbaum, the director of research at the United States Holocaust Memorial Museum, writes in the foreword to the book:

> This cookbook . . . must be seen as yet another manifestation of defiance, of a spiritual revolt against the harshness of given conditions. . . . Recalling recipes was an act of discipline that required them to suppress their current hunger and to think of the

---

6. Cited in the introduction to Cara De Silva, ed., *In Memory's Kitchen: A Legacy from the Women of Terezín* (Northvale, N.J.: Jason Aronson, 1996), xxvi–xxvii.

ordinary world before the camps — and perhaps to dare to dream of a world after the camps.[7]

The women did not survive. But their poems, letters, and recipes, their words and imagination, did survive. The important thing is to inherit and practice the hope, the defiance, and the binding that these women practiced. We learn not so much from those who have but from those who have lost, have had what is dear to them taken away. The Christian Community Bible's notes on our passage from Mark state:

> We often speak like Judas of *giving to the poor.* Yet the Lord's command is not to give but to love. To love the poor is to reveal to them their call from God, and to help them grow as persons by overcoming their weaknesses and divisions and by fulfilling the mission God entrusted to them. The poor will be the ones to live the Gospel and witness to it in the world. If we are not among them, we need conversion and true poverty to discover with them the Kingdom. How can we really love the poor unless we have passionate love for Jesus? When we do not, we prefer to speak of giving to the poor, whatever be the biblical reading on which we are commenting.

The poor are found in every country, among every religion and group. They are universal reminders of what is lacking in our love and our religious lives, and we are called to learn from them and be converted by them to a life that is based on love, justice, and an economy of sharing, hospitality, and gratitude. Just as the body of the crucified one convicts us, so the bodies of the poor convict us and remind us of what is necessary if we are to love and to be called the children of God. In our liturgy the words ring out: "Do this and remember me!" Do this: take all your excess and lavish it on the poor. Do this: give up your place and position in your own household and economic bracket and become a servant somewhere. Do this: speak up on behalf of those who side with those who are conspired against and killed, slowly by systems or outright by institutions that legally but unjustly practice the death penalty. Do this: confront those who use theology and religious sentiment to belittle the deeds and expressions of those they do not respect. Do all this (and more) and you, like Mary, Martha, and Lazarus,

---

7. Michael Berenbaum, foreword to *In Memory's Kitchen,* xv–xvi.

will know resurrection and the joy of having dinner with the Lord of life. Do this and others may come to believe in Jesus.

There are many traditions and stories of those who do these things. One comes from the Buddhist tradition; it is a well-known story about Rengetsu, a nun who spent most of her life on pilgrimage, like the Buddha, seeking enlightenment and practicing compassion for all beings, living simply and sharing even what she begged from others with those who were poor:

> One night she was on her way home after years on the road and she was dirty, tired and cold. It was almost spring. The days warmed up but the nights still had the hard edge of winter in them. She arrived in a village and went from door to door seeking shelter, food, warm drink, a blanket, whatever they would spare for the evening. No one let her in or gave her anything. One look at her and she was neither nun nor worthy of attention.
>
> Finally, exhausted, she climbed a hill outside of town, and as it was fast becoming night and colder still she wrapped herself in her thin, well-worn cloak and curled up in a ball, asleep. She slept, unawares, under a cherry tree, surrounded by an orchard of cherry trees. In the middle of the night she awoke from the bitter cold and the hard ground under her. It was a night of the full moon and the sky was filled with light. She was entranced and then slowly came to realize that the tree under which she slept had blossomed in the night, under the light of the white moon. The tree was filled with wild blossoms and the night was filled with the overwhelming scent of the flowers in the cold night air. It took her breath away, warmed her heart and stirred her to rise. Standing under the tree, she turned toward the inhospitable town and bowed slowly and reverently toward them all sleeping in their beds, unaware of the mystery that covered her. And she prayed aloud this poem-prayer of thanksgiving:

> > Through their
> > kindness in refusing
> > me lodging
> >
> > I found myself
> > beneath the
> > beautiful blossoms

on the night of
the misty moon.

The story was told to me by a Jesuit who had been in Japan for over forty-seven years, and he added that even though the people's hearts had been "hard as cherry stones," the nun was willing to be poor and would not exclude them from the hospitality of the kingdom of human dignity and eternal life. She knew the doorway would open to them in her heart full of gratitude.

Another universal story comes to mind. O'Henry wrote a version called "The Last Leaf," but the account I love to tell is by a woman named Flora Sasson, who lives in a village in the north of Lebanon called Hamadin. She does not name it as far as I know. This is the way I tell it:

Once upon a time a widow and her only child, a daughter, lived together. Their life was simple but good, and they had all that they needed. And they had one another's love. But the girl became ill, desperately ill, and was bed-ridden for weeks. She slowly drifted away, looking out her window at the tree that dropped its leaves and slowly became barren and empty. Fall came early and was almost harsh, though brilliantly bright in its change of colors. The girl loved that tree. It was her life-line. She clung to it and knew every branch and twig, every leaf and sound as it moved in the wind.

One day, as she was feeling terrible, her mother sat beside her, and the girl spoke: "Mother, look at my tree. It's losing all its leaves. When the last leaf falls, I will let go too. I'm tired, and I want to die." The mother was distressed and now watched the tree in horror, watching also her daughter slipping away from her. She was desperate. She stopped sleeping, wondering what to do to keep her daughter from dying. She couldn't stop the seasons turning, and she couldn't stop the leaves from falling.

One night she awoke from an exhausted sleep in the midst of a dreadful wind storm. The tree! The leaves! She knew what to do. It was cold; the wind was harsh and bitter; the air was full of dampness and wet dew. But she was oblivious to the weather and to its biting at her skin and lungs. There was a low wall in front of the tree, and on it she painted a leaf on a twig, on a branch. In her love and need, the drawing was almost real: one leaf, a bit ragged, a hole in one side, a bit rusty-looking. The day came when the girl counted the last leaves. And then there was just one, the one her mother painted on the wall. She watched it, waiting for it to fall. But it stayed. It held. It refused. It clung to the branch, and she found herself clinging to life, wanting to stay.

It took time. All through winter the leaf held fast, and she fought her way back and recovered. But during that winter her mother became ill. She had caught a chill the night she had painted the leaf. She grew weaker, gradually getting TB, becoming less and less able to see her daughter. And finally the mother died. The girl grieved and then went to look at her tree more closely and try to understand the tenacity of that last leaf. It was then that she learned the wisdom of her mother, her imagination and passionate devotion to her daughter's life. The gift of the last leaf was the gift of her mother's strength. Now she grieved for her mother's love that gave her back her life at the cost of her own.

Mary has a glimpse that this is Jesus' gift not only to her brother Lazarus but to her and her sister Martha and to everyone. She has witnessed resurrection and comes to believe that nothing will ever be the same again, that life can now blossom forth even out of death, out of inhospitality and dishonesty, out of murder and hate. This man Jesus and his Father now stand behind her life and the lives of all people.

Leave her alone! She is truly at home for the first time in her life. And for a moment while she anoints his feet and wipes them with her unbound hair, bent over his body at table, Jesus also is truly at home. God has been given welcome in the hearts and household of his three friends, Mary, Martha, and Lazarus. All other holds are broken.

TWO

HANNAH

H ANNAH'S STORY is found in 1 Sam. 1:1–2:10. Samuel was Hannah's first child, the child asked of God that opens her womb. Her relationship to her child is much like that of Mary with Jesus, and there are many places where the stories overlap. Both women bear children who are prophets, and both are prophetesses in their own right.

Hannah's story is about determination, about prayer, about rightful demands upon God, about mature relationships in a society that is still immature, and about how to be human and a person in your own right in a culture where men are allowed more than one wife and where women are kept at the fringes of cultic religion. It is a story, too, about who God takes note of in such a society and how God works in history in spite of its evils and divided loyalties. The story takes place at a time when the Israelites — after the nomadic time in the desert — are demanding a king like the other nations. The tribes are scattered and sensing the need for a unifying authority and a structure that they can control more surely than the inspired judges. Samuel is the last of the judges and the first of the prophets to call forth a king in Israel, who will be Saul. And his mother, Hannah, is a link between families and tribes, as well as between individuals who are struggling to change and to grow into the covenant that Yahweh, the Holy One, has made with the people.

The story begins in the hills of Ephraim, with a man named Elkanah, son of Tohu, son of Jeroham, of the clan of Zuph. The clan and tribe identifications are given to emphasize that what is about to happen is of great import not only for the individuals involved, but for the people of Israel. And the set up is ancient, acceptable in past societies and still in some places today: "He [Elkanah] had two wives,

Hannah and Peninnah. Peninnah had children but Hannah had none"
(1 Sam. 1:2).

The simplicity is devastating. One woman has standing in the family and community. The other has none. One woman has worth. The
other has none. One woman rules in her domain, however limited, and
the other is suffered and allowed to stay. But the situation is worse
even than this preliminary description would attest:

> Every year Elkanah went to worship and to sacrifice to Yah-
> weh of hosts at Shiloh. The priests there were the two sons of
> Eli, Hophni and Phinehas. Whenever Elkanah offered sacrifice,
> he gave portions to his wife Peninnah and to all her sons and
> daughters. To Hannah, however, he gave the more delightful
> portion because he loved her more, although she had no child.
> Yet Hannah's rival used to tease her for being barren.
>
> So it happened every year when they went to Yahweh's
> house. Peninnah irritated Hannah and she would weep and
> refuse to eat. Once Elkanah, her husband, asked her, "Hannah,
> why do you weep instead of eating? Why are you sad? Are you
> not better off with me than with many sons?" (1 Sam. 1:3–8)

This clarifies the meaning of the old phrase, "Insult is added to injury." Hannah must bear the daily taunts and patronizing disdain of the
other wife as well as be treated as a child by her husband, who loves
her but does not see her pain, her grief, and her exclusion from the
life of the family. He does not realize that his preferential treatment of
her with delicacies and the best portions only increases her sense of
uselessness and reinforces her relationship to her husband as a mere
child. Elkanah forgets that any woman in Israel is only deemed desir-
able and worthwhile if she bears children. Hannah has none, and her
doting husband treats her as his personal girl-child wife. And this has
gone on for years, each year the burden growing heavier and Peninnah's vicious teasing more destructive. She is so debilitated by the
abuse of her family that she cannot eat and weeps constantly. She is
desperate, and it is this desperateness that leads her to prayer, prayer
that is public in the house of Yahweh in Shiloh:

> After they had eaten and drunk in Shiloh, Hannah stood up not
> far from Eli, the priest: his seat was beside the doorpost of Yah-
> weh's house. Deeply distressed she wept and prayed to Yahweh

and made this vow, "O Yahweh of hosts, if only you will have
compassion on your maidservant and give me a son, I will put
him in your service for as long as he lives and no razor shall
touch his head." (1 Sam. 1:9–11)

Her prayer is heartrending. A more literal translation of the text reads:

Her spirit was greatly pained, . . . and she wept profusely, . . . and
she prayed: "O God of Hosts, if you will look upon and see the
plight of your servant, if you will not forget but remember your
servant and give your servant a son, then I will dedicate him to
God for all the days of his life."

The repetition of her identity as the servant of Yahweh both reveals
knowledge of herself and also reveals the discordance she experiences
as barren, and the anguish born of misunderstanding. Her husband
misunderstands her, and Peninnah is without compassion or understanding of her plight. And the misunderstanding spreads, next to the
priest Eli, who witnesses her prayer without any semblance of respect
for her and assumes the worst about her condition:

As she prayed before Yahweh, Eli observed the movement of
her lips. Hannah was praying silently; she moved her lips but
uttered no sound, and Eli thought Hannah was drunk. He, therefore, said to her: "For how long will you be drunk? Let your
drunkenness pass." But Hannah answered: "No, my lord, I am
a woman in great distress, not drunk. I have not drunk wine or
strong drink, but I am pouring out my soul before Yahweh. Do
not take me for a bad woman. I was so afflicted that my prayer
flowed continuously." Then Eli said, "Go in peace and may the
God of Israel grant you what you asked for." Hannah answered,
"Let your maidservant deserve your kindness." Then she left
the temple, and when she was at table, she seemed a different
woman. (1 Sam. 1:12–18)

She knows who she is: a woman in anguish. She stands her ground,
on the edges of the temple and before the priest in Shiloh. She knows
that what she asks of God is a prayer to be esteemed and honored in
all of Israel. And her prayer is a stream, an outpouring, a prayer of
the Spirit. Her prayer is that God will give her a child, a son, and that
she in turn will give the child back to God for all the days of his life.

The child will come through her to the service of the Holy One. She lays no claim on him, and her love for him will be bound to her love for God. She is a faithful woman in Israel, more than many are. And we are told that "Yahweh took compassion on her and she become pregnant" (1 Sam. 1:19–20). In other translations, Yahweh remembers her, or favors her, and she names the child Samuel (Shemu'el) because she asked (*she'iltiv*) God for him. The child's identity is bound to his mother's identity and relationship to God. He will be her only son, handed over, sacrificed to Yahweh, more surely than any animals that her husband sacrificed yearly at Shiloh.

The following year when Elkanah returns to Shiloh to offer sacrifice, Hannah does not go with him, remaining behind and keeping her child with her until he is weaned. That means Hannah could have stayed home with the child for three, even four or five, years. And then Hannah goes on pilgrimage to Shiloh alone with her own offerings to sacrifice: a three-year-old bull, a measure of flour, a flask of wine, and her child. We are told, "The child was still young" (1 Sam. 1:24). She hands him over to Eli, the priest, announcing who she is and that Yahweh who wanted her to have this child now wants the child and is asking the child of her as once she begged and asked. The Hebrew rendering makes the radical shift in Hannah's relationship with Yahweh very clear: "Hannah will lend Samuel to God because God has, as it were, lent ear to her voice and granted her request." She is now as gracious and responsive to God as God was to her. They are in mutual understanding and agreement, and Hannah can now, as a mature believer, teach her community Israel what she has learned in her prayer with God. Rainer Maria Rilke has a line that encapsulates Hannah's life up to this point: "Let my hidden weeping arise and blossom." And Hannah sings a song to Yahweh.

This singing in response to life, both joyful and exultant as well as in distress and fear, is the tradition in Israel, even before David the poet-king prays the Psalms. The Spirit of God comes upon individuals, streaming into them, causing them to sing, to praise and to honor God and to prophesy and teach the people the ways Yahweh works in their lives. The songs tell us that the God of Israel has a tenderness for the cast-offs, those rejected by the people. In Isaiah we hear the song:

Rejoice, O barren woman who has not given birth;
sing and shout for joy, you who never had children,

for more are the children of the rejected woman
than the children of the married wife, says Yahweh. . . .

Do not be afraid for you will not be deceived,
do not be ashamed for you will not be disgraced.
You will forget the shame of your youth;
no longer will you remember the disgrace of your widowhood.
For your Maker is to marry you:
Yahweh Sabaoth is his name.
Your Redeemer is the Holy One of Israel:
He is called God of all the earth.
For Yahweh has called you back
as one forsaken and grieved in spirit.
Who could abandon his first beloved? says your God.
For a brief moment I have abandoned you,
but with great tenderness I will gather my people.
For a moment, in an outburst of anger,
I hid my face from you, but with everlasting love
I have had mercy on you, says Yahweh, your Redeemer.

(Isa. 54:1–2, 4–8)

Hannah is prophet to her nation. She offers a hymn that will be treasured and cherished in Israel, one that Mary, from the hill country of Judea, will know by heart. Luke will put phrases of it in Mary's mouth as she praises God for what her Redeemer has done for her and what is in store for Israel and all the world. Now Hannah, who once was silent, has found her voice, and it is bold and sure. She once prayed privately, but it is time for all to hear what she has learned of God. (A difference to be noted between Hannah and Mary: Hannah sings her song when her child is born and she has brought him to Shiloh to serve God; Mary sings her song while her child still is in her womb.)

Once Hannah stood at the doorway, cloaked in misery. We have the sense now that she stands proudly and publicly in the sanctuary of the temple of Shiloh and begins to sing and praise God, in a place where women's voices were not often heard, or tolerated. She is prophetess now and priest. She lets her voice fill the sanctuary of Shiloh and prays her heartfelt prayer. This is the way she has always prayed: now she teaches it to the people and the priests. She was insulted when she prayed silently. Now there is the sense that she is respected.

The rabbis of the Jewish tradition credit Hannah with many changes and developments in how the community prays. The Babylonian Talmud asserts that she is the one who introduced petitional prayer, debating and pleading with God in the manner of the early leaders, Abraham and Moses. "In fact, the Talmud compares the assertiveness, or almost insolence, of her manner of prayer to that of Elijah and Moses. All of them, Hannah included, were judged to be justified in their arguments and tone."[1] In her petition to Yahweh she calls God "Lord of Hosts" (Zeva'ot), and the Talmud credits her with giving God this name.

Leila Leah Bronner, in her chapter on Hannah in her book *From Eve to Esther: Rabbinic Reconstructions of Biblical Women,* writes of the connections between the meaning of Hannah's name and her life and prayer:

> The rabbis also attribute to her the quality of grace, which fits with the primary meaning of her name, "to show favor" or to "be gracious." To expand upon this etymology, the secondary meanings of her name — "yearn toward," "long for," "be merciful," "be compassionate," "be favorable," "incline toward," "seek or implore favor" — all suggest the phenomenon of prayer. Some meanings, such as "yearn toward," express the posture of the supplicant; others, the attitude hoped for on the part of the deity. The meaning "long for" also fits exactly Hannah's long years of yearning for a child — the impetus for her prodigious act of prayer.[2]

What is remarkable is that this woman is offered as a model for prayer and self-defense in rabbinic Judaism, even in her silent prayer and her explanation to Eli, the priest, for what she is doing. Marcia Falk writes:

> Her act is all the more extraordinary in that, by all accounts, she is the first woman — indeed, the first "ordinary" person — to pray in any sanctuary, at this point in time before institutionalized prayer has replaced sacrifice as the means of public

---

1. Leila Leah Bronner, *From Eve to Esther: Rabbinic Reconstructions of Biblical Women* (Louisville: Westminster/John Knox Press, 1994), 97.

2. Ibid., 97.

worship. In so acting, Hannah stands poised to become a symbol for rabbinic Judaism, providing for the early rabbis — the Amoraim — a model of authentic prayer, which is to say, "the prayer of the heart" — although all Hannah meant to do is to speak her *own* heart and to be heard. We may call her intentions spiritual, but the result of her action is both spiritual and political. Hannah discovers her own voice and legitimates that voice.[3]

And Falk has more startling things to say of Hannah:

> Hannah has self-respect, and she means to be heard. Her protest — do not condemn a person until you have stood in her place, until you are sure she is guilty — is a political act. From it the rabbis will later devise the ruling that one must not let a false charge to oneself go uncorrected: One must defend oneself and not be apathetic to what others think (*Babylonian Talmud, Tractate Berakhot* 31b).
>
> So impressed were the rabbis with Hannah's prayer *and* with her defense of it to Eli that they interpolated the following words into those of the Bible story: "Hannah said to him [Eli]: You are no person of authority in this matter, and the Spirit of Holiness is not upon you, since you have been suspicious of me in this matter," and further, "You are no person of authority, nor is the Divine Presence of the Spirit of Holiness with you, since you have presumed me guilty rather than innocent. Are you not aware that I am a woman in anguish?" (*Babylonian Talmud, Tractate Berakhot* 31b).[4]

The rabbis are — amazingly — predicating authority as intimately connected to the understanding of others' inward anguish. However, although they wrote of Hannah's singular authority with Yahweh, as Marcia Falk says, "they neglected to give Hannah's daughters — the women of Israel — a place in it." Just as Eli missed an experience of knowing this "prayer of the heart," much of Judaism and of Christianity has missed it also. Hannah's child, Samuel, however, learns well from his mother, even though he is only with her for a short time. We are told in chapter 2 of 1 Samuel that Samuel listens, even as boy, and

---

3. Marcia Falk, "Reflections on Hannah's Prayer," *Tikkun* 9, no. 4: 63.
4. Quoted in ibid., 64.

is fine-tuned to the Spirit and voice of Yahweh. But not many in Israel or in Christianity have listened or let Hannah's daughters teach them of heart-prayer.

Walter Brueggemann writes:

> Real criticism begins in the capacity to grieve because that is the most visceral announcement that things are not right. Only in the empire are we pressed and urged and invited to pretend that things are all right either in the dean's office or in our marriage or in the hospital room. And as long as the empire can keep the pretense alive that things are all right, there will be no real grieving and no serious criticism.

In short, we need to learn to practice Hannah's method of grieving heart-prayer. Elie Wiesel speaks eloquently of grieving in relation to the suffering of the Jewish people in the Holocaust: "In the face of suffering, one has no right to turn away, not to see. In the face of injustice, one may not look the other way. When someone suffers, and it is not you, he comes first. His very suffering gives him priority.... To watch over a man who grieves is a more urgent duty than to think of God."

Peter Daino, a Marianist brother who has spent much time in Africa, was interviewed in Kenya about what he has learned from the women, especially those he met and worked with in East Africa. Peter told the following about a woman named Sarah. The story appeared in the *Catholic Telegraph* and is also quoted in a brochure for IMANI (an acronym for Incentive from the Marianists to Assist the Needy to Be Independent). In Swahili *imani* means faith. Here is the story:

> Sarah, a poor woman from one of the slums, walked into our agency one day and began to tell me about her life. I listened to her problems and request and made a quick mental review of the different categories of assistance which our agency provides. I realized that her petition did not fit into any of our categories or programs. I told her that we did not deal with what she required and suggested a few other agencies. Sarah did not play her part. She was supposed to say thank you and leave. Instead, she sat there. I tapped my fingers on the desk. I cleared my throat. Still she sat there. I stood up, shook her hand and pointed to the door. She wouldn't budge.

I was beginning to feel annoyed. Finally I told her that she had to go. She refused and bluntly replied that she was not budging until I helped her. We played a waiting game. I pretended to do desk work, looking up now and then to see if she was getting tired. She sat there like a rock. What was I going to do? I had reviewed all our programs and she didn't fit any of them. Her case was rejected. We had a whole file of rejected cases. Why couldn't she accept that?

That day I realized that even our wonderful service agency for the poor was a fallen creature, just like other fallen institutions. The beauty about Sarah was that she refused our easy categorization of her. She wouldn't accept the status of a rejected case. In fact, finally she grabbed a broom, started sweeping and got herself hired as the cleaning lady for the agency. Because of her innate self-esteem, she rightly rejected my labeling of her.

I, at Maria House, often need to be reminded of the very purpose for which we were founded. *Imani* is a Swahili word which means faith. We wish to teach the people faith in themselves. Our motto is to "believe in the God who believes in me."

Sarah and Hannah would have understood each other perfectly, though Peter was much more humble and open to learning from Sarah than Eli or Elkanah or even Peninnah was with Hannah. How open are we, men and women of the church and the twenty-first century, to learning from the Hannahs and the Sarahs today in our society? Marcia Falk states the question thus:

> We might take it upon ourselves to pick up where the rabbis left off. We could begin by asking what it might mean for us — as individuals and as communities — to hear Hannah's voice today. We might also ask what it would be like to create a community of empathy, where silent pain is given a voice. What, indeed, would it be like to have a truly inclusive spiritual community, a community of equals, where all could pray together in the language of the heart? What might communal prayer sound like if it included everyone's voice?[5]

---

5. Falk, "Reflections," 64.

Hannah's heart has been stretched by sadness. Her first prayer of sorrow, often called *mara,* in its silent screaming has led her to prayer that is intent on the deliverance and liberation of all her people. This silent ache that seeps throughout one's whole person is "the cry of the poor" as surely as any scream that shatters and drowns out the talk in our ears. This woman scorned and thought drunk, treated as a child without adult desires, now sings as a prophet. To use a contemporary phrase, she sings of a new world order, and she becomes the spokesperson for all those who have been despised, ridiculed in their hope, and demeaned by religious people who in their shallow faith and self-secured positions look down on others. Look and listen to what she has to say now:

> My heart exults in Yahweh,
> I feel strong in my God.
> I rejoice and laugh at my enemies,
> for you came with power to save me.
>
> Yahweh alone is holy, no one is like you;
> there is no Rock like our God.
> Speak proudly no more;
> no more arrogance on you lips,
> for Yahweh is an all-knowing God,
> he it is who weighs the deeds of all.
> (1 Sam. 2:1–3)

Hannah begins in joy, exulting as once she was bent and reduced to wordlessness, and her words are sure in their description of Yahweh as the Rock who shares strength with her and gives her the power to laugh at those who persecuted her with arrogance and insensitivity. Now she knows who this God bends to, listens to, and affords protection and solace to:

> The bow of the mighty is broken,
> but the weak are girded with strength.
> The well-fed must labor for bread,
> but the hungry need work no more.
> The childless wife has borne seven children,
> but the proud mother is left alone.
> Yahweh is Lord of life and death;
> he brings down to the grave and raises up.

> Yahweh makes poor and makes rich;
> he brings low and he exalts.
> He lifts up the lowly from the dust,
> and raises the poor from the ash heap;
> they will be called to the company of princes,
> and inherit a seat of honor. (1 Sam. 2:4–8)

Hannah has known radical upheaval and reversal in her life because of Yahweh's taking note of her pain, and now she is voice to the many in Israel and in the world whose only experience is being outcast, condemned, assumed lacking, presumed guilty of sin or personal weakness. Her song is of universal, widespread, and institutional reversals in society between the strong and the weak; the well-fed and the hungry; those who do not work for what they have and those who struggle and come up with little or nothing; those who are secure in their children, their futures, and old age and those who are left alone; those who know life and those who know death. Hannah knows of these reversals in her own life and encourages those who are still waiting on the power of God to make themselves known. She continues:

> The earth to its pillars belongs to Yahweh,
> and on them he has set the world.
> He guards the steps of his faithful ones,
> but the wicked perish in darkness,
> for no one succeeds by his own strength.

> The enemies of Yahweh are shattered,
> against them he thunders in heaven.
> Yahweh rules over the whole world,
> he will raise his own king.
> His anointed feels strong in him.
> (1 Sam. 2:8–10)

Now her prophetic prayer, born of her heart's anguish, reaches beyond the borders of her own nation out into the world. The power of her God has authority over all creation, history, and the only two really definitive groups of people and nations: the wicked and the faithful. The reversals and the vindication encompass all and everything. And then she speaks to the present historical issue in Israel: the naming of a king. She proclaims Yahweh "will raise his own king. His anointed feels strong in him." This raising of a king will be the work of her child, Samuel.

Hannah has turned the history of Israel toward its future, turning Israel itself to face Yahweh, its God, more maturely, expanding the people's horizon. So particular and universal are the themes of Hannah's prayer that it is now included as part of the *haftarah* reading in the New Year service. The tradition now recognizes that two of God's characteristics are a reversal of fortunes as well as attentive care of those found on the fringes of society.

Hannah's prayer of the heart is passed on to her child, Samuel, and to the prophets who come after, who will know the agony of the entire nation's unfaithfulness and the pain of the poor disregarded by the covenant, an insult and injury to the very heart of God.

This is Hannah's moment, her turning point, and her gift to Israel in its time of being weaned from the leadership of the judges so that it can grow into a more unified people under the guidance of the prophets and the kings. We hear about her only once more — that she accompanies Elkanah and Peninnah and her family on the yearly pilgrimage, bringing with her clothes for her child, who now belongs to the service of God, fulfilling her vow. Now it is Eli who prays that Hannah will have more children, "for the sake of the boy she asked for and then gave to Yahweh" (1 Sam. 2:20). Hannah bears five more children, three sons and two daughters, while "the boy Samuel grew in the presence of Yahweh." There is the sense that the rest of Hannah's life, as well as the life of her people Israel, will be bound to the child who released her from being barren in the midst of a family. Hannah evoked the Spirit of God, pleading for Yahweh's power in her personal life, and now that portion of Spirit is growing to maturity in the world in the person of her child, Samuel. Her prayer has taken on her flesh by the tenderness of Yahweh, her God.

And what of us today reading Hannah's story and listening to her prayer? Perhaps a story will turn our hearts toward a deeper perception of Hannah's power for us today. It is a Native American story from the Salish Indian community, originally based in the far northwest of the United States and deep into the southwestern portion of Canada, extending to the Pacific Ocean. I am indebted to Joseph Bruchac for his collection of Native American stories about indigenous plants of North America. This is the way I tell it. The title will be found in the ending of the story. It is a story told to prepare people for winter, for the hard task of survival:

Once upon a time there was an old woman. She had many children and many more grandchildren. She loved them all, loved her whole tribe. She'd seen many changes of season and many winters, but this winter seemed the worst in her long memory. The first snows had come early and they had come and come and come without a break. The hunters could not go out for game. The stores were low, for it had been a hard spring with a thin harvest. Now everyone was hungry: the children, the old; even the hunters' hands that pulled back the bow would tremble with weakness. . . . Everyone needed food.

Finally the snows stopped and the ground began to thaw. All in the village breathed a sigh of relief. But then the snows came back with ragged biting winds and freezing cold. Everything was solidly encased in ice. The people, wearied and exhausted, tried chopping through the ice and the hard ground. And the people started dying, the old, the children, everyone. The old woman could bear it no longer, watching the young, her own grandchildren and others, dying of hunger. And she decided it was time for her to die. She said goodbye to all in her family and clan, left those she loved, and went outside.

In the tradition of the ancient ones, she went to a place she had long loved, a place that was lovely in springtime. It was a small stream that flowed nearby her village. She went and knelt down on the ground by the frozen spring and began to sing her death song. And she wept, for her children and grandchildren, for all the others and for her people, the whole village that was so hungry and suffering so. She poured her tears into the ground and cried out: "Great Spirit, hear my prayer. It is not right that the children die with their mothers and grandmothers, with their elders. It is not right that so many go hungry while so many care for one another."

And the Great Spirit heard her prayer and had mercy and pity on the people. He sent the woman her spirit helper — a red bird, bright and startlingly red in color. He swooped down and landed on a branch above the old woman's head. And it sang at the top of its lungs, speaking to her. She raised her head and was startled by the bright red color against the stark gray of the sky and the dark of the dead branches. The bird spoke to her: "The Great Spirit has heard your prayer and has heard the compassion you have for your people, and has seen your tears that have fallen onto the hard earth. Your tears have made a new plant. It will bloom right in front of you. It will have red petals that open in the bright sunlight. They will be red, like my red feathers and breast, and they will have silver and grey lines in them like your hair grown long and born of wisdom and endurance." She looked and all around her in the snow were plants, flowers tightly closed. The sun rose at just that moment, and the plants opened, blossoming brilliantly red with silver lines like the bird and her own hair, just as her spirit helper had said.

She asked the bird: "I have never seen this plant before. What do we do with it? How do we prepare it and eat it?"

And the bird replied: "Dig them out by the roots. You can eat every part of it. Boil it, chew on it, cook it any way you want. Its taste will be bitter, but it will keep your village alive until the other plants begin to grow above ground, until the thaws come. Call it anything you want. It will bloom only after the snows have stopped and the icy winds return. It will be enough to feed the hunters and hold you all until you can find food in the spring."

And she gathered them, digging them out. From that day on the plant was called Bitter Root. The stream where she knelt is called the Bitter Root River, and the valley is called Bitter Root Valley. The flowers only bloom in the first sun of February or March, even as late as April, after the icy winds of the north blow down. The people dig them up and eat them. And they remember the taste of the bitterness and the sorrow and anguish of one grandmother, but the memory is sweet in their hearts. The plant, they know, is born of the heart's anguish, mourning, and a woman's death song. That's the way it always is — what feeds the future is the anguish of the old women's death songs. The bitter root.

This story, like Hannah's, is about a world order that is not right. What is given in the Indian woman's story is born of her pain and sorrow, which reveal the pain of an entire village and its people. Even the gift given — the nourishing plant — bears the bitterness of the moment and the experience of the people. It comes as gift when the woman goes freely to die. The flower is food, born of her tears. This is a universal symbol, for we in Christianity speak of the tears of the poor and those who struggle for justice, of the tears and sweat of the workers and farmers, and of the bread of justice that is Eucharist, sweet in our mouths at long last.

The grandmother, like Hannah, goes before God to pray with self-respect, placing her anguish and that of her people before the Great Spirit. She knows her own and her people's immediate needs but also knows from long experience that the snow and ice, the hard spring of the previous year, and the weakness of the hunters are interconnected in many ways and that the Great Spirit's plan is all of a piece. She relates to the Great Spirit as a member of her people, not primarily as just an individual. She is a grandmother, and her experience, the experience of her people, is a tragedy, and yet she still approaches all of life, this hard time included, with reverence. And it is her prayer and her tears that call forth food, a new thing, a plant that will carry her people all through the future, in the hard times, in between winter's last ferocious blast and spring's slow beginnings.

Both stories might lead us to ask ourselves and others three questions. First, What is the greatest anguish of your life? Or in other terms: What is the bitter root of your life? It must be something that is consistent, is sustained, and does not go away. For Hannah it is lack; it is barrenness, the emptiness of living without connections to family, to the future, to her people's hopes, to the covenant with Yahweh. For the grandmother, it is the lack of food and of time for the young. We answer with other things: insecurity, powerlessness, the fear of abandonment, an awareness of the shallowness and the arbitrariness of our commitments. . . . It is these that we — like Hannah and the Indian woman — must take to God and the Great Spirit. As Hannah's petition was taken up by Yahweh and transformed into her son; as the Indian woman's tears were taken up by the Great Spirit and turned into food, so God will listen to our pain and transform it into meaning not just for us but others as well.

The second question is: What is it that we lend God? Or how do we return the favor of God's own favor to us? Hannah lends Yahweh what is most treasured in her life, what Yahweh gives in response to her grief, her child, her son. The grandmother lends the Great Spirit her compassion and her tears, and in return she is given a plant, food for her people. Both are given gifts, and once they give the gifts back to God, the gifts are then shared with the people. The answer to the question, then, is that we must give back to God whatever we treasure most. That done, God will take our gift and transform it into nourishment — "bitter root" — for many.

The third question has both personal and political repercussions. Who is it that we judge most harshly? Often it is people and institutions that exhibit characteristics and behaviors that we cannot abide: arrogance, self-centeredness, an inflated sense of self, violence, slander, dishonesty. Oftentimes our sense of what is wrong is connected to what we think is the worst thing that we could do or that could be done to us. Sometimes we harshly judge those who are close to us, who do what we do, only do it differently or better, wounding our sense of self. And we can judge not only in words and actions but also by ignoring people and behaving as if they simply aren't there: like the homeless, the sick, those who speak another language, those who hold opinions different from ours, the poor, and so on. Eli, Elkanah, and Peninnah all harshly judge Hannah, and within each of us there lives an Eli, Elkanah, and Peninnah. To counteract that, we need to develop a spirit like that of Hannah.

For Hannah's spirit is not selfish or small, vindictive or destructive, not even angry or enraged. It grieves. It is misunderstood, ignored. But it persists, gathers strength, and eventually bursts into song. She matures from a woman wanting a child and acceptance to a woman who is a prophet of her people. Hannah's prayer begins as an instinct of need and matures into awareness of a people's need, their deepest need — connection to God.

Hannah's song reveals that she now knows God, and it is only God that she fears. But her fear is the profound religious fear of God that is the root of wisdom. One of the Orthodox fathers, Theophan the Recluse, tells us about this fear of God that is the result of prayer. He refers specifically to the Jesus Prayer, which is brief and direct: "Lord Jesus Christ, Son of the Living God, have mercy on me, a sinner." He comments:

> Our task is the art of the Jesus Prayer. We must try to perform it quite simply, with our attention in the heart, always preserving the remembrance of God. This brings by itself its own natural

fruit — collectedness of mind, devoutness and fear of God, a recollection of death, stillness of thought, and a certain warmth of heart.... We should always hold fast to the fear of God. It is the root of all spiritual knowledge and all right action. When the fear of God rules in the soul everything goes well both within and without. Try to kindle this sense of fear in your heart every morning before you do anything else. Then it will go on working by itself as a kind of pendulum....

The remembrance of God is the constant companion of the state of grace. Remembrance of God is never idle but invariably leads us to meditate on the perfection of God and on His goodness, truth, creation, providence, redemption, judgment, and reward. All those together comprise God's universe or the realm of the spirit. He who is zealous lives always in this realm.[6]

Hannah learns this fear of God from grief that purifies and directs prayer single-heartedly. It is a discipline that she submits to rather than chooses of her own accord. The poor and those in terrible grief, those who are lacking and those who are belittled by others, often know this prayer of the heart. And today there are many Hannahs, without children, barren, and worse — hungry, condemned to live as factory and agricultural workers, illiterate, and the first victims of war and repression. A few statistics help illuminate this: 60 to 70 percent of the world's poor are women; two-thirds of the world's illiterate people are women; and 70 to 80 percent of the world's refugees are women and children.[7]

If women are to struggle out of these conditions, they must, like Hannah, speak out with confidence. They must tell their stories and listen to others. William Stringfellow puts it this way:

We are, each of us, parables. Theological exploration of biography is congruent with the definitive New Testament insight and instruction: the Incarnation. Listening is a rare happening among human beings. It is a primitive act of love, in which a person gives him or herself to another's word, becoming accessible and vulnerable to that word.

---

6. From Timothy Ware, ed., *The Art of Prayer: An Orthodox Anthology* (London: Faber and Faber, 1966), 125, 130–31.

7. See *Challenge: Faith and Action in the Americas* 5, no. 3 (Washington, D.C.: EPICA, fall 1995).

One of the crucial words in this quote is "biography," not "auto-biography." Often in a climate of individualism the focus is kept on "my" story rather than on another's. Our own particular story is but a word, a bit of punctuation, in the larger story that must be shared and written. Muriel Rukeyser's famous line is apropos: "The universe is made of stories, not atoms." But these stories must be conjunctions, links with other stories and networks, as Hannah's story catapults her into the stories of the poor, the weak, those outside the covenant and her nation. Martin Luther King Jr. put it succinctly: "Injustice anywhere is a threat to justice everywhere. We are caught in an inescapable network of mutuality, tied in a single garment of destiny." All our stories come down to one task and question: How to relieve suffering? Another way of expressing it comes from the realm of science: "There is a tendency for living things to join up, establish linkages, live inside each other, return to earlier arrangements, get along wherever possible. It is the way of the world" (Lewis Thomas).

Hannah's story is a biography worth telling. In some ways, it is the story of Hannah overcoming a lack of kindness. Elkanah and Eli are not kind enough to listen to her pain. Peninnah, a woman with power, resources, and acceptance in society, refused to show kindness to Hannah in her grief. (The Dalai Lama has a simple universal creed for all practitioners of every religion: "My religion is kindness.") Yet Hannah refuses to be negated by this lack of kindness. She persists.

There is a simple historical story of what can happen on such a personal level. This piece was given to me by a lover of literature:

Once upon a time there was a young husband and wife: Sophia and Nathaniel. They were struggling, working hard and barely making ends meet. But Nathaniel had a job, though one he detested: working in a customshouse. Sophia too worked as a seamstress when she could. He complained often that it was a dead-end job and that there was no possibility of advancement or a place to use his real talent, which was the crafting of ideas and words. But she always listened and always encouraged him.

And then came the day when Nathaniel arrived home early, laid off from his low-level job. He was frantic. Now there was little or no income. What would they live on? But Sophia listened and then spoke up clearly, and with obvious excitement and joy. "Now you can write," she announced. "Yes, I guess so," he answered. "But what will we live on? I will always be worrying about food, the rent, money for the coal, and how to provide for you, and I won't be able to concentrate."

She left for a moment and soon returned from the bedroom, unwrapping a handkerchief. Out spilled a substantial amount of money! "The last time I counted it," she stated, "there was enough for us to live for about a year, ... maybe a bit more." Nathaniel looked at his wife dumbfounded. "Where did you get it?" She smiled. "I listened to you every night when you came home, and whenever you gave me the money for the house and our expenses I took some and put it aside. We've been living on less and less so that I could save more and more. Now," she beamed delightedly, "you can write!"

And write he did. Within the year, Nathaniel Hawthorne completed *The Scarlet Letter,* and Sophia and Nathaniel, while never rich, were also never poor and struggling again. All because someone listened and acted. Sophia listened not to the complaining but to the heart of the one she loved, and she believed in his heart's dreams. Yahweh listened to Hannah and listens to the hearts of all who pray, even to those who do not pray, who have no words and no heart left. The more we learn the wisdom of God's listening, the more imaginative and creative the world becomes. The more we listen not only to our own hearts but to others, the more possibility there is for community, equality, and justice for all, beginning with simple human kindness.

But this listening project must also happen on a more communal, national, and global level, just as Hannah's sorrow tuned her ears to the cry of Yahweh's forgotten people. In an ecology workshop in a farmers' cooperative in El Salvador, one woman spoke up and announced: "We are the root from which the whole people sustains itself and grows." She was speaking of those who raise the crops and do the harvesting and taking to market, those who literally feed the people of a nation. But she was speaking about those at the bottom of the ladder, those with no hope of upward mobility, those who live in the realm of daily survival because of national and global systems of injustice.

The problems are huge. The outlook bleak. The immediate future for many threatened. The long-term prospectus dim. But Hannah's story proclaims hope, encouragement, and dependence on God. Hannah learned firsthand that "God guards the steps of his faithful ones ... and that the lowly are the ones picked up from the dust of the earth, and the proud are the ones who will be left alone." This is what our prayer must teach us, what our listening must help us mature into, and what must be the root of our actions. Hannah the prophet calls to us across the centuries and declares that grief is the bitter root that blossoms into a perfect tree: an order conceived by God out of the cries, the prayers, and the tears of the poor and those who are weak in the world. She who "vowed a vow" in her heart and who knew the prayer that is only given in grief can teach us and pass on to us a portion of that spirit that she lent to her child Samuel and so lent to God. Like Hannah's time, now is a time for the prayers of the servants of God to rise and for history to experience an opening that brings forth men and women whose spirits are tuned to the pain of others and who speak on behalf of the many in the world whose human misery is far greater than our small personal sorrows. Now is the time for a shift to a new world order of the Holy. And our hearts will know strength and exultation in our God.

THREE

THE WOMAN BENT DOUBLE
FOR EIGHTEEN YEARS

PERHAPS ANOTHER TITLE for this story would be the one that Jesus himself uses to describe this woman: the daughter of Abraham. She is nameless, not only as many women are nameless, but as the majority of human beings in the world are nameless. Yet Jesus praises her as a daughter of Abraham! Abraham received the promises of Yahweh for a people yet to be born. Abraham was reckoned as a friend to God. And Abraham used that position for leverage, even on behalf of cities that were notorious for their inhospitality, wantonness, and misuse of human beings. After Abraham has sought to obey the command to sacrifice Isaac, the son he truly loves, the Angel of Yahweh tells him what God will do for him and those who are his true descendants:

> By myself I have sworn, it is Yahweh who speaks, because you have done this and not held back your son, your only son, I will surely bless you and make your descendants as numerous as the stars in the sky and the sand on the seashore. Your descendants will take possession of the lands of their enemies. All the nations of the earth will be blessed through your descendants because you have obeyed me. (Gen. 22:16–18)

Abraham is thus the father of faithfulness whose story roots the age-old promises of a land, a people, and a way of life for those who follow after. The woman in our story is a daughter to this hope. She is daughter and granddaughter to Abraham and so to Isaac, the sacrificed one, bound on an altar, and to Joseph, sold into slavery in Egypt. She is the child of that people who were dealt with warily, . . . with taskmasters set over them to oppress them with forced labor, . . . who became ruthless in making them work. They [the Egyptians] made life bitter for them in hard labor with bricks and mortar and with all kinds of work in the fields . . . and treated them harshly. (Exod. 1:10–14)

And she, in her own time, is one of the myriad nameless people who live in occupied territory, a conquered people in their own land who are expendable workers, bearing the burden of injustice and poverty. Yet she is a daughter of Abraham, and so she too in her lifetime lives on the promises of the Messiah, the savior who will liberate her and her nation. She is of the race of long-suffering and believing people, as countless as the stars of the sky and the sands of the seashore, who know the stories of old and stake their day-to-day lives on their coming true, perhaps even in their own lifetimes. She would have heard the readings in the synagogue services, one of them from Exodus:

[The children] of Israel groaned under their slavery; they cried to God for help and from their bondage their cry ascended to God. God heard their sigh and remembered his covenant with Abraham, Isaac, and Jacob. God looked upon the sons [and daughters] of Israel and revealed himself to them.

(Exod. 2:23–24)

So, as we listen to the story, we must listen as one in a long line of memory to sense what happens when Jesus, an itinerant preacher, stands up in this synagogue on a Sabbath to remind the people of Israel of the covenant that their God initiated with them and is still intent on completing, with their agreement and obedience. Let us listen:

Jesus was teaching in a synagogue on the Sabbath and a crippled woman was there. An evil spirit had kept her bent for eighteen years so that she could not straighten up at all. On seeing her, Jesus called her and said, "Woman, you are freed from your infirmity." Then he laid his hands upon her and immediately she was made straight and praised God. (Luke 13:10–13)

The story is given here in only four sentences. In those four sentences worlds are overturned. The woman bent double for eighteen years is straightened up, can now stand and look the world and her community in the eye and hold her head up with dignity. The scriptures say that it was an evil spirit that had kept her bent for so long.

What was that evil spirit? Many assume that it was a crippling disease. But maybe it was not a disease at all, but a condition brought on by a lifestyle, by back-breaking work, by being stooped over for so many hours in a day that eventually her body revolted and she could not straighten up. Had she been no more than a slave, a farmworker, a beast of burden?

I remember distinctly the first time I traveled to Nicaragua in the early 1980s and stayed in a poor, make-shift area of Managua. By American standards it was a slum, but in reality it was well-ordered and had been meticulously organized into small groups that met for scripture study, for liturgy, for food distribution, and for community decision making. One afternoon and evening a week people would come in from all over the countryside to sell their produce and wares, to exchange information, to talk strategy for resisting the government, and to share how they were just surviving. They came bent over, doubled up, bowed down, with enormous loads on their shoulders and backs, all of them: men, women, and children carrying their barter, their food, their books, cement blocks, firewood, and clothing. And when I traveled back with them into the countryside and mountains I learned for the first time what it meant to be "heavy-burdened."

And again, more recently, on my first trip to Japan, I noticed older men and women so stooped and bent that they were unable to stand up. They were given seats in the trains and deferred to by those who were middle-aged. But it wasn't until I traveled to the countryside that I realized these were farmers who had grown up in the rice fields, bent over and hand-sowing, weeding and reaping the rice harvest. They had spent their lives standing in wet fields raising the staple food of a densely packed nation.

In our own country, those who do the back-breaking work of picking grapes, lettuce, and other produce are young, the women, and those most in need of work. They work long hours for the meagerest wages, suffering from conditions brought on by the weather, malnutrition, pesticides, lack of decent housing, and lack of health care. They constitute a lower caste that provides the undergirding of a society of wealth that depends upon them, yet ignores and oppresses them.

The woman was bent double for eighteen years. In Israel's history, an eighteen-year period has special significance in two instances. In Judg. 3:14, we read that after eighteen years of Moabite oppression, Israel was finally set free. After that, there was a time of peace in

Israel that lasted eighty years. And in Judg. 10:8, we are told that the Israelites

> treated Yahweh badly; and they served Baals and the Ashtaroth, the gods of Aram and Sidon, the gods of Moab, the gods of the Ammonites and the gods of the Philistines. They abandoned Yahweh and no longer served him, ... and for eighteen years all the Israelites living on the other side of the Jordan ... were disturbed and oppressed. ... Then they put away their strange gods and served Yahweh. And he could no longer endure the suffering of Israel. (Judg. 10:1–18)

After eighteen years, they were rescued from the Ammonites.

Even more to the point theologically, the Hebrew word *chai* (life) has the numerical value of eighteen. This story is about life, about freedom, about God no longer being able to endure the suffering of those who are faithful to the covenant and who worship only the true God of life. The woman has endured with faith and hope, and that in itself cries out to God, who cannot abide, cannot endure, the suffering of his own people. The coming of Jesus into the world is charged with immediacy, especially for those who have waited, waited for the coming of hope into their midst. This bent and bowed woman is in the tradition of others in Israel, the remnant that responds to the presence of Jesus, always with praise.

At the very beginning of Luke's gospel, when Mary and Joseph bring the child Jesus to the temple to consecrate him to the service of the Lord and to offer sacrifice and fulfill the requirements of the law, they are met by Simeon and Anna, both of whom are possessed by the Holy Spirit when they look upon and see the child. We are told that Anna, a prophetess, had continually been serving in the temple, fasting and praying, and that she was eighty-four. "Coming up at that time, she gave praise to God and spoke of the child to all who looked forward to the deliverance of Jerusalem" (Luke 2:36–38).

This bent woman is one of the remnant who has remained faithful to the teachings of the law and the prophets, whose life is seen in relation to God's promises. They literally lived on hope!

Jesus, we are told, was teaching in the synagogue. His teaching has been made clear by Luke in chapter 4, when Jesus stands up in his hometown of Nazareth on the Sabbath in the synagogue and declares forthrightly that his presence has inaugurated a new harmony in the world: "The Spirit of the Lord is upon me. He has anointed me to bring good news to the poor, to proclaim liberty to captives and new sight to the blind; to free the oppressed and announce the Lord's year of mercy" (Luke 4:18–19).

Jesus' words, voice, and presence are imbued with the power of the Spirit, the power of authority and truth that is often accompanied by healings, forgiveness, and freedom for those who experience being imprisoned by illness and prejudice. It is vital to note that in Jesus' quotation from Isaiah 61, the one new phrase he inserts is "to free the oppressed," which is lifted from Isaiah 58. In that text, the prophet is declaiming injustice in the land while the people claim to practice the rituals of fasting. He declares:

> Is that the kind of fast that pleases me,
> just a day for a man to humble himself?
> Is fasting merely bowing down one's head,
> and making use of sackcloth and ashes?
> Would you call that fasting
> a day acceptable to the Lord?
>
> See the fast that pleases me:
> breaking the fetters of injustice
> and unfastening the thongs of the yoke,
> setting the oppressed free
> and breaking every yoke. (Isa. 58:5–6)

As Jesus is teaching he "sees" the woman. Immediately upon catching sight of her, Jesus stops his discourse and calls out to her, "Woman, you are freed from your infirmity." Jesus' message to the woman is precisely what he has just said is God's message for all people. She will be not only a model of his words, but a living, straightened, and wholly liberated incarnation of his good news to the poor! He lifts her yoke and unfastens the thongs of the yoke that has bent her over all these years.

And then "he laid his hands upon her and immediately she was made straight." Perhaps she felt his touch before she realized he was speaking to her, before she lifted her head so that she could see him. Her first sight upon rising would have been his face. And she breaks into praise of God, into song and psalm for all to hear.

In many synagogues men and women gathered together, though in separate areas on the ground floor, especially if the synagogue was poor. Jesus would have seen her as he looked around at those listening to his words, but he would have had to go over to her to lay hands on her. Does the weight of his hands on her shoulders break the weight of long pain, work, and her own sense of worthlessness? Any infirmity was bound in the Jewish people's minds to sin and punishment, to a penalty exacted for failure to obey the law or for transgression. The law unfortunately was often used by those who had power in the community to break even the spirits of those already heavily burdened with poverty, illness, or the inability to pay taxes. And sometimes the poor disobeyed the law and suffered the penalties out of ignorance or weariness. What was meant to free the spirit was now used by some to bolster their own sense of ego while pushing others down. Did Jesus' hands laid on her lift her up, raise her head, and touch the foundation of her soul that had served as her own hope and meaning for living?

However it happened, the gesture of Jesus' connecting with her so intimately and publicly in the midst of the synagogue ritual would have disrupted the service, and everyone would have reacted visibly and verbally. After all, she starts praising God, probably loudly. A marvelous poem written by Denise Levertov, paradoxically called "A Man," describes perhaps what would have ensued:

> "Living a life" —
> the beauty of deep lines
> dug in your cheeks.
>
> The years gather by sevens
> to fashion you. They are blind,
> but you are not blind.
>
> Their blows resound,
> they are deaf, those laboring
> daughters of the Fates.
>
> But you are not deaf,
> you pick out
> your own song from the uproar
>
> line by line,
> and at least throw back
> your head and sing it.

Most likely for awhile there was bedlam. We know that the reaction of the ruler of the synagogue was swift and furious: "But the ruler of the synagogue was indignant because Jesus had performed this healing on the Sabbath day and he said to the people, 'There are six days in which to work; come on those days to be healed and not on the Sabbath'" (Luke 3:14–15).

Now the controversy begins. Initially it will be over the division between work and worship. The woman had come to the synagogue on the Sabbath to worship. We know that because the verb used to describe her praise or her glorifying of God in response to her knowing liberation in her body is in the form that connotes a continuation of an action already begun. Her praise out loud has been triggered by Jesus' healing, but it is a continuation of what she was doing in silence as she was bent and bowed before. Even Jesus' words to the woman ("You have been freed" [*apolelysai*]) have the sense that it was already an established fact before Jesus intervened to make it noticeable and felt in her person. He announced it, and it manifested itself in fullness! But the ruler of the synagogue, who speaks for the religious leaders opposed to Jesus, posits his indignation in terms of Jesus' breaking the Sabbath injunction not "to work," but "to rest" on this seventh day. The ruler of the synagogue was usually the teacher in the community, and here he moves in to pull the group back together, to reestablish control over the scene, and to use the moment to teach according to the usual interpretation of the Sabbath code.

The ruler of the synagogue would have had in mind the commandment of the Sabbath rest. He may have intoned it for the people's benefit at this point. It is found in the Decalogue:

Take care to keep holy the Sabbath day, as Yahweh, your God, commands you. You have six days to work and do your tasks. But the seventh day is the Day of Rest in honor of Yahweh, your God. Do not do any work, you or your child, or your servant, or your ox, or your donkey, or any of your animals. Neither will the foreigner who lives in your land work. Your servant will rest just like you. (Deut. 5:12–14)

Most probably he would have neglected to add the part of the exhortation that explains the connection between obedience to the law and the people's gratitude for and memory of what God had done for all of them. It follows immediately after the above text: "Remember that you were once enslaved in the land of Egypt from where Yahweh, your God, brought you out with his powerful hand and outstretched arm. For that reason, Yahweh, your God, commands you to observe the Sabbath" (Deut. 5:15).

This connection between remembering Israel's slavery and resting — a rest that is to be extended to everyone in the land — undergirds the command of the Sabbath. On the Sabbath the memory of liberation is to take precedence over all else, and that liberation is the reason for praising God. The dramatic story of God bending down to earth and hearing the cry of the oppressed, of sending Moses to lead the people out in his name, and of drawing them to himself as their protector is the reason they can work and rest, and so honor the one who remains the true leader in Israel. But it seems that the ruler of the synagogue is concerned with the barest bones of the law, not with its meaning and its power to free.

The ruler ignores the woman and the powerful expression of freedom that has just occurred. The official is concerned only with setting the people straight in regard to the demands of the law and what is correct theology.

It is Jesus who now turns indignant and responds with a prophet's righteous rage:

> But the Lord replied, "You hypocrites! Everyone of you unties his ox or his donkey on the Sabbath and leads it out of the barn to give it water. And here you have a daughter of Abraham whom Satan had bound for eighteen years. Should she not be freed from her bonds on the Sabbath?" (Luke 13:15–16)

Jesus goes to the heart of the matter: freedom is the soul of the law, the Sabbath, and the community. It is a quality of life that belongs by right to every human being and even to animals. Jesus, then, has done the only work that is fitting to the Sabbath, the work that constitutes true worship of God: he has set a human being free so that she can rest and honor God in her body, mind, and heart.

This is good news to the poor. Jesus is clear: his role is to break the yokes of servitude, poverty, disease, and prejudice. His words and hands break the boundaries that separate one human being from another, one group of human beings from others, whether the boundaries be of gender, race, religion, class, or culture. In response to this Sabbath work of Jesus, the woman praises God. Perhaps she cried out the praise of God from Psalm 72 (71):

> He delivers the needy who call on him,
> the afflicted with no one to help them.
> His mercy is upon the weak and the poor,
> he saves the life of the poor.
> He rescues them from oppression and strife,
> for their life is precious to him. . . .
>
> Praised be the Lord, God of Israel,
> who alone works so marvelously.
> Praised be his glorious name forever;
> may the whole earth be filled with his glory. Amen. Amen.
>   (Ps. 72 [71]:12–14, 18–19)

This psalm, called the "King of Peace psalm," comes at the end of David's prayers. It comes as a dream, as a hope after so much obstinacy, murder, hatred, and injustice. There will be one who comes whose presence in the world will do justice for the humble and will draw together those who desire peace. The notes in the Christian Community Bible explain what this psalm sings of:

> The King of Peace brings good news to the poor (Luke 4:18). He defends the rights of the lowly. He proclaims a new age when God will reconcile humanity; the weak have the right to live and there is food for all.
>   Our world is far from the realization of the universal charter of human rights, and it is not for us to wait passively for this reign. God is so thoughtful toward humanity, created in his image, that he wishes humans to be associated with all his works, including the realization of the eternal city.
>   This will be, evidently, a gift of God, but not a simple gift as was the apparition of the universe. It will be the crowning of what humans have begun to do on earth.

The ancient prayers and promises are clear that no one and no group is to be treated as inferior or relegated to a second-class life. This is the heart of the good news, and it is what Jesus proclaims in the synagogue by liberating the woman from her affliction. The reaction within the synagogue is clearly stated in the story: "When Jesus said this, all his opponents felt ashamed. But the people rejoiced at the many wonders that happened through him" (Luke 13:17).

Jesus' ministry proceeds along battle lines. For now his opponents have been foiled, dismayed, and even shamed in public while the people rejoice. And the story is followed immediately by two of Jesus' short parables that seek to describe Jesus' own following, the community that will be a corrective to religion that separates life from worship, justice from prayer, people who are not acceptable from those who have institutional power:

> Jesus continued speaking, "What is the kingdom of God like? What shall I compare it to? Imagine a person who has taken a mustard seed and planted it in his garden. The seed has grown and become like a small tree, so that the birds of the air shelter in its branches."
>
> And Jesus said again, "What is the kingdom of God like? Imagine a woman who has taken yeast and hidden it in three measures of flour until it is all leavened." (Luke 3:18–21)

In a real sense this is just what Jesus has done. He has planted a seed in the heart of his garden, his people gathered together in the synagogue on the Sabbath. It is the seed of hope, a seed that will grow into a community of those once bent, broken, and bowed down. That community will be the tree that shelters, that offers hospitality to the birds of the air, and especially to those bereft of home, of love, of recognition, and of worth. The fruit of a mustard seed is, in fact, not a tree but more a bush that grows wildly and can take over fields, gardens, even growing in dirt roads. It grows incredibly quickly and is hardy, pushing out other plants. Birds do indeed flock to it, hiding in its thick, sturdy cover. You can often hear the birds loud in their songs and cries back and forth to one another inside the bushes. Flocks leave to forage for food and return in droves as nightfall comes. It is not exactly a welcome plant to farmers and gardeners, but definitely is so to bird-watchers and bird-lovers. This is Jesus' kingdom. Those he has healed, freed, and praised along his route are a diverse and sometimes scraggly lot. He has given them welcome and shelter from the harsh realities of their lives.

The second image is homey: that of a woman about the work of feeding her family and neighbors their daily bread. She takes yeast and hides it in three measures of flour, much like the birds hide in the thick, overgrown branches of the mustard plant. But she works it in, kneading it and rolling it until it disappears utterly, so that it cannot be detected at all. And it is the yeast that will cause the bread to rise and expand, to take on the shape that the woman's hands will lend to it before it bakes. It is work, hard work, like the work of liberation, of giving hope, of lifting burdens. It is a work of transformation, of uniting, and of nourishing others. Jesus' kingdom is thus about nourishing and feeding with the bread of justice and inclusion.

Jesus has just singled out a woman hidden in the synagogue community and lifted her up, liberating and freeing her to praise God. She is yeast in the community, now active and churning through the whole group. Jesus has been kneading dough and making bread by his healings and touch, his hands-on lifting up. Now the kingdom and the church will be the place where these hidden people of society can impact others. In fact those once thought to be "unclean" and certainly undesirable are now the ones who will permeate the whole group and cause it to grow past its borders and boundaries. This is the experience of Luke's community as described in Acts. Not only are Gentiles entering the church, but others are entering as well — those who were often considered lax in the practice of the law because they were diasporan Jews, living at a distance from Jerusalem; and those who were poor, enslaved, or defined as sinners.

But there is more to the image. We are told very clearly that the woman hides the yeast in the flour. This image was used before in Gen. 18:1–10, where Sarah tells her servants to take three measures of flour and make cakes for their visitors, who bring with them good news of the coming birth of a child for their old age. The visitors hide their true identity from Abraham and Sarah.

This verb "to hide" (*krypto*) appears in some parables in Matthew, like those regarding the treasure hidden in the field and Jesus proclaiming to his disciples that they are being given access to what has been hidden from the very foundations of the world. And the verb appears also in Luke 10:21:

> At that time Jesus was filled with the joy of the Holy Spirit and said, "I praise you, Father, Lord of heaven and earth, for you have hidden these things from the wise and learned, and made them known to little children. Yes, Father, such has been your gracious will." (Luke 10:21–22a)

Later in the gospel, when Jesus laments over Jerusalem and the entire nation of Israel, he prays: "If you, even you, had only recognized
on this day the things that make for peace! But now they are hidden
from your eyes" (Luke 19:42; NAB). And when he is trying to teach
the disciples about the mystery of his passion, what he says is "hidden from them" (Luke 18:34). This hiding of the yeast in the dough,
this hiding of the kingdom among those who are poor, insignificant,
and lost in their communities, is part of the mystery of God. And surprisingly this imagery also suggests that this God who hides, this God
with the floured hands, is a woman![1]

We are told that "Jesus went through towns and villages teaching
and making his way to Jerusalem" (Luke 13:22). This is Jesus' intent:
Jerusalem. Even before this chapter of Luke is finished Jesus will cry
out his anguish in regard to his own people and their obstinate refusal
to accept the good news of freedom and mercy for all. He cries out:

> O Jerusalem, Jerusalem, you slay the prophets and stone your
> apostles! How often have I tried to bring together your children,
> as a bird gathers her young under her wings, but you refused!
> From now on your temple will be left empty for you and you
> will no longer see me until the time when you will say: Blessed
> is he who comes in the name of the Lord. (Luke 13:34–35)

Jesus as prophet declares that he will not set foot in the city and
the temple until it is time for him to enter Jerusalem to face his own
death at the hands of the powerful. In the previous line he reveals
what he is about: "I drive out demons and heal today and tomorrow, and on the third day I finish my course" (Luke 13:32). He is
sending a message to "that fox, Herod," and declaring that many in
Israel who have considered themselves righteous before God because
of their careful observance of the law will be left outside the kingdom of God, excluded from the table because they did not observe
their neighbors' need and suffering with the same devotion as they did
the demands and details of the law. Even on the cross Jesus will be
taunted:

---

1. For other ideas related to this image, see Barbara E. Reid, "A Woman Mixing
Dough," in *Choosing the Better Part: Women in the Gospel of Luke* (Collegeville, Minn.:
Liturgical Press, 1996), 169–78.

The people stood by watching. As for the rulers, they jeered at him, saying to one another, "Let the man who saved others now save himself, for he is the Messiah, the chosen one of God!"

The soldiers also mocked him and when they drew near to offer him bitter wine, they said, "So you are the king of the Jews? Free yourself!" (Luke 23:35–36)

This is Jesus' religion: to free those who have been bound or enslaved by others. Such religion is an act of profound courage. It is the courage of the bent woman whose eyes may be focused on the ground beneath her feet and on the feet of those around her, but her heart is focused on God's goodness and coming salvation. Graham Greene once said: "People talk about the courage of condemned men walking to the place of execution. Sometimes it needs as much courage to walk with any kind of bearing toward another person's habitual misery." This is the courage of those who are faithful to the good news, helping it to slowly and fitfully become a leaven in society and a tree sheltering those in need of refuge.

Un-chi, an Asian poet and priest, once put this in a simple statement when asked about his religion and philosophy: "I have no doctrine to give people — I just cure ailments and unlock fetters." This too is Jesus' work. Indeed, the woman he cures, this true daughter of Abraham, has much to teach us in her infirmity — her graceful endurance, her faithful waiting, and her response to the burden of her life and her release. She teaches us about overcoming servitude and a crushing daily grind. There is a marvelous story from the Native American Mandan people that weaves together the themes of heavy work, of trees and birds, of shared survival, and of song that praises; the story also speaks of the freeing of all those who are around a person who learns what it really means to be free. The Mandan people were bound to the grasslands and prairies, nomadic to a degree, gathering their food from the land. It was primarily women's work, backbreaking, daily, and done no matter the season or the weather. It was a necessity for survival. A version of this story called "The First Basket" appears in a book of Native American stories collected by Joseph Bruchac and Michael Canuto.[2] I have heard it in various versions among other

---

2. Joseph Bruchac and Michael Canuto, *Keepers of Life* (Golden, Colo.: Fulcrum Publishing, 1994), 149–50.

peoples and include some other details, but basically it is the story in Bruchac and Canuto's collection:

Once upon a time, long ago when life was hard, but life was sweet, there came a time when just finding enough food seemed a heavy burden. It fell to the women, who would go forth from their villages early in the morning while it was still dark to forage and look for roots, berries, herbs, and plants that they could cook and eat. They dug for roots, picked berries, and collected nuts and plants, leaves and stems, but it was always difficult to carry what they found back to their tents. They tried large leaves, pieces of cloth, the bottoms of their skirts, pieces of bark from trees, but none worked well.

One day, a woman who was weary from all the walking and gathering sat down to rest under a sprawling cedar tree. She dozed and was awakened by the sound of birds. She looked up and high above her in the branches she saw two birds building a nest, with scraps of twigs and leaves, string and moss. She smiled as she watched them work. She was still in a state of being half-asleep and half-awake and realized that the tree that she was leaning up against that was easing her sore and tired back was speaking to her. It was saying: Watch the birds. They are building nests, small dwellings for their little ones. That is what you need to do — build nests to carry and hold what you find and collect in your hunt for food. I will help you. Take your digging stick and go out to the edge of my branches and dig. You will find roots that are tough and sinewy yet slender and pliable. Weave them together like the birds in their nest-making. My roots will help you carry your load and make your burden lighter.

The woman was wide awake. Of course it would work! She dug, found the slender, strong roots, and worked them together, plaiting them like her hair as she had seen in her dream, making them into the shape of a bird's nest. She remembered that she should give thanks for such a gift and took corn and a piece of her own hair and buried them in the ground, covering up the hole and blessing the cedar tree for sharing its dream, its idea for the basket. The basket was perfect, light and strong. It would carry many nuts, seeds, roots, and plants. Then she went to work gathering roots and herbs, acorns and seeds. Soon her basket was overflowing. She stooped to lift it and found how heavy it was. She groaned under its weight and was soon crying in frustration and exhaustion.

This time it was the cedar basket that spoke to her. Do not weep woman, it said. Didn't my mother tell you that she would help you ease your work and that this would be a good thing? Pick up the basket and let it rest on your shoulder. If you will sing while you carry it, then I the basket will carry your load for you. The sound of your song will remind me of the birds' happiness and I will bear your burden for you. The woman obeyed and lifted the basket and began to sing. The basket was lighter! She stood straight and returned to her village singing. From a long way off the other women heard the song and came out to see who sang and what this new song meant. After all, they could never remember any woman returning in song from working all day on the prairie.

They saw the woman and this new thing, her basket. And in response to their questions she told them of the cedar tree's dream and her observation of the birds, and how the tree taught her to make the basket of its own roots, and how the basket itself told her to sing and it would remember its old home and would carry the burden while the woman walked. All of them begged her to show them how to make this thing. Soon all the women had their own baskets, differing sizes, shapes, depths, each with its own signature and style, though all in the form of the birds' nest, woven of roots and now reeds and strong stems. And now when they returned from working all day, they seemed to stride across the prairies with strong steps. They all sang as they came home with their burden that was light, food for their families and neighbors. They all gave thanks in their own lodges for such a marvelous gift from the cedar people.

But one day when a woman was out foraging she came upon a cache that the Mouse People had stored for the hard months ahead. She could not believe her good fortune, though in fact her response was an act of greed. And she stole from the Mouse People everything that they had collected for their families, all the seeds, beans, nuts, and plants. She left them nothing and gleefully returned carrying their food. She had broken the Mandan People's unwritten covenant with the Mouse People. You were allowed to take some of the Mouse People's food, but you must leave some behind — otherwise they would starve, and it was not right that others, any of your relations, should suffer because of your greed and laziness. But this woman left them nothing. In the tall flowering grasses of autumn the Mouse People were crying. Their granary had been found, invaded, and emptied out. They would starve. All their hard work had been destroyed by one greedy woman. But the woman didn't even notice them. She was off on her way thinking of what she'd do with all this store of food.

The woman had been thinking of what to do with her full basket, and she forgot to sing as she carried the basket on her shoulders. When the basket grew very heavy, she tried to sing, but she found that she couldn't remember the song that would ease her burden and let the basket carry the load. Exhausted, she put the basket down, and then found she couldn't pick it up. It was too heavy. She tried to remember the song, sitting down to think, but nothing came. She then tried picking up the basket again, but she could not move it. Then she grew impatient and angry and kicked the basket but it would not move and would not lift her burden or help her with her load. The woman cursed the basket, but the basket did not move and did not speak again. The song was gone.

The woman had forgotten the gift of the cedar tree and how it gave of itself to help the women with their burdens. The woman had stolen from another and added to the burden of those who already had worked hard. The basket would have no part in her stealing from those smaller and weaker than her. Finally the woman had to empty the basket — until it was less than half full. Then she could lift it. She was still angry at having to leave behind all those seeds and nuts, such good food. She thought, Maybe I can mark the place and return with my basket again tomorrow. But the Mouse People quickly discovered their food and hid it well so that she could not steal from them again. When she returned, there was no trace of any of the food. And ever since that time, all the baskets have refused to help the people. The song was lost, and now people must carry their burdens without help from the baskets. What a pity! So much was lost because of one person's greed.

Jesus is much like the cedar tree, offering the woman bent from long labor and suffering a dream, a vision, a hope. Jesus chooses to bend before her, before a woman, and that was radical in his day, breaking all the customs and accepted rules of behavior in synagogue and society. Like the limbs of a sheltering tree, he bends over one in need of rest, of Sabbath, of refreshment. He bends over one who had borne the burden of her society's injustice, one of the expendable, unnamed, uncounted, and disregarded ones. She had carried the cross for eighteen years, years of faithfulness and hanging on to the word of God that had been given to her people; hanging on to her tradition, though it was in rags and tatters, only a remnant of what it once was; hanging on to belief in a God who listened, who heard the cries of those in distress, and who would send someone to lift her up and give her cause to sing.

Like the woman, we have been given the good news of liberation: "Woman [and man], you are freed from your infirmity!" It is the wood of the cross, the bending of God before us, that has liberated us and set us free. We wonder what the woman, once freed, did with the next eighteen years of her life. And we wonder about ourselves: What are we going to do with the next eighteen years of our lives? What of all the bent-over men, women, and children of our world, still waiting for our words and presence in their lives that will announce the reality of their freedom? Are we prepared to become interruptions in the life of a society that refuses to acknowledge that many among us are not free, are not standing up straight, and are not singing for joy because the glory of God has visited them?

Since we have been talking about plants and weeds, mustard seeds and those who work in fields, perhaps it is apropos that we end with another image of nature, that of the flower named anemone. With the onslaught of spring on the west coast of northern California comes wind that batters and howls and beats down everything in its path. It is exhilarating, but after a while it becomes exhausting. The Pacific coast can begin to belie its name. Wendy Johnson, who works the gardens of the Green Gulch Farm in California — a Zen mountain retreat, meditation center, and monastery — has written about these anemones:

> "Only the winds of Spring," wrote Pliny the Elder, early in the first century, "can open the anemone." In the simplicity of

their petals sleeps an old mystery. Anemone flowers are called "daughters of the wind." Growing in the cool shade of wind-swept forests, they have a long association with sorrow and death. Greek legend describes the god Adonis dying on a bed of anemones, changing the pale white flowers to blood red. In early Christian symbolism, the anemone is linked with the crucifixion of Christ, and in Byzantine mosaics Jesus is shown standing in a windy field, surrounded by drifts of anemones.

Anemones have been in cultivation since antiquity, but they are ephemeral flowers. Grown from a black, claw-like mass of roots planted in the late autumn, the roots of the anemone pene-trate to the bottom of the garden, where death moans below the cultivated roots. Unvanquished, the anemones drink up death and rise out of the ruin of their own stalks and stems. The wreathed petals of the flower encircle an inner crown of dark stamen. Unique in the plant community, anemones bloom with startlingly blue clouds of pollen.[3]

In the Bible these flowers, anemones, are sometimes referred to as "lilies of the field." Jesus tells us that, like the birds of the air, the wild-flowers of the field are reminders that God cares for all his creatures and will "clothe us, people of little faith, with so much more" (Luke 12:27ff). We are not to worry. We are to seek rather the kingdom of God, and all else will be given to us. We are to

> not be afraid, little flock, for it has pleased your Father to give you the kingdom. Sell what you have, give alms. Get yourselves purses that do not wear out, and make safe investments with God, where no thief comes and no moth destroys. For where your investments are, there will your heart be also.
>
> (Luke 12:32–34)

Are our hearts grounded in the kingdom of freedom for all? Are our hearts, like the roots of the anemone, grounded "where death moans below"? Are we invested, with Jesus, in the remnants of the earth's people?

In his preaching, Jesus often quoted or alluded to a text from Isaiah, a text that puts our choice clearly:

---

3. Wendy Johnson, column in *Tricycle, A Buddhist Review* (spring 1997): 90–91.

If you remove from your midst the yoke,
the clenched fist and the wicked word,
if you share your food with the hungry
and give relief to the oppressed,
then your light will rise in the dark,
your night will be like noon.
Yahweh will guide you always
and give you relief in desert places.
He will strengthen your bones;
he will make you as a watered garden,
like a spring of water
whose waters never fail.
Your ancient ruins will be rebuilt,
the age-old foundations will be raised.
You will be called the Breach-mender,
and the Restorer of ruined houses.

If you stop profaning the Sabbath
and doing as you please on the holy day,
if you call the Sabbath a day of delight
and keep sacred Yahweh's holy day,
if you honor it by not going your own way,
not doing as you please . . . ,
then you will find happiness . . .
and you will feast joyfully. (Isa. 58:9b–15)

This story is foundational. The Sabbath was made for human beings. No law — no matter how holy it is considered, how traditional, or how long in practice — is allowed to be applied ever in such a way that it oppresses a human being. This is the pillar of God's law and the pillar of Jesus' kingdom of compassion and truth. Every law is to be broken, bent and molded so that it serves those most in need of the common good and the law's justice. In this case, the faithful daughter of the covenant must be released from bondage on the Sabbath so that she can truly praise God and keep the commandment to rest, to do no work, and to bless God for freedom and the chance to live without oppression and shame, without exclusion and suffering, if it lies in the realm of possibility and grace. This is foundational to any ritual or tradition of worship. This is, in fact, the worship that God finds most holy and acceptable — to lift up those bowed down and to straighten the backs of the bent, and if we cannot, then to bend with them, sharing their burden, picking up their cross and shouldering it awhile so that they might walk with a bit of ease and dignity. In Luke's gospel, when Jesus goes out carrying his cross, there is another who lifts that burden for him: "When they led Jesus away they seized Simon of Cyrene, who was coming in from the fields, and laid the cross on him to carry it behind Jesus" (Luke 23:26).

We are to bear one another's burdens, to relearn the songs that lighten loads and help others bear their sorrow and pain. And we are do to this with enduring grace, for eighteen years or more, and we are to do it singing! Let us end with a prayer, "A Prophecy of an Asian Woman," based on another woman's song of freedom, the Magnificat. It was given to me by a Japanese sister:

> All the broken hearts shall rejoice;
> all those who are heavy laden,
> whose eyes are tired and who do not see,
> shall be lifted up to meet with
> the Motherly Healer.
> The battered souls and bodies
> shall be healed;
> the hungry shall be fed;
> the imprisoned shall be free;
> all earthly children shall regain joy
> in the reign of the just and loving one
> coming for you, coming for me,
> in this time, in this world. Amen.

May all on earth know this in our presence on earth, for we have been freed and live now in the freedom of the children of God. We are those marked by the sign of the cross, marked by the wind of the Spirit, and marked by our bending before one another in devotion and reverence, so that all may rise and stand in the presence of God and sing.

FOUR

DAUGHTERS OF WISDOM

A God-Fearing Woman
and a Woman of Great Love

I T MAY SEEM STRANGE to put together these two stories, that of Susanna, a God-fearing woman whose story is told in the book of
Daniel, and that of an originally unnamed woman in Simon's house
whom Jesus describes as a woman of great love. But the stories and
the women themselves share many similarities.

The background of both stories is concerned with the presence and
power of a prophet in the midst of the people. Susanna is accused unjustly by elders in her community and is condemned to death. She
cries out to God, her last resort, and is answered when the young
prophet Daniel refuses to be a part of her death and uses a simple
questioning process to expose the lies and evil of the elders and to
vindicate Susanna's own truthfulness and fear of God. And in Luke's
story the entire chapter is about Jesus being a prophet who sees truly as
God sees. In this story set in Simon's house Jesus will use a parable —
simple and direct in its structure and questioning — to expose what is
hospitality, what is sin, and what is forgiveness and love, vindicating
the woman whom others look upon with disdain. Both stories involve
a reversal brought about by God's interfering in the situation and revealing the power of truth and justice already inherent in the people;
the exposure of evil and revelation of what is deeply hidden but true
nevertheless; a dividing and separating out with God taking obvious
sides. In both, justice is done; the truth is told; there is hope for the
future; and there is an awareness that God is present in every situation. In both, the presence of the prophet of God alters the outcome
and is a force that must be reckoned with, for it reveals a rift in the

universe where grace, mercy, and forgiveness rush in and transform reality.

One of the differences is that while Daniel is a young prophet and this is one of his first appearances in Israel, Jesus is *the* prophet of God, the fullness of truth who sees with the eye of God and whose very presence announces the good news of forgiveness and mercy as normative in society.

Susanna

The story of Susanna begins with a description of her. We are told that "there lived in Babylon a man named Joakim, who was married to a very beautiful God-fearing woman, Susanna, Hilkiah's daughter, whose pious parents had trained her in the law of Moses" (Dan. 13:1–3). This, then, is a story of people in exile in Babylon, awaiting return to Israel and struggling to live faithful to the covenant in an environment that is hostile to their belief, culture, and traditions, even their survival. But we are told in the next line that Joakim, Susanna's husband, is very wealthy and greatly respected, and their house and garden are places where the elders gather to discuss and dispute points of the law. The exile in Babylon was long, and some in Israel rose to places of power and influence, living well and adapting to the Babylonian lifestyle and culture while retaining their hope of return to their own homeland and obeying their own religious customs.

The story goes sour very quickly with the description of the two judges: "Wickedness has come forth from Babylon, through the elders appointed judges, who were supposed to govern the people" (v. 5). They are acquainted with Susanna because of their visits to her husband's garden. And they have already fallen low: "Forgetting the demands of justice and virtue, their lust grew all the more as they made no effort to turn their eyes to heaven" (v. 9). Each wallows in his lust, both possessed of the same passion. They are ashamed of their desire, but they continue watching her. Both individually plot to have their time alone with her, bump into each other, and share their common lust for her. They are described as so degenerate that now they both will approach her and seek to possess her. They bide their time and know exactly what they are going to say. They begin with a threat: "We desire to possess you. If you refuse to give in, we will testify that you sent your maids away for there was a young man here with you" (vv. 20b–21). This is a calculated set up. She is trapped.

Susanna knows she is caught in a dead-end, and she knows that if she refuses the men, it will mean her death. She clearly recognizes what is at stake, and she replies: "I would rather be persecuted than sin in the eyes of the Lord" (v. 23). This is followed by yelling, shrieking, people running back and forth, accusations put forward, and dismay. We are told even the servants are "taken aback" by the elders' accusations, because they had never heard anything like this said about Susanna before.

Things move quickly. The next day there is a meeting at the house, and now the two elders are "vindictively determined to have Susanna sentenced to death." She is sent for and arrives with her husband, parents, children, relatives, and neighbors. She is veiled but is forced by the elders to unveil, and then they have the gall to lay hands on her head. But Susanna, we are told, is "completely trusting in the Lord; she raised her tearful eyes to heaven." They tell their fabricated story of seeing her with a young man and raising the alarm, trying to catch him, but he escaped, and so they caught her and asked her who he was, and she refused to answer. They end with: "This is our statement, and we testify to its truth" (v. 41).

The assembly takes their word, and Susanna is condemned to death. This is the law, an extension of a society in which the word of a man, especially an elder, took precedence over the word of a woman. Susanna has no recourse under the law and so turns to God, her last and only resort. She prays aloud: "She cried aloud, 'Eternal God, nothing is hidden from you; you know all things before they come to be. You know that these men have testified falsely against me. Would you let me die, though I am not guilty of all their malicious charges?'" (vv. 42–43).

That is all she prays. In her prayer Susanna sounds much like Abraham in his words with God when he seeks to intervene on behalf of the people of Sodom and Gomorrah. Abraham prays: "Will you really let the just perish with the wicked? . . . It would not be at all like you to do such a thing, and you can't let the good perish with the wicked, nor treat the good and the wicked alike. Far be it from you! Will not the judge of all the earth be just?" (Gen. 18:23, 25).

This is the tradition: God does not allow the people of earth to practice injustice with impunity. This just God, we are told, hears Susanna's prayer: the cry of the poor, the innocent unjustly accused, the one persecuted for righteousness. And on the way to Susanna's execution, Daniel appears and loudly refuses to participate in her death. Daniel is a wedge driven into the process of death. He boldly speaks to the people: "Standing in their midst, he said to them, 'Have you become fools, you Israelites, to condemn a daughter of Israel without due process and in the absence of clear evidence? Return to court, for those men have testified falsely against her' " (vv. 13:48–49). In response, the people return with Daniel to court. They separate the elders so that Daniel can question each of them and catch them in their lies. Daniel's ruse is deceptively simple: "If you really witnessed the crime, under what tree did you see them do it?" The first one answers, "Under a mastic tree," and the second one answers, "Under an oak." They have fallen over their own words and have revealed a discrepancy in their testimonies. Daniel has prefaced each interrogation with a condemnation of their behavior, of their lies, and of what they had become long before they approached Susanna. And both times Daniel speaks on Susanna's behalf, describing her as an innocent and just woman who will not be put to death and as a daughter of Judah who would not tolerate the elders' wickedness.

The community then turns against the elders, and they are condemned to death, convicted by the word of their own mouths (v. 61). "In accordance with Moses' law, the penalty the two elders had intended to impose upon their neighbor was inflicted upon them. They were sentenced to death" (v. 62). In a sense this is the epitome of Jewish justice as recorded in the Torah, that of "an eye for an eye." It vindicates the just yet is not vindictive. And the story seems to end happily ever after.

> Thus was the life of an innocent woman spared that day. Hilkiah and his wife praised God for the justice given Susanna, and so did Joakim her husband and all her relatives, for she was not found guilty of any shameful deed. Daniel was greatly esteemed by the people from that day onward. (vv. 62b–64)

Both Susanna and Daniel, then, are models of life for the people in exile. They are teachers, a woman and a man who exhibit the characteristics and virtues necessary for survival in an alien environment and who continue to pass on their faith to their children and generations to follow.

Susanna is known and remembered for her resistance to evil, for her steadfast trust in God in the face of persecution, and for her prayer to the God of justice who hears the cry of the innocent and poor. She is holy according to the covenant and her community. She is the living Torah in the community and carries the oral and written tradition within her person. Her presence reminds the people of God's faithfulness to them and his promises for the future. Susanna validates the people's faith. Daniel is her backup, God's witness to her witness of life. It is Susanna who has judged rightly, who is the elder in the faith, to be looked up to, honored, and respected as a true believer. She is a daughter of Israel who is faithful to the God of the covenant.

And Daniel is the prophet of God who defends her and teaches the people how to resist evil by imitating Susanna in her goodness and God-fearing behavior and prayer. The prophet is concerned with three things: the honor of God, the coming of justice, and the care of the poor. In reality these three issues are one — single-hearted worship of God and obedience. This involves loving only the one true God with all your heart and soul and mind and strength and loving others with the same. This is loving much. And Susanna, her family, relatives, and neighbors are grateful for God's remembrance of them and his keeping them in his justice. Susanna and her relationship with the Holy One are the focuses of the story. She who fears God loves much.

Susanna has learned what Hildegard of Bingen will sing about thousands of years later when she writes of God:

I, God, am in your midst.
Whoever knows me can never fall.
Not in the height, nor in the depth, nor in the breadth.
For I am love, that the vast expanses of evil can never still.

A Woman of Great Love

Now we move to the gospel of Luke and another story of a woman accused of "being a sinner" by someone in authority. Jesus defends her honor and behavior so that she is revealed as one to be imitated and learned from because of her actions. The background of the chapter is crucial, for this is the last in a group of stories. It begins with elders of the community in Capernaum coming to Jesus and asking him to intervene on behalf of a foreigner who has been good to them. This man is a captain, a Roman who built a synagogue for them. He is described as loving "our people" (Luke 7:5).

Jesus responds to this man's love for the people by healing his servant from a distance, and Jesus' admiration for the man's depth of faith and obedience is publicly proclaimed: "I say to you, not even in Israel have I found such great faith" (Luke 7:9). Jesus continues on his way from Capernaum to Naim and at the gates of the city is moved to deep compassion for the plight of the widow whose only son is being buried. He raises him from the dead and gives him back to his mother — a story with parallels to that of Elijah the prophet raising from the dead the child of the woman who befriended him and fed him in exile.

In 1 Kings 17 the story is told of how God listens to Elijah's pleading and gives breath back to the child. "Elijah then took the child and brought him down from the upper room. He gave him to his mother and said, 'See, your son is alive.'" The woman's response confirms Elijah's identity and mission. She replies: "Now I am certain that you are a man of God, and that your words really came from Yahweh" (1 Kings 17:23–24).

This too is the story of an outsider whose faith is greater than those in Israel. And the widow of Naim is a nobody, just another widow in Israel who is given an extension of life in the life of her only child. By law, an only son was required to care for his widowed mother until he was thirty years of age. Without him, she would be left without kin, without a place of security or respect within the community. She would have to fend for herself and most likely be sold into servitude or die begging among the tombs if no one would take her into his home. Jesus in raising her son from the dead gives both of them life. When the people witness what Jesus has done, their reaction is expressed in terms of the presence of a prophet in Israel: "A holy fear came over them all and they praised God saying, 'A great prophet has appeared among us; God has visited his people'" (Luke 7:16).

The people are not described as fearing God because of Jesus' deeds. Susanna, however, is described as God-fearing, and this characteristic is at her very core, not just a momentary occurrence because of a specific deed. The people of Israel experience this fear of God when Daniel's ruse keeps her from execution and turns the tables on the evil elders. Such fear is a mixture of awe, wonder, and unsurety, and it causes the question to arise: Who is this man?

Jesus is approached by John the Baptist's followers while John is in jail with the question: "Are you the one we are expecting, or should we wait for another?" (Luke 9:19). John is the herald of the coming prophet, the Messiah, but Jesus is not behaving in the same tradition as the earlier prophets in many regards. And yet Jesus' answer to John is couched in words of the prophet Isaiah: "Go back and tell John what you have seen and heard; the blind see again, the lame walk, lepers are made clean, the deaf hear, the dead are raised to life and the poor are given good news. Now, listen: Fortunate are those who encounter me, but not for their downfall" (Luke 9:22–23). This echoes Simeon the prophet's words to Mary about the child Jesus when he is brought to the temple in Jerusalem to fulfill the law. The prophecy was spoken: "See him; he will be for the rise or fall of the multitudes of Israel. He shall stand as a sign of contradiction, while a sword will pierce your own soul. Then the secret thoughts of many may be brought to light" (Luke 2:34–35). Jesus is this sign of contradiction, of questioning, and of disorientation in the nation; he is an interruption, a visit from God. He is a prophet.

This theme of prophets and their relation to wisdom arises in the line that precedes our story. Jesus says: "But the children of Wisdom always recognize her work" (Luke 7:35). Jesus is commending those who repent and come to listen to his words — the words of a prophet — as children of Wisdom.

The book of Wisdom is all about the just ones, about seeing rightly, and about abiding in the justice of God in the face of persecution. The book begins with the words: "Love justice, you who rule over the world. Think rightly of God, seek him with simplicity of heart, for he reveals himself to those who do not challenge him and is found by those who do not distrust him" (Wisd. 1:1–2).

The wise and the children of Wisdom are contrasted with evil-doers and the godless whose thinking is perverse and wicked, cold-bloodedly so. They are described with horror:

> Let everyone take part in our orgy; let us post everywhere the signs of our joy, for that is our due, the lot assigned to us.
>
> Let us oppress the upright man who is poor, and have no thought for the widow, or respect for the white hair of old age.

Let our strength be our right, since it is proved that weakness is useless. Let us set a trap for the righteous, for he annoys us and opposes our way of life; he reproaches us for our breaches of the law and accuses us of being false to our upbringing.

He claims knowledge of God and calls himself son of the Lord. He has become a reproach to our way of thinking; even to meet him is burdensome to us. He does not live like others and behaves strangely.

According to him we have low standards, so he keeps aloof from us as if we were unclean. He emphasizes the happy end of the righteous and boasts of having God as father. (Wisd. 2:9–16)

The text continues with descriptions of the evildoers' intent to torture, humble, and inflict pain on the one who believes and stands fast, to test and ascertain whether God is with him. It could easily be a description of Susanna and her persecutors, the two elders who have become godless in their designs and deeds. And, of course, it is a description of what the nation's leaders will do to Jesus when they seek false witnesses against him and have him condemned to death in collusion with Rome. The next chapter goes on to encourage those who are just and who die: "Those who trust in him will penetrate the truth, those who are faithful will live with him in love, for his grace and mercy are for his chosen ones" (Wisd. 3:9). This too describes Susanna and those who imitate her life, and as we will see, it is a marvelous description of the woman in Simon's house who comes to the banquet uninvited but seeking to express her gratitude to Jesus, the prophet.

Prophets are about change, change that is not an option, but absolutely essential and necessary. Their very appearance announces that things must change, that things are intolerable to God, and that life among the people of God has reached a level that is lacking in integrity and is an insult to the God of justice and truth. They are, generally speaking, adamant, definitive, sure of themselves, and forthright in their conversations and their attempts to make the blind see in regard to sin and its effects on others.

They perceive reality not as others see it, and certainly not as those who are in authority or power perceive it, but from the vantage point of the eye and heart of God, which is wisdom. Their primary concern is the will of God and that it be obeyed, and the will of God is very specific: honor God, care for the poor, and make sure that justice is done.

Prophets are in love with God, with God's justice and mercy, with God's passion and truth, with God's compassion and unrelenting pursuit of us in word, deed of history, and presence. Their sight blinds us and reveals our dimness and blurred focus and insensitivity to suffering and our capacity to ignore our own sin while highlighting that of others. They are merciless with the truth and merciful beyond imagining with God's forgiveness, peace, and reconciliation.

A Jewish story, a Hasidic tale called "The Judgment of the Messiah," pulls many of these ideas together and tries to make us see differently than our usual ways. It is a glimpse of the way Daniel sees and a long glance at the way Jesus sees:

> Once upon a time there was a young man of marriageable age who loved the study of the Torah. He had gone off from home at an early age and had studied with the Great Maggid, pouring over the word, the commentaries, the Midrash, and steeping himself in the conversation and company of those whose life was the understanding of God's word. That was his life, and he was not really interested in marrying, but it was expected, even required of him, and he was brought before the tribunal and pledged to a woman of his town. It was witnessed, and there was rejoicing among the families. He gave his word that he would honor her and stay at home and be a good husband.
>
> Time passed and the love for the Torah overcame him again. He spent more and more time studying, finding books to borrow, and cornering people to talk about the scriptures. Finally, he ran away from home, leaving his wife behind, but he was once again taken from the company of those in the study house and returned to his wife. This time it was his father-in-law, not his own father, who instructed him in the law and his responsibilities to his wife and family to come. He pledged again that he would stay. He did, for a time, and they had children: two, three. He worked hard, but spent his nights praying and studying, falling asleep during the day from exhaustion. His real life was his love of the Torah.
>
> Finally in desperation his wife approached the judge and declared grounds for divorce. She was in need of the basic ne-

cessities of life. He just spent too much time studying instead of working in these hard times. His first duty was to his family, and his pledge could not be trusted. The divorce was granted according to the law. This left the poor man with nothing, his family with the house, land, harvest, savings, and so on. And the woman married again, going on with her life. But the man had no way to live, no food or place to stay. It was winter, and he soon died of starvation and cold.

Now, the story goes that when the Messiah comes, justice will be done! And this man who loved the word and the wisdom of the Lord will ask that justice be done toward his own father, his father-in-law, his wife, the judge, the tribunal, and the towns-people who let him die. And the Messiah will gather them all together and call them to defend their behavior that resulted in the man's suffering and death. The father will use scripture to defend his case that a man must leave his family and cleave to his wife, and they are to be fruitful and multiply in obedience to the will of God. And he will be vindicated. Then the father-in-law will defend his case with the tradition of the community that exhorts the in-laws to intervene and do all that is possible to keep a family together, even threatening and bribing the one who is lax in his duties. And he will be vindicated. And the wife will come before the Lord and defend her case by calling on God to witness that she was responsible for the children's welfare and that the demand to provide for one's children required that she divorce him. And she will be vindicated. And the judge will be called to state his reasons, and he will appeal to the word of a rabbi, who will quote the word of the law and its commentaries. And he will be vindicated. And the people will come before the Judge of all the Earth and be questioned on why they were not generous in sharing their resources to keep the man alive, and they will appeal to their own families' needs in a hard time and to the fact that they gave to others in more desperate situations, and they will be vindicated.

And lastly the man himself will be brought to defend himself before the Lord and all the people, and he will be asked why he gave his pledge repeatedly and did not in the end honor it, al-ways leaving again and again to return to the study of the Torah. And he will have no defense, no appeal, and no one to back up the reasoning for his behavior. He will, at first, keep saying: "You don't understand. I had to. I had no choice. I had to study the Torah. I just had to." And then he will fall silent and stand there weeping. And then the Lord of the Universe will make the judgment upon his behavior. All will be justified by their own words, defense, the law, the word of others that had more authority, the community's need, and even what was the common good and expected. But the man who broke his pledge will have no justification.

But the Master of the Universe will watch while the Messiah will run to the man and embrace him warmly and hold on to him declaring for all to hear: "This is why I have come! I have come for those who have no defense, no appeal, and no justification. I am their hope, their savior, and their defense!" And indeed, the Messiah will have come.

This is the picture of Jesus that is developing prior to the story that takes place in Simon's house. And the above parable that throws us off-guard is nothing in comparison with Jesus' words, deeds, and very presence that are the parable of God's forgiveness, liberation, and mercy. Jesus has been fulfilling the claims he had made: he has been healing, raising the dead to life, preaching good news, giving sight to those who are blind to the presence of God among them, and drawing back into the embrace of the community those who have been exiled by sin and lifestyle. Now Jesus the parable of God will use a parable to try to open the eyes of Simon the Pharisee.

The setting is a dinner party. Jesus has been invited to Simon's home to share a meal, and he is reclining on a sofa as he eats. So many of Luke's stories about forgiveness, healing, and hope take place at meals, and all are bound in some intimate way with the feast of forgiveness, the Eucharist, the banquet of mercy. It is a public meal, not unusual. The wealthy would often invite a teacher or a person of some note to a meal for a chance to have a conversation, to ask questions, and to be seen in his company. It could be a gracious encounter, an awkward jousting, or a setup. From the discussion that ensues between Jesus and Simon it appears that the meeting is an attempt on Simon's part to watch Jesus at close range so he can decide for himself who Jesus is and whether he will listen to him. As Barbara Reid comments on the scene: "The issue is how one evaluates what one sees and hears concerning Jesus: does it draw you to faith in him, or do you take offense?"[1] The story begins at a fast pace:

> One of the Pharisees asked Jesus to share his meal, so he went to the Pharisee's home and as usual reclined on the sofa to eat. And it happened that a woman of this town, who was known as a sinner, heard that he was in the Pharisee's house. She brought a precious jar of perfume and stood behind him at his feet, weeping. She wet his feet with tears, she dried them with her hair and kissed his feet and poured the perfume on them. (Luke 7:36–38)

Dinner is interrupted by an uninvited guest! But, again, this is not unusual. The wealthy often made space for those not invited at their public dinners. The food and the formal dining area would have been in a courtyard of a large house, and there would have been space around the tables for on-lookers, the curious, disciples, and opponents to listen and afterward eat the leftover food. It would have been public knowledge that Jesus was invited, and many obviously cared to see the teacher-prophet, to see what he would do and what Simon would do as well. The woman enters and goes straight to Jesus. She is single-minded and single-hearted.

She has heard that Jesus is there and knows of him. In fact, there is the sense that she has encountered him before. She does not care what people think of her or what she is doing. She sees only Jesus and goes straight to him. She is wealthy and has brought a jar of perfume to use on Jesus' feet. But when she finds herself behind him, at his feet, she begins to weep. Next, she bends with her head over his feet and dries the tears on his feet with her long hair. She kisses his feet, wetting them again, and pours the ointment on them, leaving the ointment to dry on his feet and perfume the whole courtyard and outlying rooms of the house. It must have been an awkward couple of minutes — people gaping at her in disbelief, in horror, tongues waiting to wag, with murmurs and gestures of disgust, with shock and perhaps even admiration for her boldness.

We are told nothing of Jesus' reaction. He remains reclining on the sofa and lets her weep and dry his feet with her hair and pour the oil over them. He makes no gesture of offense or rejection or distaste. But

---

1. Barbara E. Reid, *Choosing the Better Part: Women in the Gospel of Luke* (Collegeville, Minn.: Liturgical Press, 1996), 109.

one thing we know for sure is that he looked at her; he gazed at her with intensity and acceptance. We know this from what follows and the words he uses to speak about her to Simon.

And the reaction is immediate. In the very beginning we are told that this woman "was known as a sinner." In other translations she is called a sinful woman in the city, or sometimes a public sinner, all of which are terms loaded with insinuations. Later even Jesus will describe her as one who has many sins, and she is therefore presumed to be known as such in the city. Remember Jesus has been accused of consorting with public sinners, his own behavior labeled as wanton and excessive, like her own actions right now. The heart of the issue is found in Simon's own mind and heart. His thoughts, kept to himself, must be showing on his face: "The Pharisee who had invited Jesus was watching and thought, 'If this man were a prophet, he would know what sort of person is touching him; isn't this woman a sinner?'"

Simon's judgment is swift, using her presence and behavior and Jesus' apparent acceptance of her touch and expression of reverence as disavowing any worth to either of them. He is merely witnessing the encounter between a sinner and a false prophet or teacher. What the rumors say is true: he consorts with public sinners and is friend to them, eating and drinking in their company, careless of the law. His reasoning follows the pattern: see the sinner, assume the sin, judge the sinner, dismiss the sinner and anyone who would associate with her, condemn them and turn away in disgust, and seek to keep oneself pure by avoiding contact with them. He is wise to be wary, to perform only the bare civilities. Now he can extract himself from the company and have good reasons to denigrate Jesus' person. The woman has been helpful in showing Jesus for what he really is.

But there are two things worth mentioning about the woman, because they can make us think twice about who she might be. Barbara Reid has something very crucial to say about the woman's condition of sinfulness. She writes:

> Verse 37 does clearly say the woman was a sinner, but the imperfect verb *en* has the connotation "used to be"; she is no longer the sinner she once was. That she had been forgiven before this dinner party is clear from verse 47. How or when the woman's sins were forgiven is not narrated. In verse 47 the perfect tense

of the verb *apheontai,* "have been forgiven," expresses a past action whose effects endure into the present.[2]

The woman's actions follow on her forgiveness. They are a response to what she has already experienced from Jesus. In a word, they are an expression of thanksgiving, of overwhelming gratitude for what has been given to her and what she has known from Jesus already. She has been forgiven, radically changed, and she is no longer what she was. She is something new altogether.

The way the woman approaches Jesus shows that she reverences him as one worthy of great respect and honor. In many cultures today kissing is acceptable, especially in ritual situations or when entering a house, even if you do not know the hosts well. It is done on one cheek or on both cheeks. But to kiss someone's hands is more telling. It is a sign of humility, of respect, and of the person's authority, power, even holiness, and your own acceptance of and relation to that power. And to kiss someone's feet in certain cultures is the highest form of offering honor and reverence. It is a ritual act of submission, of welcome, of belonging in some way to that person or what that person does or stands for.

I will never forget working in a poor parish during Holy Week in a valley in California. The parish was primarily made up of migrant families, all illegals who were being hounded by the Immigration and Naturalization Service and preyed upon by other groups. But they were devout, kind, generous people trying to work and raise their families and live with integrity and dignity. I was an outsider, and all during the week at the services, talks, and prayers I was acutely conscious of being a guest, though I was the one giving the talks, pulling the prayer services and the rituals together, and often leading the prayers. Many of the people were new to the United States and to the ways we do the Holy Week liturgies, specifically the Holy Thursday liturgy of the washing of the feet.

After many meetings we decided to do the traditional Mexican version of the stations of the cross in the streets of the town, coming back to the church for the rest of the service of the Word and the honoring of the cross, as they had always celebrated it. But we would do the Holy Thursday celebration the way it was often done in parishes in

2. Ibid., 113.

California, both Anglo and Hispanic. And so members of the community, men and women, young and old, were chosen to have their feet washed.

Choosing the people was the easy part. It was obvious who were the leaders, beginning with an old woman, whose name was, believe it or not, Sophia. She was ninety-one and had prepared the church for every service since she had come to the States six years earlier. Getting Sophia to agree to have her feet washed, however, proved to be nearly impossible. Finally, it was decided that the only way to convince her was to have the pastor order her to do it, leading the way for the others to follow in her wake. At last, she agreed, though obviously not at ease with being in the sanctuary during the liturgy and having her feet washed first. The pastor knew her though and carried it off with grace, even bending to kiss her feet in respect and thankfulness for all she was for the parish. Sophia accepted having her feet washed, dried, and kissed stoically, never moving a muscle on her face.

The rest of the service went back and forth with Mexican and U.S. traditions, language, and symbols mixed. And finally we neared the end of the Easter Vigil. The kiss of peace had been saved for the last, after Communion, when the newly baptized could be welcomed by the community. The pastor said the words, inviting people to give one another the kiss of peace, and after embracing the deacons, he came down the steps to Sophia in the front row, who was glowing by this time. He took her hands in his and kissed them, and she immediately took his hands in her gnarled brown hands and bent to kiss them. Then she turned to me, standing beside her, and there was a long, awkward moment when everyone waited and watched to see what would happen next. Whatever she would do would decide for the whole community.

I didn't see it coming. The tears were running down her face, and before I could stop her she was down on her knees, kissing my feet and murmuring her gratitude through her tears. We were both in tears as I lifted her up. She was tiny, thin, delicate, but tough. Then, when she was on her feet again, she took me by the hand and brought me to each of the leaders to kiss their hands, while everyone in the church applauded.

In our long talk afterward what stood out for her was the power of having her feet kissed. It was not so much the washing as the touch of lips on the skin of her weary feet that destroyed, she said, any resis-

tance that was in her and unleashed a sea of gratitude at the greatness
of God, who bent before his friends.

This is what the woman who had been a sinner is doing with Jesus.
This is what Jesus sees, as opposed to what Simon thinks he sees.
Simon is blind to the woman's gratitude, reverence, and honoring of
Jesus. He sees it as vile, base, and in bad taste.

The other important note in regard to the woman's past has to
do with what was considered sinful according to the laws of Israel.
First, any prolonged contact with outsiders, with Gentiles, anyone who
wasn't Jewish, was considered sinful. If one's work and livelihood demanded such contact, then it was likely one would be cast as a sinner.
The duties of midwives, weavers, dyers, tentmakers, musicians, and
others that entailed economic or professional encounters with Gentiles made them known sinners, persons who were consistently lax in
obeying the law.

Israel was occupied territory, oppressed harshly by its Roman oc-
cupants, who despised the Israelites as a whole, dealing only with
individuals who usually curried favor and were considered traitors by
their own people. Many people who were considered sinners were
merely poor, destitute, and caught in structures of oppression, like
slavery and prostitution, which were not chosen but forced upon huge
groups of people at the bottom of the social ladder by necessity, violence, and the need to survive. A woman theologian from Brazil
wrote an essay on this segment of Luke's gospel called "Jesus, the
Penitent Woman, and the Pharisee." Someone gave me a copy, unfortunately torn out of the journal it appeared in. The theologian's name
is Tereza Cavalcanti, and her article deals with this woman in fasci-
nating ways. She states that being a prostitute in the ancient world was
often the result of political and sociological factors. Prostitutes could
be slaves, daughters sold or rented out by their parents, wives rented
out by their husbands, poor women, divorced women, widows, single
mothers, prisoners of war or of pirates, women bought by soldiers, and
so on. They and other downtrodden persons were precisely those who
both heard the good news and, being poor, took it to heart more than
the better off, who found it more disconcerting than liberating. Jesus
proclaims that the seats in his kingdom will be given on a first-come
basis and that these downtrodden folk will be given precedence over
the priests and Pharisees (Matt. 21:31).

So even if the woman was "that kind of woman," she no longer is, and Jesus sees her and her heart and her gratitude to him for what they are, and there is no judgment of her. She remains standing there, and Jesus turns to say something to Simon. She becomes the context, the parentheses, around his discourse with Simon.

> "Simon, I have something to ask you." He answered, "Speak, master." And Jesus said, "Two people were in debt to the same creditor. One owed him five hundred silver coins, and the other fifty. As they were unable to pay him back, he graciously canceled the debts of both. Now, which of them will love him more?" (Luke 7:40–42)

It may seem strange to tell a story about debts, money, creditors and in the same breath ask about love. But Simon is thinking in just these terms. Sin is a debt that is forgiven, according to the law, through sacrifice, tithing, and almsgiving — in terms of money. Jesus knows exactly how to talk to Simon, and Simon walks right into the trap and answers Jesus' question correctly, as Jesus expected him to:

> Simon answered, "The one, I suppose, who was forgiven more." And Jesus said, "You are right." And turning toward the woman, he said to Simon, "Do you see this woman? You gave me no water for my feet when I entered your house, but she has washed my feet with her tears and dried them with her hair. You didn't welcome me with a kiss, but she has not stopped kissing my feet since she came in. You provided no oil for my head, but she has poured perfume on my feet. This is why, I tell you, her sins, her many sins, are forgiven, because of her great love. But the one who is forgiven little, has little love." (Luke 7:43–47)

Jesus then turns his back on Simon to face the woman while asking Simon, "Do you see this woman?" There is no time for a response because the answer is no — Simon does not see her. He sees what he has always seen, wants to see, just as he does with Jesus, with religion, with the law, and with God.

Simon has assumed her sin. Now Jesus honestly lists Simon's sins: no water, no kiss, no oil, no hospitality, no honesty, no concern for his well-being or respect for his person. Even in Jewish society this would have been a severe breach of custom and of what was expected of a host, especially of a Pharisee. She has made up for his lack generously. She has paid his debt for his failure to observe the laws. She is held up as a model for him to see, to watch, and to imitate, and perhaps she could also teach him about love, about gratitude, and about how to change.

Her sins are behind her. Now she stands behind Jesus and at his feet. She is his disciple, publicly proclaiming her allegiance and her joy at being called to change and repent. Her debt was great, and now so are her gratitude and love. Simon's debt is great too, but he cannot see that because there is no space in him for mercy, for forgiveness, or for wisdom.

Jesus has made his appeal to Simon. Now it is left to him to decide whether or not to see, to repent, to acknowledge his own great lack and debt, and to open a place inside himself where God's goodness can enter. Jesus, now facing the woman who is still kissing his feet, speaks to her alone: "Then Jesus said to the woman, 'Your sins are forgiven.' The others sitting with him at the table began to wonder, 'Now this man claims to forgive sins!' But Jesus again spoke to the woman, 'Your faith has saved you; go in peace.' "

Joachim Jeremias in his book on the parables has said that to kiss a person's feet was to acknowledge that this person had saved you from death, from servitude and oppression, literally saved your life. This is what Jesus has done for the woman. She is forgiven, pardoned, and she responds in love. Jesus' words come as a shock to everyone around him, including the Pharisee Simon. We are back once again to the issue of the chapter in Luke: Who is this man? Is he a prophet? Has God visited his people? Are his words true? Can he really forgive sin and raise people from the dead?

Jesus tells the woman to go in peace. In some translations it is better put: "Arise and go in peace." She has known the power of his presence and grace. She has been accepted into his community. She lives now, in the liturgical words, "no longer for herself alone, but hidden with Christ in God," and her life is to be lived in faith and in peace. He has responded to her with mercy, as generously given and shared with her as her perfume was lavished on him. They have exchanged gifts.

In earlier stories of the prophets, mercy (*hesed* in Hebrew) is the overwhelming characteristic of God, who hears and sees the suffering of those who are condemned on earth by other human beings. God is a God of justice for those who truly are sinners: those steeped in evil and adamant in their sin, lying to themselves, to others, and even to God, and doing harm to others, especially if they do it and think themselves religious. But God is a God of mercy and tenderness to those who once were sinners but who now are forgiven, repentant, and healed. Simon is being invited to show mercy, like God, to this woman. Jesus is trying to open his eyes to the reality of compassion — of concern for another's pain and struggle, of solidarity with another who has been harmed but who is worthy of respect and being looked at with love. This is Jesus' year of favor, the year of mercy from the Lord. Jesus is telling Simon to look at the woman so that he can get a glimpse of that mercy and favor and what it looks like in another's actions.

The woman is a child of Wisdom. She sees and knows Jesus as Jesus sees and knows her. She is a disciple, a believer in his word.

This is important. Jesus sends her off in peace, with a blessing for her new life. What follows in the next lines is the description of women who followed Jesus and their response to Jesus' presence in the world:

> Jesus walked though towns and countryside, preaching and giv-ing the good news of the kingdom of God. The Twelve followed him, and also some women who had been healed of evil spir-its and diseases: Mary called Magdalene, who had been freed of seven demons; Joanna, wife of Chuza, Herod's steward; Suzanna and others who provided for them out of their own funds. (Luke 8:1–3)

This is testimony to the reality of women disciples who traveled with Jesus and provided for his needs and those of his other male dis-ciples. The women were converted to the good news and put their resources at the service of the preaching and teaching of the gos-pel. All three of the women are named here, one associated with a town, Magdala, and described as healed of seven evil spirits. Seven is a whole number used to describe enormity or depth, wholeness. It can, in this context, mean she was healed of a terribly serious illness and also can mean that she is now sevenfold converted and responsive to Jesus' call. Joanna's husband, Chuza, is described as Herod's stew-ard, telling us that she is wealthy herself or has access to a good deal of money, influence, and power. Suzanna, in contrast, is not connected to anyone; presumably she is single, a widow, no longer connected to her past.

Often in literary pieces, the one named last in a series is the one who had been referred to immediately above. Perhaps, then, this

Suzanna is the woman who had been in Simon's house, the woman freed from her past, her connections, and even her sin. Perhaps she now dwells in Jesus' community, following behind him and ministering to him on a daily basis. She too is a daughter of Wisdom who sees and recognizes the justice and mercy of God that have visited the world in the prophet Jesus. After all, Jesus has told Simon to follow her example and that she could teach him about hospitality, graciousness, and gratitude. Perhaps in her new life she continues this hospitality that Jesus extended to her: she dwells in mercy.

She would understand Therese of Lisieux, who once said:

> After earth's exile, I hope to go and enjoy you in the fatherland, but I do not want to lay up merits for heaven. I want to work for your love alone.
>
> In the evening of this life, I shall appear before you with empty hands, for I do not ask you, Lord, to count my works. All our justice is blemished in your eyes. I wish, then, to be clothed in your own justice and to receive from your love the eternal possession of yourself.[3]

Susanna of Daniel 13 and Suzanna of Luke's gospel are both God-fearing, God-faring daughters of Wisdom, acquainted with mercy and God's justice. Both are witnesses to God's Word. Both are faithful and have known the intervention of God in their lives. Both merit to be held up as disciples and models of life, refusing to sin in the face of persecution and lies and liberated from sin for a life of freedom and ministry. God provided for these women, and they, in turn, seek to return the favor of God's gracious visit to their lives in providing for those people who are still looking for God's intervention in their lives.

The questions are still the same: Do you see this woman? Do you see this prophet? Do you see what is true and just? Do you see what really is sin and ingratitude? Do you see only what you want to see? Do you see as God sees? Do you see your own sin that blinds you to the goodness of others and the goodness of God? Let us end with a prayer by Sheila Cassidy, a doctor, a healer who was jailed and tortured for taking care of wounded people who were considered dangerous to the law in Chile in the 1970s. She prays:

---

3. Quoted in *America*, March 28, 1998.

> Lord, teach us to forgive;
> to look deep into the hearts
> of those who wound us,
> so that we may glimpse,
> in that dark, still water,
> not just the reflection
> of our own face
> but yours as well. Amen.

For we are all sinners, have all been sinners, and yet we have all been touched by the forgiveness of God in the person of Jesus who has visited the earth in incarnation. And now we are all invited into the feast of forgiveness and the banquet of mercy. And it is still "the children of Wisdom who recognize her work." These are daughters of Wisdom, those who see truly and dwell in the realm of God's mercy.

FIVE

DAUGHTERS

*The Only Daughter of Jairus; the Daughter of Jesus;
and Sara, the Only Daughter of Ragouel*

Jairus's Daughter and the Daughter of Jesus

THE STORY OF JAIRUS'S DAUGHTER appears in all three of the Synoptics: in Matt. 9:18–26, Luke 8:40–56, and Mark 5:21–43. In Luke it comes almost immediately after Jesus' description of his family as those who "hear the word of God and do it" (Luke 8:19–21), and so it is about being true kindred of Jesus. It also follows Jesus' calming the storm on the lake, when his disciples wondered, "Who can this be? See, he commands even the wind and sea and they obey him!" (Luke 8:26). They had been buffeted by strong winds and had been fearful. But Jesus, asleep in the boat, roused by their panic, had been more concerned with their lack of faith. They had told him that they were sinking, but Jesus' words to them in reply had been: "Where is your faith?" (8:25). The entire chapter is about who really follows him and who really hears his word and understands with faith.

This chapter also contains the description of the women who followed Jesus and the account of the wrenching reordering of the man called the Gerasene demoniac. Jesus' power to right what is insane and demented instills fear in the people who witness the event, and they want him to leave them. Jesus does. He returns to the other side of the lake but not before telling the man who has been given back his sanity and his life to remember "how much God has done for him" and to return to his own people as a witness to Jesus' works. He confesses and witnesses to Jesus' power in his own body and mind.

Prior to this healing and the stilling of the storm, Jesus has narrated the parable of the sowing of the seed in various kinds of ground. Following that, he states: "No one, after lighting a lamp, covers it with a bowl or puts it under the bed; rather he puts it on a lampstand so that people coming in may see the light. In the same way, there is nothing hidden that shall not be uncovered; nothing kept secret that shall not be known clearly" (Luke 8:16–17).

Jesus is trying, it seems somewhat in vain, to make the people aware that the kingdom, the realm of power, peace, and healing that he is announcing, is in their midst already. Because of his presence in the world, nothing is as it appears. All the rules have changed, and all things — the sea, the wind, the very ground — now obey him. But his disciples, for the most part, totally miss the implications and the wide-ranging ramifications of Jesus' word and presence.

Even though they have been told that "to them is being revealed the mysteries of the kingdom and the secrets of God long hidden," they, like their contemporaries, are "seeing but not perceiving and hearing they are not understanding" (Luke 8:9–10). The parable has ended with the imperative: "Listen, if you have ears to hear!" They are listening not with open hearts and minds, but with well-formulated expectations of their own and their nation's hopes. Still, the rest of the chapter makes it clear that some are hearing and are beginning to realize that there has been a shift in history, that Jesus might be the long-awaited answer.

Both of the people involved in our story — Jairus, an official of the synagogue, and a woman who has been afflicted with a disease that causes her physical distress and also results in her being ostracized — are desperate. Jairus is frantic over the impending death of his little daughter, his only daughter, and the woman is at the end of her hope and her resources. It is in situations such as these that the presence of Jesus is most capable of bringing forth fruit a hundredfold. Perhaps, the evangelist is telling us, faith begins at the very edge of despair and fear, and at death's ragged razor edge.

In Matthew's gospel the story appears in a chapter where Jesus heals a paralytic who is brought to him by friends, but he heals him only after he publicly tells the man: "Courage, my son! Your sins are forgiven!" (Matt. 9:2). Jesus then calls Matthew the tax collector to be a disciple, and surprisingly Matthew drops everything and obeys him. He lays aside his job, his career, his savings, and his sins and promptly responds to the invitation of Jesus who "sees" him. Matthew then throws Jesus a party and invites all of his old friends: other tax collectors and sinners, those who were known to be lax in their obedience to the law and the accepted behaviors of righteous believers. Jesus' response to and association with such people are questioned, and his own motives and person are disparaged. Jesus replies with words of startling clarity that are reminiscent of the prophets: "Healthy people do not need a doctor, but sick people do. Go and find out what this means: 'What I want is mercy, not sacrifice.' I did not come to call the righteous but sinners" (Matt. 9:12–13).

The major difference in the stories of Luke and Matthew is that in Luke, Jairus's daughter is close to death when Jairus approaches Jesus, while in Matthew, the synagogue official is not named and his daughter is already dead. In the latter, the official requests that Jesus "come with him and place his hands on her and she will live" (Matt. 9:18–19). This, of course, is an important difference: it is one thing to cure someone close to death, another altogether to bring someone back from the dead.

The account of the woman who comes up behind Jesus to touch his cloak as he passes by on his way to the official's house is told simply, without any of the details that are found in Luke or Mark. This is true also of the account of Jesus raising the young girl to life. Both sound like routine experiences, with Jesus going about his work of healing as though it is second-nature to him. And he is concerned that others join him in this work, this harvest that is so abundant, but others are slow to join him in this work that he has been entrusted with by the master, God (Matt. 9:35–37).

In Mark, the story comes very early in Jesus' ministry. Again it follows the announcement of who Jesus' true family is: those who hear and do the will of God are "brother, sister and mother to me" (Mark 3:34). Then Jesus tells the story of the sower and the seed, the parable of the lamp, and the story of how the seed grows of itself once it is planted. The next story speaks of the tiny mustard seed that has grown into an unwieldy bush that shelters the birds of the air. Then follow the stories of Jesus calming the storm on the lake and of the man from the Gerasene region whom Jesus frees from his chains and commands to go home to his people and bear with him the story of what God has done for him.

In all the gospel accounts, Jesus arrives in the midst of despair, into a world grown callused and used to suffering, a world devoid of pity and lacking in hope, a world that isolates those who suffer and condemns them to the realm of being victims of their own or their relatives' sin. Even among religious people there is a hardness of heart and an insensitivity to those who are broken in body, suffering from diseases that destroy the flesh.

A Muslim story describes the human condition that Jesus in his incarnation enters:

Once upon a time there was a beggar who came with her begging bowl to a great king and asked for alms, for food, for anything that he would give. The king gestured to one of his advisers, and the beggar's bowl was filled with grain. But to the adviser's dismay, no matter how much he put in the bowl, it was still empty, as though it was bottomless. The king repeated his order, and the man sought to fill the bowl again and again and again. Finally, in desperation, the man cried to the king that the bowl seemed to eat everything that it was given.

The king looked at the beggar with different eyes, seeking to understand. The woman stood there with her empty bowl and patiently held it out for the offering. They both stood looking at each other, and the king finally asked: "Who are you and why have you visited my kingdom?" The beggar looked at the king and held out her begging bowl. She answered: "This bowl is the bowl of human wants and needs. It is impossible to fill, but it is the work of all those who believe in Allah, the most Compassionate One, to try. Is this the work of your kingdom?" And the beggar left the bowl on the floor in the middle of the great hall of the king. And she left.

This is our world still, the world that Jesus entered. Jesus is the most compassionate of God's children. He has come with the mission of making sure that even if the bowl is not filled, the hand of the one who holds it out is reached for and held with tenderness and strength.

This background is important for the stories of the two women, both called "daughters," who are about to leave their families, countries, and previous existences and be initiated into Jesus' family. We will look at the story as it is told in Mark because of its details and humanness and because in Mark the experiences of the women overlap more clearly than in the other accounts.

In relating the two stories, Mark uses images from Isaiah to describe Jesus the prophet. In Isaiah, in the first song of the suffering

servant of Yahweh, the servant is described as the one who will be
accepted and heard by the minority, while the majority of people will
harden their hearts and steadfastly refuse in their blindness to see or
acknowledge the power of God that comes among them in ways they
are not expecting. This song introduces us to an image of God among
us that reveals Jesus as the one chosen and upheld by God:

> Here is my servant whom I uphold,
> my chosen one in whom I delight.
> I have put my spirit upon him,
> and he will bring justice to the nations.
>
> He does not shout or raise his voice;
> proclamations are not heard in the streets.
> A broken reed he will not crush,
> nor will he snuff out the light
> of the wavering wick.
> He will make justice appear in truth. . . .
>
> I, Yahweh, have called you for the sake of justice;
> I will hold your hand to make you firm;
> I will make you as a covenant to the nations,
> to open eyes that do not see,
> to free captives from prison,
> to bring out to light those who sit in darkness.
>
> (Isa. 42:1–2, 6–7)

In other translations, verse 6 contains the lines, "I will grasp you by
the hand" and "I have called you for the sake of justice." This is Jesus'
mission: to grasp those who draw near to him by the hand and hold on
to them for the sake of justice, for the sake of holiness and wholeness,
for the sake of what is right and good on the earth.

The other portion of Isaiah that is pertinent to Mark and to these
stories in particular is found in Isaiah 61:

> I rejoice greatly in Yahweh,
> my soul exults for joy in my God,
> for he has clothed me in the garments of his salvation.
> He has covered me with the robe of his righteousness,
> like a bridegroom wearing a garland,
> like a bride adorned with jewels.

> For as the earth brings forth its growth,
> and as a garden makes seeds spring up,
> so will the Lord Yahweh make justice and praise
> spring up in the sight of all nations. (Isa. 61:10–11)

This portion follows the famous lines that Jesus will quote in the synagogue of Nazareth when he announces that he heralds the coming time and that the present day is the time of God's visitation. These servant songs describe Jesus as reaching out and grasping people physically, grasping them by the hand. But they also describe the mantle, the cloak or garment, that hides him from eyes that do not want to see and from people who do not want their lives touched or altered by his presence among them.

In the very first chapter of Mark, Jesus is brought to Simon's house where his mother-in-law is sick in bed with a fever. We are told that "Jesus went to her, taking her by the hand, raised her up, and the fever left her, and she began to wait on them" (Mark 1:31). Thus, Simon's mother-in-law is described as ministering in the kingdom, as a disciple of Jesus. In Mark, Jesus is always stretching out his hand or asking that others stretch out their hands toward him in obedience so that they can be healed, freed, and released from what holds them. Other examples are the curing of the leper (Mark 1:41), the healing of the paralytic who is lowered through the roof to reach Jesus (Mark 2:4), and the cure of the man with the withered hand who is commanded by Jesus to stretch out his hand (Mark 3:3–5). In fact, Jesus is God's hand stretched out to us, reaching for us, to grasp hold of us and hold fast until justice and truth are planted in our hearts and on the earth. This is salvation. This is the glory of God being made manifest.

And this is what happens when Jesus has contact with the woman who has been hemorrhaging for twelve years. The woman is in profound need of Jesus' healing physical presence. She, according to the custom and laws of the time, was impure because of her disease. Indeed, anything that had to do with death, or the body of one who was sick, or the body of a dead person, was ritually isolating. In the case of someone who was diseased, this enforced isolation was in part the result of fear of contagion, but it was also in part a religious sanction that condemned both the behavior and the person who was afflicted. It was tantamount to an announcement that God had abandoned that person because of sin. The assumption was that sickness was an outward manifestation of individuals' failure to obey the law, of their sin, of their unholy position before God the Holy One.

Whole sections of the code of purity dealt with disease, mildew, childbirth, lepers, clean versus unclean slaughter and eating of animals, and the presence of any discharge from the body. In regard to the woman who had been suffering from a severe loss of blood for twelve years, the law would have been devastating, adding to the grief caused by her physical condition. The law would have literally isolated her from the community, from any kind of normal life, and from any sense of worth or meaning. She was cursed, humiliated, and avoided as though any contact with her would sully others. The law reads brutally:

> When a woman has a discharge of blood, and blood flows from her body, this uncleanness of her monthly periods shall last for seven days. Anyone who touches her will be unclean until evening. Any bed she lies on will be unclean; any seat she sits on will be unclean.
>
> Anyone who touches her bed must wash his clothing and take a bath and will be unclean until evening. Anyone who touches any seat she has sat on must wash his clothing and take a bath and will be unclean until evening. If there is anything on the bed or the chair on which she sat, anyone who touches it will be unclean until evening....
>
> If a woman has a flow of blood for several days outside her period, or if her period is prolonged, during the time this flow lasts she shall be unclean as during her monthly periods....
>
> When she is cured of her flow, she will let seven days pass; then she will be clean. On the eighth day she is to take two turtle doves or two young pigeons and bring them to the priest at the entrance to the Tent of Meeting. With one of them the priest is to offer a sacrifice for sin and with the other a burnt offering. This is the way in which the priest will perform the rite of atonement over her before Yahweh for the flow that made her unclean.
>
> (Lev. 15:19–23, 25, 28–30)

The life of the woman in our story would have been a constant accusation, a hell that never ended, a life without meaning, without human contact, without simple human companionship. She would have been seen as defiled and as defiling the people, as abhorrent to God. Misery and despair would have been her only lot. Hers is a story within a story, a story of a woman redeemed and brought back to life after twelve years within the context of the story of a young girl, only twelve years old, who is brought back to life. The young girl has lived as long as the woman has been plagued with her infirmity and isolation:

> Jesus then crossed to the other side of the lake and while he was still on the shore, a large crowd gathered around him. Jairus, an official of the synagogue, came up and seeing Jesus, threw himself at his feet and asked him earnestly, "My little daughter is at the point of death. Come and lay your hands on her so that she may get well and live."
>
> Jesus went with him and many people followed, pressing from every side. (Mark 5:21–24)

The story begins in desperation, in a father's fear of losing his child, with a man who is willing to sacrifice his place in the community, his reputation, for the sake of his daughter. He is willing to publicly beg the teacher, the itinerant preacher, on his knees for help for the one he so cherishes. He throws himself at Jesus' feet, in the midst of the crowd, humbling himself before this man who might be able to help his daughter. It is love that drives him, love that propels him toward Jesus. He begs on behalf of another, his child. She is at the point of death; he is at the point of trying anything, absolutely anything, that might work. And without any ado, Jesus, we are told, went with him.

Now, usually stories such as this are about sons. But this is a girl-child, and it is on this point that we move back to the story of Sara, related in Tobit 3.

Sara

The story of Sara is one of the only girl-child stories in the First Testament. Sara, the only child of Ragouel, is plagued and cursed by the death of seven husbands, each on her wedding night. Her plight bears resemblance to that of both daughters in Mark's story. Sara is maligned by her own servants, taunted, and told to go and join her husbands in death. She is even cursed: "May we never see a son or daughter of yours!" (Tob. 3:7–9). Sara is so distressed that she seriously considers hanging herself to escape the horrible insults and

meanness of even her own household. What stops her is the thought
of her own father and mother and what they will have to endure if
she does such a dishonorable thing. So, instead, she just prays that she
will die:

> She thought better of it, and said: "If people ever reproached my
> father and said to him: 'You have an only daughter whom you
> cherished and she hanged herself because she was unhappy,' I
> would cause my father in his old age to die of grief. It is better
> for me not to hang myself but to ask the Lord that I may die and
> not live to hear any more insults." (Tob. 3:10)

She continues with a prayer that links her to the woman who will sneak
through the crowd and reach out for Jesus' garment in her desperation:

> At that moment she stretched forth her hands towards the win-
> dow and prayed, saying, "You are blessed, O Lord my God, and
> blessed is your holy and glorious Name throughout the ages.
> May all your works praise you forever. Lord, I have turned my
> eyes and my face towards you. Command that I be set free from
> the earth and that I may hear no more insults. You know, O Lord,
> that I am pure of all contact with man; that I have not defiled my
> name, nor my father's name in the country of my captivity. I am
> my father's only daughter. He has no other son or daughter who
> can inherit from him; neither has he a close relative who can be
> given to me as a husband. So, after my seven husbands are dead,
> I have no one to live for. If it does not seem good to you, O Lord,
> that I should die, command that people will respect me and that
> I may hear no more insults." (Tob. 3:11–15)

We are told that the Lord of Glory hears her prayer and the prayer
of Tobit, Tobias's father, who has also been praying in desperation.
The angel Raphael is sent to heal both Tobit and Sara. Their prayers
are separated by distance and seem not to be connected at all, yet they
are both bound in God's hearing, and they will both be healed and
further bound to one another in mysterious ways. Many things will
come together from the prayers of two distinct people in terrible pain
and isolation. We are told:

> The Lord in his glory heard the prayer of Tobit and Sara and he
> sent Raphael to heal them both — to give back his sight to Tobit

and to give Sara, the daughter of Ragouel, to Tobit's son Tobias, as his wife. Also Raphael would enchain the wicked demon
Asmodeus so that Sara would be the wife of Tobias. (Tob. 3:16)

The prayers of both, the lives of both, will become intimately intertwined by the intervention of Raphael, sent by God to heal, to enchain
the demon that kills and causes such suffering, and to set in motion a
future undreamed of by either of those in such distress now. Families
will come together because of God's attending to their pain, and God
will draw the larger history of his people together by using that pain
and their dependence and continued belief. The great and wonderful
works of God will be revealed in the lives of those who turn to God.
This is the import of the stories of Tobit and Sara and Tobias. Now,
once again, the lives of people will come together in the power of
God's answer to their prayers. Communion, community, will be a gift
added to the more immediate and pressing requests at hand.

Jesus' True Family

This kind of interruption — initiated by faith, responded to by God,
and culminating in binding people in communion — is at the heart
also of our story in Mark. After Jairus's pleading, Jesus turns to go
with him, and the crowd goes along:

> Among the crowd was a woman who had suffered from bleed-
> ing for twelve years. She had suffered a lot at the hands of many
> doctors and had spent everything she had, but instead of get-
> ting better, she was worse. Since she had heard about Jesus, this
> woman came up behind him and touched his cloak thinking, "If I
> just touch his clothing, I shall get well." Her flow of blood dried
> up at once, and she felt in her body that she was healed of her
> complaint. (Mark 5:25–29)

We are really told a great deal about this woman who has no name.
She is untouchable. She has known this life for so long that she would
have a faint memory of any other. Not only was she plagued by a mysterious illness — she was also at the mercy of doctors who made her
suffer with their impotent attempts at cures and their ravenous eating
up of her money. We know, then, that she had been wealthy, though
now she is at the end of her money. But she has heard about Jesus. This

line is crucial. What has she heard? Has she heard the story of the man who lived among the tombs? Has she heard hearsay about Jesus controlling the weather? Has she heard other stories about healings? Has she heard about Jesus breaking the rules of cleanliness by associating with Gentiles and sinners and others who were condemned like her because of their bodies' betrayals? She is determined, and she breaks the codes of purity by pushing her way through the crowd to get near Jesus. She wants to get near enough, just near enough, so that she can touch his clothing, the hem of his garment. And she, who is probably very adept at being invisible, at being unnoticed, gets close. She reaches out and touches his cloak. And in that moment of cloth and fingers touching she knows! She feels it deep inside her. She knows she's whole again. The shift, whether it was subtle or sudden and strong, is visceral. Was it a shudder like that sunlight can evoke on cold skin? Was it like an electrical charge, a current that ran through her? Was it more like a whisper of comfort, her own body sighing in relief? Was it like a singing through her bones startling her back into life and awareness of what is around her? Or was it like the line from the spiritual "A Balm in Gilead"? And all she's done is touch his cloak! But that cloak, that hem of a garment, has a history in Israel, a history of prayer and closeness to God, of intimacy with God when one approaches the Holy. Whenever believers in Israel come to prayer, they wrap themselves in a *tallit,* a prayer-shawl, and as they wrap the cloth around their head and shoulders, they pray the traditional blessing:

> Here I envelop myself in a prayer-shawl of fringes
> in order to fulfill the commandment of my creator.

This blessing and the wrapping of oneself in the shawl draw together one's intention to pray, to concentrate solely on the person of God, and to bind oneself to the Holy One. Such prayer is an incredibly private act, but the preparation for it is more public, taking place in the larger community. The ritual is an ancient tradition that connects and ties one to the larger community of Israel, to its prayers, and to worship of the Holy One. The Hebrew word for tradition is *masoret,* meaning "to hand on, to deliver, to hand over to another what one has received." In this case, one hands over to God what one has received from one's ancestors in faith and prayer, and one also hands over oneself, which is the basis of all prayer. In doing this, one is made whole, and the community is rebound, retied as one.

For centuries, the *tallit* has been a separate cloth donned for the occasion of prayer, but before that, for many generations, the poor couldn't afford an extra cloak, so their everyday cloak and the one worn for prayer were the same. The cloak was hemmed with fringe. Was this true of Jesus? Was the cloak Jesus wore when he walked the streets the same one he drew close around him when he came before God to pray?

The cloak the woman touches certainly is prayerful, imbued with holiness. Jesus knows that someone in that huge crowd pressing around him knows him and has touched him at the source of his person:

> But Jesus was conscious that healing power had gone out from him, so he turned around in the crowd and asked, "Who touched my clothes?" His disciples answered, "You see how the people are crowding around you. Why do you ask who touched you?" But he kept looking around to see who had done it. Then the woman, aware of what had happened, came forward trembling and afraid. She knelt before him and told him the whole truth.
>
> (Mark 5:30–33)

Again, there is much more going on here than meets the eye. The disciples do not have a clue that something has happened. This reveals an awful separation between them and Jesus. They are always in his company, at ease in touching him, eating with him, sleeping in the fields with him, even praying with him on occasion, yet they do not often touch him or know him as this woman has, by just reaching for his cloak. Her intent, her devotion, her need, her hope, her pain have opened a door for her to something deep inside of Jesus, and he immediately knows that someone has touched his spirit, his power, his soul. And now Jesus is determined to find out who is now bound closer to him than his own disciples by her single-minded and single-hearted intent to draw near to him.

The woman realizes the enormity of what has happened. Her body starts to react by trembling. She is healed. In an instant the twelve years are gone. Whoever this teacher is, he has the power to heal without seeing who it is, without consciously directing his attention to the one in need. And so she comes to him, comes before him, as one would in prayer, and "kneels before him and tells him the whole truth." The words have a sense of confession, of an outpouring that combines emotions, thoughts, and awareness that has suddenly flooded through her along with the disappearance of her sickness. The flow of blood that is destructive and life-threatening has ceased. And in its place there is a surge of life that now courses through her body, mind, and soul. This is what she pours out: who she is; how she has had to endure pain, humiliation, shame, and despair; the prayers; the lack of anyone to help her, to ease her anguish; her great need for God, to be touched, accepted; and the fact that she broke the law to get to Jesus. It would have been a confusion of confession of sin, guilt, fear, awe, thanksgiving, delight, freedom, and praise, her words falling over themselves as they came out. They probably sounded crazy, and probably her mouth was full of laughter and tears, the way we get when we are at a loss to explain what has happened. She is on her knees before Jesus, surrounded by the crowd.

But there are only the two of them in this moment. "Then Jesus said to her, 'Daughter, your faith has saved you; go in peace and be free of this illness'" (Mark 5:34). He calls her "daughter," a term of endearment, intimacy, and relationship. In chapters 3 and 6, which follow, the stories are all about Jesus' true family and who belongs with him and to his community. For Jesus' family is bound not by blood ties, ancestry, or marriage. No, Jesus' true family is bound by faith, by hearing his Word and doing it, by discipleship and baptism, by desire, and by his blood on the cross. These are new ties, new kinship lines, new relations, and new ways of being intimate with God. She has been drawn into his family by her reaching out in faith. So he calls her "daughter," signifying her close association with him. As he is son to the Father, she is daughter. And he announces to her that it is her faith that has saved her. She is free of illness and association with sin. She is free now to go in peace because she is free to dwell in holiness, in wholeness, in shalom, and in his community of believers. She is now a disciple. She would, one would think, stick close to him and follow as near as she can to him as he is pulled on by the arrival of Jairus's servants telling him that Jairus's daughter is dead.

The story continues:

> While Jesus was still speaking some people arrived from the official's house to inform him, "Your daughter is dead. Why trouble the Master any further?" But Jesus ignored what they said and told the official, "Do not fear, just believe." And he al-

lowed no one to follow him except Peter, James and John, the brother of James. (Mark 5:35–37)

Jesus' words to Jairus are a command: "Do not fear, just believe." This is the kind of faith that the woman who trembled before him had had. Now Jairus must grab hold of this kind of faith, and so must Jesus' disciples. For now it is death that must be wrestled with and a lack of faith that is even more deadly than the physical reality. Death interrupts, and Jesus turns his attention solely to what is at hand, even though the others are saying that a teacher or master is useless now in the face of death. There is lack of faith everywhere Jesus turns. But the group heads toward Jairus's house together, this small community:

> When they arrived at the house, Jesus saw a great commotion with people weeping and wailing loudly. Jesus entered and said to them, "Why all this commotion and weeping? The child is not dead but asleep."
> They laughed at him. But Jesus sent them outside and went with the child's father and mother and his companions into the room where the child lay. Taking her by the hand, he said to her, "Talitha kumi!" which means: "Little girl, get up!"
> The girl got up at once and began to walk around. (She was twelve years old.) The parents were astonished, greatly astonished. Jesus strictly ordered them not to let anyone know about it, and told them to give her something to eat. (Mark 5:38–43)

Jesus knows what he faces: not only death but ridicule and disbelief as well. But as Jesus commanded the wind and waves to be still, so he strides toward the child lying asleep. He commands that life return, that the child's spirit — still so near, in physical proximity — come back into her body. He will reach out and take her by the hand, touch her, and draw her forth. In response to her father and mother's faith, need, and love, he will reach and grasp the child's spirit and draw it back. His words to her, "Little girl, get up!" are also translated "Arise!" Her spirit obeys him. She arises and walks around. She is probably disoriented, in a daze, unaware of what is going on, slowly coming back to life and consciousness, like awakening from a dream.

And they are astonished. Amazed. Probably speechless, paralyzed, just standing or sitting by the bedside watching her, with her hand in Jesus' as she stands up and walks around, alive. Jesus, holding her hand, was introducing her to the dance of life again, leading her in the steps back into her family, her newly extended family. Now Peter, James, and John are witnesses to the raising of the dead. Jesus is trying shock treatment on the lifeless state of his own disciples' belief.

This, then, is a story about the followers of Jesus — about those who are asleep to his real nature and about awakening to it. And so the proclamation of resurrection and the presence of Jesus alive in the community are followed immediately by the sharing of food. The child is given bread to nourish her, but surely it was a meal shared by the mother and father, Peter, James, John, and Jesus, like other meals shared among Jesus' followers, like that shared by Mary, Martha, Lazarus, and the disciples with Jesus as told in John's gospel. This is Eucharist, the meal of thanksgiving for life, for the transformation even of death, because of Jesus' presence among those who believe in him.

In the very next story Jesus will be rejected in his hometown, by his own neighbors and relatives, and because of their lack of faith there will be very few miracles or healings. Jesus cannot do the work of the kingdom, the work of bringing life, because of their narrow-mindedness and insistence that they know who he is: the son of the carpenter. Only those who are believers really know who Jesus is: the one who has power over all things and has brought all things to fullness of life; who can break the hold of death and forgive sins; who can calm the storms of earth and those raging violently in people's hearts and bodies.

I imagine the woman who spent the last twelve years of her life in isolation and pain meeting with and coming to know the young girl on the verge of becoming a woman at twelve years of age. This is the traditional age of the ceremony of bar mitzaph, and more recently bat mitzaph for a young woman. The two women would have naturally shared their stories about Jesus with their families and those who would rejoice in their newness of life. Jesus' community is reaching out and extending into new places, crossing boundaries and lines of economic and class distinctions, breaking barriers to real community, and drawing together those who have been touched by forgiveness, healing, wholeness. This is Jesus' new family, and he is trying to bring his own disciples, Peter, James, and John, into that community of believers, like Jairus and his wife and daughter, and the woman who touched Jesus in the street. These are the fringe folk. Where life has been unraveling is found at the fringe, the tassels of the new prayer-shawl that God is using to wrap around the new family born of Jesus' Spirit. From place to place Jesus is picking up his rag-tag followers, bringing together his church. And these are the people that Jesus will, in turn, send out to continue his work. It is interesting to note the wording: "Jesus then went around the villages teaching. He called the Twelve to him and began to send them out two by two, giving them authority over evil spirits. . . . They drove out many demons and healed many sick people by anointing them" (Mark 6:6b, 13). The Twelve go two by two. These twelve are his disciples, as are the woman he cured, Jairus, his wife, and his daughter. The early church would do what the disciples were commanded to do — share in Jesus' own power, call people to repent, heal, and gather in those who heard the good news and came to believe. The first pair that Jesus sends out (two by two) are these two unnamed women. But even more important, they are described by their relation to Jesus' — they are both daughters, daughters of hope, born of anger and courage.

This is a story about how one person's faith relates to another — Jairus, after all, needed to see and experience the faith of the woman who had been bleeding to death for over a decade. And Jairus's faith in turn saved his daughter, who would have come to faith in Jesus, who raised her from the dead. Faith is shared just as we share together in the meal, the Eucharist, feeding each other food that keeps us awake, alive in faith and walking about in faith. But lack of faith is present in the story also. Both power and weakness are there, reminding us that we either are alive to the needs of others or are dying and dead. We are either companions of Jesus or among those caught in the grip of the crowd that flocks to the scene of death. We are either daughters and sons by faith, disciples sent out two by two, or those caught weeping and wailing in the great commotion surrounding death. Brushing against us, those in need feel either a surge of life or death's cold.

Jesus bluntly tells Jairus: "Do not fear, just believe" (Mark 5:36). He is to ignore what everyone else says. We are to do the same. We are not to fear, just believe! What is this faith? Once, years ago, I watched one of my nieces learn to walk. She was fast on all fours, crawling and scurrying around and under everything. But one day as I was sitting in a chair across the room from her she grasped the coffee table and pulled herself up. She was wobbling and shaking but standing on her own two feet. She looked over to me, caught the look on my face, and

laughed delightedly. I reached out my arms to her, and without another thought she let go of the coffee table and with arms outstretched
took a few headlong steps toward me, falling flat on her face. But she
looked up at me again, and because I was smiling, she was too. She
immediately tried again, and this time when she went to fall, I caught
her. She got more and more adept at it. That is faith!

Faith is looking to God, in Jesus, from the heart of Jesus' family — it is looking to someone you already have a relationship with
and reaching, walking, falling forward, relying on their reaching back
to you. This is what we are sent out two by two to do for one another.

So this is also a story about making family, about bringing together
people separated by structures, laws, customs, economic classes, disease, about making strangers in a crowd, bound only by need and
suffering, into a family, a church, a new people born of the Spirit of
Jesus. It is a story about touch, about power, and about how it is used
and experienced. It is a story about basic changes in relationships, in
regard to intimacy and knowing. It is about women and men who are
bound in faith and desperate need in a new kinship tie. It is a story of
making church.

These stories reveal characteristics shared by members of Jesus'
true family. The Gerasene demoniac, who after being cured was "fully
clothed and in his right mind" (Mark 5:15), wanted to accompany
Jesus, but he was sent home to make clear to others what God's mercy
has accomplished in him. Like him, members of Jesus' true family are
those who have been baptized, clothed in the garment of resurrection,
and given a right mind and soul. They are now given a mission. They
are to go out and proclaim to all in the surrounding cities the marvels
of God. They are the ones who know now that fear is useless and only
faith is sound.

Like the woman who touched the hem of Jesus' garment and was
cured, the members of Jesus' family are those who have heard the
Word and do the will of the Father with Jesus, now on earth. They have
touched the fringe of Jesus' garment, the seamless garment of life, the
cloak of justice, and know that healing goes out from these edges to
others in need. The power of the Spirit is known among them to work
most strongly as it dwells in the community and in the simple touch of
one human's hand on the hand of a person in distress, rejection, and
bodily suffering. The members of Jesus' family are thus found on the
margins, the borders, the fringes, ignoring society's fear of contagion

and insisting that those who are deemed unacceptable are precisely those God goes looking for and touches. It is these outsiders whom Jesus "gives birth to first" in resurrection.

The true members of Jesus' family are determined. Not long ago I read a marvelous interview with two women: Denise Curry, a sister of Notre Dame de Namur, and Debbie Polhemus, who, with Denise, directs a program called Spanish Education for Women in Guadalajara, Mexico. They were interviewed in Washington, D.C., where the offices of SEW are located. Debbie wrote a book entitled *Cuando Una Esta Decidida,* which literally means "when you are determined." They say: "The title comes from stories that a women's group in Lima, Peru, developed as a kind of self-help book for women who go out with carts to sell food to workers during break times. The full sentence runs, 'When you are determined, nothing can hold you back.' "[1] The family of Jesus is determined — in the presence of hard realities, of disease, unemployment, hunger, and lack of resources — to reach out, even for the fringes and edges of hope, for transformation and freedom, like the woman determined to just touch Jesus' cloak.

And there is the story of Josephine Butler, a member of the Church of England who relentlessly worked to reform attitudes toward prostitutes and the lives of these women at the fringes. More than a hundred years ago, this sickly woman embarked on a crusade against a social ill — one still prevalent today — that causes harm, sickness, death, and a demeaning life of abuse, exclusion, and condemnation. Mary Grey, a British theologian, has said this about Josephine Butler:

> She was a tireless campaigner for women and very young girls, forced into prostitution in England, France and Belgium. . . . She was a woman, happily married, with children; she was a deeply committed Christian, sensitive and mystical in her spirituality and yet passionately involved in social action.
>
> But it is from the aspect of a philosophy of connection that I want to see her. Josephine Butler was from an upper-class English family, who had every opportunity for a pleasant, cultural and social life, untouched by the social injustices and the oppression of women of the time. But — initially driven to seek out the misery of other women because of grieving over the death of her

---

1. "The Gifts of Tongues" (interview with Denise Curry and Debbie Polhemus), *America,* September 12, 1998, 13–14.

own small daughter, she entered into the degradation of women and young girls, most often dragged into prostitution by abject poverty. At first she reacted on a personal level of individual effort: she brought them to live and die — with her, then founded new homes, visited the sea-ports, pleaded with sailors.

But the struggle was then pursued at an institutional level, both nationally and internationally, at great personal risk. Once Josephine Butler was smuggled out of a hotel just before it was burnt to the ground. Such was the fury of conventional opinion: first, that a decent woman should even *speak* about prostitution, and secondly, that she should try to rock the boat of an institution, which, it was claimed, actually protected the health of institutional marriages!

My point is this: first, that the ability to absorb the interconnectedness of the plight of all suffering women with her own situation clashed with the ethic of separation, which told the "decent woman" to have nothing to do with the prostitute. Secondly, Josephine Butler was empowered to do this by a faith which refused to separate spirituality from political action, and which found its inspiration from the Christ event.[2]

Individuals touched by death and personal affliction, but also touched by faith and resurrection, are commissioned — as members of Jesus' family — to reach out to others caught in society's strictures that contribute another level of misery to their already desperate plight. Men and women trapped in prostitution, those afflicted with AIDS and HIV-related diseases, and those enduring contagious and long-debilitating illness are especially vulnerable in societies that already discriminate in regard to health care and medical support services.

Mary Grey quotes Josephine Butler herself, who wrote:

Search throughout the gospel history and observe his [Jesus'] conduct with regard to women, and it will be found that the word *liberation* expresses above all others the act which changed the whole life and character and position of the women dealt

2. Mary Grey, *Weaving New Connections: The Promise of Feminist Process Thought for Christian Theology* (Nijmegen: Katholifke Universiteit Nijmegen, n.d.), 23–24; the pamphlet is the text of a lecture given at the Katholifke Universiteit Nijmegen.

with, and which ought to have changed the character of men's treatment of women from that time forward.

In a note on this text, Mary Grey comments: "She [Josephine Butler] was equally convinced that this liberation, this explosive breaking of legalistic boundaries, had been totally obscured by subsequent Christian history." The text from Butler then continues:

> When anyone tells me that the Church or Christianity teaches this or that with respect to women and their social positions, I go back to the words of Him who is acknowledged to be the Head of the Church and the author of Christianity, and I frequently find very little likeness indeed in any of his teaching . . . to those views, which, propounded by Councils, Fathers, or Decrees, have so greatly influenced the history of men, women and nations, since Christ came upon the earth."[3]

Both Mary Grey and Josephine Butler are specifically referring to the in-house situation of the church, but outside — in the much harsher and broader world — the case must be made first for the majority of all human beings in regard to health care and survival, especially in the area of contagious disease. And then, even more so, the case must be made for two groups of women: young girls and older women.

Amnesty International in the spring of 1998 launched actions to raise global awareness of children's rights, especially girl-children, and specifically in South Asia. The materials noted, however, that the experience of these 539 million children under the age of eighteen (out of 1.2 billion people) constituted the problems of children in the world at large. Generally, governments of the region — in Bangladesh, Afghanistan, India, Nepal, Pakistan, and Sri Lanka — agreed to and have ratified the UN Convention on the Rights of a Child, but "in the face of this promise, South Asia's children remain subject to a long list of human rights violations by state agencies and armed opposition groups, as well as abuses committed in the private realm of community and family."[4]

All the issues of gender, ethnicity, caste, and economic and religious background can exacerbate these children's situations. The girls

---

3. Josephine Butler, *Women's Work and Women's Culture* (Liverpool, 1869), lix, quoted in Grey, "Weaving New Connections," 24.

4. See "Children in South Asia: Securing Their Rights," *Amnesty Action* (summer 1998): 3; also available at http://www.amnesty.org.

especially suffer from dislocation, discontinuance of education, and slavery, while also undergoing the horrors shared by all poor children in the region: land mines, witnessing brutal acts of terror, and being "disappeared." While the boys are singled out for recruitment and maimed as combatants, the girls are targeted for sexual abuse, harassment, and rape. All suffer from economic exploitation, child labor, and a life without a future, without dignity, health care, education, or decent living conditions. Child labor leads inevitably to deprivation, abuse, prostitution, ill health, and lack of education. Worse still is another form of exploitation, "child trafficking and sexual slavery, which occurs all over South Asia. About 9,000 girls a year are trafficked form Nepal to India and from Bangladesh to Pakistan. The number of younger girls trafficked may be increasing because of the preference for virgins and fear of AIDS."[5] While this report highlights the girl-child in South Asia, the conditions are indicative of the plight of the girl-child in Africa, Central America, South America, China, and parts of First World countries where the gulf between social, racial, and economic classes is becoming more pronounced.

At the other end of the age spectrum is the status of elderly women in need of health care. Discussions of women's health care and social justice issues often focus on sexuality and reproduction for women of child-bearing age, ignoring issues faced by older women. The U.S. Census Bureau states that one in every five women in the United States is now over sixty-five, and by the year 2030 the number will be one in four. And then there is the "old old" population that is over eighty-five. This particular group is enormous in the United States and worldwide. M. Cathleen Kaveny states: "About two-thirds of people in the United States over 65 are female. That percentage climbs to three-fourths among those older than 85."[6]

She looks specifically at this issue in light of the tradition of the early church and how the first Christians cared for, included, and celebrated the elders among the women, many of whom must have been afflicted with illness and decreasing abilities. The woman who touched and knew Jesus' power in her flesh reminds us both of the shunned older women of the world and also of our need to come forward, trem-

---

5. Ibid.
6. M. Cathleen Kaveny, "Older Women and Health Care," *America,* September 12, 1998, 15–16.

bling, and to fall on our knees, worship, and tell the whole truth. We are called to confess, to express what God in Jesus and in the Body of Christ has done for us, as well as exhort the Body of Christ to awaken, to arise, and to reach out to the margins and form a life-line to those the world could care less about. Confession is a vital part of the process of healing, of being liberated, and of being drawn into Jesus' true family.

Elsa Tamez, a theologian from Latin America, writes: "To confess is to speak honestly with ourselves, with God. Confession places us in a space of vulnerability, where we are completely exposed. This is especially true when confession is born not out of the desire for absolution, but out of a bold need to speak the truth, to break the silence."[7]

The article is Elsa Tamez's confession, born of confused thoughts, insight, struggles, and an attempt to bring meaning out of life's complexities and out of the world's violence and injustice. It is her personal confession, but as a theologian it also edges into the public domain, speaking for others and with others. She knows she is delving into mystery, into God, into images of being human, and into the essence of what holds all of these together. She begins:

> I confess that I could not live without Thee, my God, any more than I could live without bread or without love.
>
> Human beings need bread and drink for survival. We must eat to live. And we live more fully if our food is prepared with time and care, with pleasure and without hurry. When beans, tortillas, corn, rice, vegetables, fruit and meat (if there is any) are transformed into a delightful meal, we live heartily.
>
> But eating and drinking alone will not sustain us. We need others with whom we can share the food and swap recipes. We need love.
>
> We cannot live without loving and being loved, without desiring and being desired, without touching and being touched. This does not mean there will never be times when we love without being loved in return, or when we are loved and do not wish to love back.
>
> We may know moments when we turn away from someone who has extended an embrace to us or times when no one is

---

7. Elsa Tamez, "Confessions," *The Other Side* (September–October 1998): 43.

there to embrace us. The trembling of our bodies during these moments of great love or great disappointment is a sign that we are living life with its laughter and tears.

The need to love and the need to eat cannot be separated. Both are bodily experiences, manifested not only in the flesh but in the spirit. Love, like bread, has flavor; both can be sweet or bitter. Just as we enjoy eating a good meal, our body feels pleasure in the presence of a loved one, or pain in that one's absence.

As the God of all life, our God is love and bread. I confess that I cannot live without God, because I cannot live without love or bread.[8]

It is a marvelous confession, well thought out, crafted, experienced and known in her own flesh, and with others. It speaks of God, of human beings, of relations and of disconnections, of survival and of loss, and ultimate loss: lack of love and death. And underlying her words about bread and love are ingredients of that bread: truthfulness, forgiveness, sin, suffering, death, community, solitude, evil, and justice. She is concerned with images of God, but her underlying and undying images are love and bread. She continues:

The other images we sometimes use for God — Creator, Judge, Father, Mother, Liberator, Warrior, King, Lord — are simply extensions of these fundamental nutrients for life, love, and bread.

Out of love, the Creator provides bread for all creatures. The Judge condemns those who take bread and leave others with none. The Mother and Father provide bread for beloved sons and daughters. Through love one liberates, governs with justice, begets life, is molded, and suffers as Christ did. Bread grounds that love in the realities of life, making sure it does not become ethereal.[9]

The stories in chapter 5 of Mark end with bread! We are told: "Jesus strictly ordered them not to let anyone know about it, and told them to give her something to eat" (Mark 5:43). Life sundered has been healed, sealed, and bonded solidly again. Life has not just been returned — it has been re-membered, reclaimed, and reconstituted,

---

8. Ibid.
9. Ibid.

and so the girl-child and those given life with her must be nourished together with bread that sustains this life.

And Jesus orders them not to let anyone know about it! It seems ludicrous. We retort: Wouldn't everyone know what happened? And yet experience tells us that disillusion reigns and disbelief pervades even religious communities. The reality of Jesus' power over death itself, over all disease, insanity, violence, and sin, cannot easily be spoken about. These experiences must be honored, and so words must be carefully chosen and shared with others before they are too easily formed and cast about among those who do not believe and who will not confess and commit themselves to following Jesus. The whole truth is not easily known or quickly expressed. The real work of sharing the mystery of Jesus' presence, of the incarnation of the Divine and the Holy in human flesh and blood, must be incorporated into our own flesh and blood personally and as a family, as the Body of Christ, the church, and as a people sent into the wider world.

Elsa Tamez knows this, and she knows that living with faith in the world requires vigilance and devotion. She ends her confession this way.

I confess that many times I have felt the need to defend God, to make up some explanation for how a loving God can allow the injustice and pain we see in our world, the lack of bread and love. There have been times when I felt that if I did not seek to defend God, I might have stopped believing in God. I have had to construct discourses and confessions to give reasons for God's silences or God's hidden presence when faced with injustices and impunities in this reality of misery.

I don't believe that these discourses lie just because they are constructed for this reason. I believe that God inspires such work, and that such efforts can help us understand the dark sides of God and of human beings, the aspects that seem incomprehensible and contrary to the luminosity with which we are familiar.

I believe God is pleased that I do theology in this manner. Not because God is "being defended" — God does not need any defense. But I believe that God is pleased when people seek to keep the light of hope burning day to day, sometimes even weakly, as we live in pursuit of the time when God's presence will be fully revealed in the love and bread that will be shared among all God's people.[10]

Mark's gospel is the confession of his community in Rome at the beginnings of the church, and it was intended to nourish and give life to those who followed the path of resurrection in the hard years that followed. It is nearly two thousand years since those words were written and since Jesus saved a woman condemned to a living death by her neighbors and religious community on his way to saving a young dead girl and her grieving parents. Their stories of faith, of hope, of determined courage, and of anger at death that is needless are our stories also. They found the words to share with others, to feed others' souls and trembling unsteady steps in faith, and we are called to dig into their stories and our own lives to find the words that will confess to God's mercy and healing in our time and history. In the early Middle Ages, an English mystic, Julian of Norwich, wrote:

> The beloved soul was preciously knitted to God in its making, by a knot so subtle and so mightily that it is united in God. In this uniting it is made endlessly holy. Furthermore, God wants us to know that all the souls that will be saved in heaven without end are knit in this knot, and united in this union, and made holy in this holiness.[11]

God in Jesus is intent on our wholeness, our life, and our liberation, no matter our ages, our genders, or our status in society. If God has favorites, it is the fringe people, found at the edges of our worlds, on the other side of our borders and boundaries.

We end with a fairy tale from Hans Christian Anderson. The story, called "The Leap Frog," can lighten our hearts and perhaps our step along the way and invite us into the dance of resurrection life, once we see it in others and know that we are all invited in:

> Once upon a time there was a king who had an only daughter whom he loved dearly. No matter what was happening in the kingdom, the king was thinking of his little girl and how it would affect her life and her future. One day there was an

10. Ibid., 45.
11. Julian of Norwich, *Showings,* trans. and ed. Eric Colledge and James Walsh (New York: Paulist Press, 1978), 284.

argument among some members of his kingdom. The king overheard the three fighting and insisting that each of them was the best, the most skilled, and the most important. The frog, the cricket, and the flea were all claiming to be able to jump the highest.

The king interrupted and declared, "Let us have a contest to see who can jump the highest, and whoever wins will get to be my little daughter's friend forever." It was agreed. A great circle was drawn in the sand and the contest began. First came flea, and he jumped so high that he disappeared altogether and was never seen again! The king declared him "out of bounds," disqualified, long gone. Next came cricket, who rubbed his legs together, pranced around, and then did his jump — right into the face of the king! He was brushed aside, swatted, declared in contempt, and so disqualified, too. Last came frog, who looked around at all the people gathered together, the king, his little daughter, and all the advisers, and promptly jumped straight into the lap of the little girl! "Ah," said the king, "we have a winner!" And the king confessed in the presence of all to hear that in his estimation, there was no one higher in all his kingdom than his beloved little daughter.

Of course the story does go on. Flea was annoyed at the turn of events and declared that people weren't fair and that he was going off to live with the animals, which, of course, we know, he did. If you spend a lot of time with cats and dogs, then perhaps you've meet the very flea! And cricket wasn't happy with the outcome either, and he decided to get away from it all, down by the creek among the rushes and weeds. And if you're ever wanting to get away from lots of people and head down to the creek or river, then perhaps if you listen and understand, cricket will tell you this story!

The story isn't that different from the gospel. Like the king with his little girl, Jesus tells us that God considers the least in our world the highest. We are all invited into this kin-dom, where there are no distinctions of class, gender, race, or economic and social standings. All sinners are forgiven; all those once possessed are back in their right mind; all those dis-eased and ill are healed and eased; and all those once dead are raised to life again. In this "rain" of God all are beloved daughters and sons, fed with bread and love, welcomed home and touched, grasped for the victory of justice, dwelling in peace, sharing the life-line of the power of God's own Spirit still at home among us. And, of course, wherever that happens, everyone is "astonished, greatly astonished."

S I X

QUEENS

Esther and Vashti

A N ANCIENT TALE told in many cultures is the basis of the most famous story in the collection *Arabian Nights*. It is the story of Scheherazade, the woman who weaves stories for 1001 nights, entertaining the king, adding days to her life, even (in some versions) raising a family. She spins out lifelines to the future for herself and others, averting the death that has come to others. She is a model of survival in a time of oppression, but it is the story and its telling that are the message:

> Once upon a time there was a king, married to a woman who betrayed him. While she escaped to live her new life, the king was embittered and enraged. He swore never to marry or to trust again. But every night he decreed that a young virgin was to be sent into him, and every morning the woman was beheaded. And it fell to his chief adviser to find these women, on pain of execution himself. The days were numbered by the murders, and the land itself lived in fear and desolation, mourning and grieving, as the young women died by decree. The king was soon hated by all, and lamentation was heard in the land. This dreadful situation continued until there were only two young women left in the whole of the country, the two daughters of the chief adviser. Only when it was his daughters' turn to die did the adviser confide in them what he had been doing and that they were next in line for this despicable end.
>
> They listened to their father and there was a deadening silence. But the elder daughter was thinking and had a plan. She spoke and though she was afraid, she offered to go to the king

herself, protecting her younger sister. She was wise, for she had listened long to her people's stories and tales, histories and hopes, and she was adroit with words. She told her father of her distress at the deaths of so many of her people and the death of their own futures and children and that she had pondered how to stop the killing and the cruelty that were its source. She declared that she would deliver them all from the king's destruction!

Her father was aghast! But she was adamant. He thought her proud and foolish, unaware of the depth of evil she was walking into that night, but she was determined. Later she spoke with her sister, Dunyazade, and told her, "When you are summoned tonight before the king, after you embrace me, ask me to tell you a story to help pass the night before I lose my head."

And so Scheherazade went and gave herself to the king, who enjoyed her beauty, her laughter, and her freedom more than anyone he could remember. But when he was finished with her and wanted to sleep, she began to weep and moan softly, like a little child. He was moved to comfort her, and she said simply, "Please, if I'm going to be beheaded in the morning could I please see my little sister for these next few hours of the night?"

The king sent for her, and when they fell into each other's arms, Dunyazade pleaded for some stories so that she could remember her sister and her words when she was gone. And so Scheherazade began:

> Once upon a time there was a merchant who was astute in his dealings, famed for his bargains and for his wealth. He traveled often looking for goods and animals and loved his journeys, the meetings with strangers, and the wisdom he culled along the way. And at the request of a long-time friend he set out again. It was a long, hot, and dry trip through arid county, and when he was thinking only of water and shade he came upon a garden. It seemed to be miraculous, appearing out of nowhere. He wondered if it was just his mind, but he entered and sat under a walnut tree, sinking deep into his cool breeze and tasting the richness of a handful of walnuts. Then suddenly . . .

The story soon caught the king's attention, and he was listening, sitting up, his eyes fixed on Scheherazade, fascinated by her words, her face, the sound of her voice, even the look upon her sister's face as she heard the story unfold. She spun sights and sounds, smells and excitement, anticipation, fear and surprise, and the time sped by. Eventually the light crept in through the bedroom curtains. When a shaft of sun hit the cloth covering Scheherazade's knees, she abruptly stopped. Dunyazade's face darkened, and the king found himself disappointed. Without thinking, he urged her on: "It's a great story. I've never heard anything like it, continue!"

But Scheherazade turned sadly to him, gesturing to the light in the window and spoke, "True, it's a great story, and so is its ending, and so it is the story I'd tell tonight, but it is time for me to die." The king was caught. He summoned his adviser and instructed him to care for Scheherazade and let her rest, feed her well, and tend to whatever she wished. He wanted another story.

The sisters and their father rejoiced. They would have another day of life! It was to be the first of many more days of life, for Scheherazade drew out the tales, teaching, nudging the listener toward hope, toward freedom and desire, toward goodness and love.

Soon all the town, then the country, knew that the king was no longer killing their young maidens and that there was one who held back his hand. They did not know that she was molding his soul, changing his mind, and softening his heart. The nights and days began to stack up. Scheherazade even bore him three children, and there were 1001 nights between them. Dunyazade had long ago stopped coming. It was now just the king and his beloved Scheherazade, his teacher, his storyteller and poet, his friend.

How long could it go on? It was Scheherazade who broached the subject. One morning as the sun rose she turned to him and asked for a favor. He was quick to answer, "Anything!" She asked for her children to be brought in, and when they arrived she hugged and cuddled them, all five of them in the bed together. "Please, my king," she begged, "let me live. Rescind your degree, and let these children have a mother, a life that is blessed with hope, and a secure place now so they may grow strong and free, true to their ancestors' traditions."

The king looked at her long and said nothing. Then he took her in his arms and declared, "Scheherazade, do you not know that you have long been pardoned, long before even our first child was conceived? Your stories told me of you, your truthfulness, your risk, your love of your father and sister, even of your people. Your stories told of wars and wisdom, hatreds and great devotion to ideals, and your stories told me the truth of my own evil and possibility for goodness. I did not want the stories to stop, or our time together to ever end. Will you marry me and become my queen so that all in the land may rejoice with us?"

And in the Islamic version, it ends: "So praise be to Allah, the most compassionate one, who in wisdom may grant us stories all our days, and at the end, a death worth dying."

Scheherazade touched the king's conscience sideways, using her people's traditions and stories to keep herself alive and eventually to convert a tyrant into a man she could love for his children and his future with her, and so she saved her people and ruled a kingdom from behind the throne.

Esther's story shares much with the intent and pattern of Scheherazade's story. There is dispute even among the Jewish people over whether Esther's story should be part of the Jewish canon. The scroll of Esther is one of five scrolls — the Song of Songs, Ruth, Lamentations, Ecclesiastes, (also called Qoheleth) and Esther — that are closely associated with feasts in the liturgical calendar and life of the Jewish people. Esther's story serves as the basis for the feast of Purim.

Esther's story is interpreted by contemporary scholars and students to reveal wildly contradictory character traits. Traditionally, Esther is the model of a Jewish woman who uses her beauty and her position within an oppressed society on behalf of her people's salvation from a decree of death. She is the heroine who unabashedly uses her sexuality to save Jewish lives. But others find her crafty and full of wiles, concealing her true identity, ruthless in her demands, no different than the man she serves in his harem, using her power to destroy women and children in revenge. For these interpreters, her redeeming traits are her courage in trying to save her people and her dedication to her race.

Others see her as a victim trapped in a harem, used sexually by a ruthless king, used by her uncle as a pawn in a political intrigue to save a nation. Here she is a devout though sequestered young woman who is unaware of her own position of power until she is led to use it on behalf of her people. She guards her true identity not only out of fear but because she secretly serves only the true God of Israel.

For others, "her conduct throughout the story is a masterpiece of feminine skill. From beginning to end, she does not make a misstep.... She is a model for the successful conduct of life in the often uncertain world of the Diaspora."[1]

Still others among feminist scholars see her as the worst of women to be emulated:

> Buried in Esther's character is... full compliance with patriarchy. In contrast to Vashti, who refused to be men's sexual object and her husband's toy, Esther is the stereotypical woman in a man's world. She wins favor by the physical beauty of her appearance, and then by her ability to satisfy sexually. She concentrates on pleasing those in power, that is, men.[2]

The story is loosely based on events at the time of Ahasuerus (also called Xerxes I), a Persian king who ruled from 485 to 464 B.C.E.. But even that is disputed. And the text does have some peculiarities. The original version never once mentions the name of God, and in later additions there are dream accounts, prayers to God, and an attempt to explain the Jews' brutal vengeance on their enemies.

Why is the text included in the canon? It is a wisdom story; it is based in the history of oppression; and it is a story that boldly sets out good and evil, exhorting the Jews to remember that even when they are slaves and in exile God is hidden in their history and their daily lives. The story points to the absolute necessity of obedience to the covenant and trust in a community for survival. Still, Esther's story presents us with as many problems as insights.

First, Esther, the hidden Jew, is a slave-queen in the harem of a ruthless despot. The story begins with what is meant to be a disgusting display of waste, immorality, and hedonism. Kathryn Darr describes it:

> Our story begins with an opulent show of self-indulgence. The scene is Susa, capital of the mighty Persian empire stretching

---

1. Sidnie Ann White, "Esther: A Feminine Model for Jewish Diaspora," in *Gender and Difference in Ancient Israel,* ed. Peggy L. Day (Philadelphia: Fortress Press, 1989).

2. Alice L. Laffey, *An Introduction to the Old Testament: A Feminist Perspective* (Philadelphia: Fortress Press, 1988).

"from India to Nubia." After entertaining his nobles and governors during a one-hundred-and-eighty-day wine feast, King Ahasuerus hosts a second celebration for all the city's other inhabitants.... Wine flows in abundance. It is, in short, an astonishing display. Meanwhile, in a nearby suite of rooms, Queen Vashti fetes the female guests.[3]

It seems in the beginning that Vashti also rules in her small realm, following the custom of separating men and women for certain feasts. But things get out of hand. In a drunken show of gross power and possessiveness, the king and his guests summon the reigning queen to appear before them. She refuses. Even she, it seems, pagan though she may be, has a sense of limits and boundaries to what is endurable.

In her book *Biblical Women Unbound: Counter-Tales,* Norma Rosen tells us a great deal about Vashti and what she reveals about women, about life in slavery, and about what it means to reach a limit and resist, even knowing the consequences:

I have never met a woman who liked the Megillah of Esther. Too many aspects of the story make us squirm.

First, what to do with Vashti? She seems a heroine of defiance, but the text doesn't recognize her. It's the genius of the midrashic rabbis that adds the essential note missing from Vashti's part of the story. When the King sent for her to appear before his carousing guests, says a midrash in *Pirke de Rabbi Eliezer,* she was to come naked.

Every Purim I have to check the text to remind myself that this searing detail is not in the Bible story. But the midrashic version, once imagined, will not go away. It has seized the text, and made itself a legitimate part of it.

The rabbis did not say that Vashti was a hero, but they heightened our sense of what was at stake for her. She was not arrogant and willful, she was self-respecting and full of courage. She upholds the sacredness of human, therefore divine, aspect in a court so debauched that any woman who enters will certainly be dehumanized.[4]

---

3. Kathryn Darr, *Far More Precious Than Jewels: Perspectives on Biblical Women* (Louisville: Westminster/John Knox Press, 1991), 167.

4. Norma Rosen, *Biblical Women Unbound: Counter-Tales* (Philadelphia: Jewish Publication Society, 1996), 170.

Vashti's behavior is noted not just as a single act of resistance. Rather, since she is the queen, her behavior can have disastrous consequences for everyone in the kingdom. Her position has enhanced and empowered her person beyond her private choices. It is decreed that she be banished, and her disrespect of the king's arbitrary wishes is written up in a decree and made law: protecting the rights demanded by "husbands, from the least to the greatest, to be honored by their wives" (Esther 2:13–20). Later, when the king's anger cools, and, one suspects, he sobers up, he remembers Vashti's disobedience but also his relationship with her, but it's too late. The king's courtiers come up with the solution that the king be given suitable young maidens for his pleasure to replace his once-cherished queen. This is all a setup for the story of Esther, who will be thrust into this sordid society, the symbol of the Israelite community subservient to the nation of Persia.

Many women want to make Vashti the heroine of the story because she is more suitable to our times: the valiant woman who stands up for herself in the face of her husband or any man who owns her as a piece of chattel, accepting banishment rather than obey an insulting command. However, although she models individual resistance to unlawful power, she is not a model for the Jewish community. Vashti is not connected to a community of solidarity, and she is without connection to a larger system of morals, laws, and structure.

The Jewish nation is concerned with its survival in the midst of slavery, oppression, exile, and the climate of genocide, not with an individual's personal sense of being affronted on a level of sexual indignity. Vashti's behavior is not unimportant, but it is the behavior of one in touch with power. Her example is thus a dead-end for a community concerned with living with hatred and the constant threat of annihilation from a hostile government as well as virulent individuals. This is a story about salvation for a people, not about an individual's level of tolerance for abuse.

Now enters Esther, but not alone. From the beginning she is accompanied by her uncle Mordecai, who raised her. She had been an orphan, and Mordecai had adopted her as his own daughter. Even in captivity the family and the nation must hold together and care for their weakest members. The picture of Esther is mixed; within a difficult situation, she uses what she has been given by nature; at the same time, she learns from her tradition and heritage to use her power and natural resources in tandem with the community's own belief. She does all this so as to strengthen the Jews' covenant and community within a hostile environment.

She is befriended and taken under the wing of the custodian of the women:

> In compliance with the king's edict, a great number of young girls were brought to Susa and entrusted to Hegai. Esther was among them. Esther pleased the custodian of women and won his favor. He not only promptly provided her with cosmetics and good food but assigned to her seven special maids from the king's household and transferred her and her maids into the best place in the harem. (Esther 2:8–9)

Who is this custodian of the women? His name, Hegai, is Jewish, connected to Mordecai. Is he part of a vast network of Jewish slaves in the king's own household? Does he, like Esther, keep his nationality and his religion secret? Hegai knows what the king likes, and he makes sure Esther suits those likes. They are working together from the start. Soon she is Queen Esther. Further, Mordecai, in the process of keeping an eye on her, overhears two eunuchs discussing an assassination plot. Mordecai tells Esther, who tells the king. The connections deepen.

Next, Mordecai refuses an order from Haman, who is the highest official under the king. Mordecai will not bow before Haman. The reason for the refusal is that Mordecai is a Jew. Haman is enraged, and his rage is kindled not just against Mordecai but against all the Jews. The threat is taking shape, and Haman has the resources and the power to act on his hatred. Haman strikes a deal with the king, and a decree is made: on "a single day, the thirteenth day of the twelfth month of Adar," there will be utter destruction of all the Jews — young and old, women and children — and the plunder of all their goods (Esther 3:12–13).

Mourning in sackcloth and ashes is rampant in the Jewish community, but Esther is outside the chain of events and has to send one of her eunuchs to find out what is happening. The messages then flow back and forth between Mordecai and Esther through eunuchs and slaves. Mordecai begs Esther to beg the king for mercy and to intercede for her people. In turn Esther relays the message that if she goes into the presence of the king without being summoned she will incur the death penalty. And she hasn't been called for thirty days. The ante is upped.

Now to disobey and appear before the king merit death. Her act of disobedience is more dangerous than Vashti's.

And now we hear what the essence of the story is about. Mordecai sends the following message to Esther:

> Do not suppose that because you are in the king's palace, you alone of all the Jews will escape. If you remain silent now, relief and deliverance will come to the Jews from another source, but you and your father's family will perish. And who knows — perhaps you have come to the throne for just such a time as this.
>
> (Esther 4:13–14)

Esther comes into her own right as Jew and as queen. She responds to Mordecai: "Go, gather all the Jews who are in Susa. Fast for me — all of you; do not eat or drink for three days, night or day. My maids and I will also fast. Then I will go to the king, even if it is against the law. If I die for this, let it be" (Esther 4:15–16).

Esther is systematically setting about to do civil disobedience on behalf of her people, with the backup and support of her people, who will, in solidarity, fast and pray with her. This is the action of a people, a revolution that will set in motion their eventual freedom and vindication by their God. It is here that the Greek text introduces Mordecai's and Esther's prayers, just as it has previously been incorporating dreams sent to Mordecai about what God has intended to do for his people all along. In the Greek telling, the entire plot has been planned from the outset, as was Scheherazade's plot to seduce the king through stories. Now the king will be seduced not primarily through Esther's beauty, though that too will play its part, but through the prayer, fasting, and faith of the Jewish people in God's providence and protection, no matter how dangerous their situation among the nations.

Mordecai prays:

> "Lord, King and Master of all, everything is under your power; no one can withstand you in your will to save Israel.
>
> "You made heaven and earth and all the marvels under heaven. You are the Lord of all; no one can resist you, Lord....
>
> "And now, Lord God, King, God of Abraham, deliver your people! Our enemies plot our ruin; they are bent upon destroying the inheritance that was yours from the beginning...."

And Israel cried out with all their might, for they were faced
with death. (Esther 13:8–18; Greek version)

And Esther too prays, alone yet bound to all her people:

My Lord, you who stand alone, come to my help; I am alone and
have no help but you. Through my own choice I am endangering
my life.

As a child I was wont to hear from the people of the land
of my forebears that you, O Lord, chose Israel from among
all peoples, and our fathers from among their ancestors to be
your lasting heritage; that you did for them, all that you have
promised.

But we have sinned, and for this you have handed us over to
our enemies; we have worshiped their god, but you, O Lord, are
just. . . .

Remember us, Lord; reveal yourself in the time of our ca-
lamity. Give me courage, King of gods and master of all power.
May my words be persuasive when I face the lion; turn his heart
against our enemy, that the latter and his like may be brought to
their end.

Save us by your hand; help me who am alone and have none
but you, O Lord. . . .

O God, more powerful than all, hear the voice of those in
despair; save us from the evil man's power, and deliver me from
my fear. (Esther 14; selected texts from Greek version)

The prayers are significant because they reveal Israel's belief and
Mordecai's and Esther's service of God above any they are forced
into in this vile kingdom. These are the desperate prayers of a people
caught in the powers of evil. In segments of Esther's prayer especially
we sense an abhorrence of her life, her servitude and position, as well
as her duties to the king. She lives under constant constraint, perhaps
in opposition to Vashti, who enjoyed at least limited power within the
kingdom.

We are told that when Esther appears before the king unannounced,
she is "radiant" after invoking "the all-seeing God and Savior." She
wears a mask of joy, love, and assured sense of self, yet her heart is
frozen with fear, and she's shaky from lack of food and drink during her fast. The fast has enhanced her beauty and power as well as

making her weak, and so more attractive to the king. We are told
it is God

> who changed the king's anger to gentleness. Alarmed, he sprang
> from his throne, took Esther in his arms until she had recovered
> and comforted her with soothing words. "What is it, Esther?"
> he said, "I am your brother. Take heart. You will not die, be-
> cause our decree applies only to ordinary people. Come speak to
> me." He raised the golden scepter, touched her neck with it, then
> embraced her saying, "Speak to me." (Esther 15:8–12)

The story reads like a novel. Esther swoons after praising the king's
appearance and power and commenting on his kindness. And now
it is the king who is distressed. Surprisingly, Esther asks permission
to invite Haman to a banquet that she has set up for that day. It's
done in an instant. Later, at the banquet, in the midst of the drinking,
the king offers Esther half his kingdom if she wishes it. She counters
with an invitation to another banquet, with Haman as guest, for the
following day.

Haman is delighted. He leaves the banquet and once again sees
Mordecai at the gate. Mordecai again refuses to bow. Haman's rage
is renewed, but he hides it, goes home, and summons his friends and
wife to boast of his place in the court, even of Queen Esther's favor. But he also is clear that none of this is enough while Mordecai
and the Jews are still alive. His wife and friends suggest building a
huge gallows on which to hang Mordecai — to ease Haman's anger
temporarily. Now they are all involved in the conspiracy against the
Jews as the Jews are all involved in their conspiracy with God to save
themselves.

That night the king can't sleep, so he has the chronicles of the
kingdom read to him — and the story of Mordecai's exposure of the
assassination attempt is retold. The king finds out that Mordecai was
never rewarded. The next day, before the banquet, when Haman arrives, he asks him how he, the king, should honor someone. Haman
thinks it is himself and suggests royal robes, a horse, and being led
through the city to the accolades of the king, in the presence of
all the people. The king immediately instructs Haman to do all that
for Mordecai. Instead of hanging Mordecai on newly made gallows,
Haman is now forced to honor Mordecai and is enraged. At home he

is morose and dejected, and his friends begin to see that the plan may be foiled.

He is escorted to the banquet. Again the king entreats Esther to claim what she wants, and this time she speaks up, asking for her own life and the life of all her people who have been slated for destruction, slaughter, and extinction (Esther 7:3–4). In response to the king's question of who would plan such a thing, Esther stands and points out Haman as "wicked, an enemy and a foe!"

The king goes into his garden in anger, and Haman approaches Esther to plead for his life. He has read his fate in the king's face. In his fear he throws himself on the bed Esther is reclining on (the custom at such dinner parties). The king reenters and is furious, thinking that Haman is seducing the queen. Another of Esther's servants, another eunuch, volunteers the information that Haman has already built a fifty-cubit gallows for Mordecai, who has faithfully served the king. The decree is for Haman now to be hung on it instead. And the king's anger subsides.

This is a story about power, hatred, intrigues, and political systems, as well as personal lives within these systems, corrupt as they are, alongside the alternative society with another code, such as the Jewish diasporan community. Now Esther reveals who she is, her connection to Mordecai, and Mordecai is honored with the king's signet ring. Esther once more weeps before the king and begs him to frustrate the plot that Haman has set in motion. The king not only grants Esther her wish but empowers Mordecai to write decrees under the king's authority and in the king's name concerning the Jews. The edicts are startling, almost unbelievable in their scope and power:

> The king's edict granted the Jews in each city the right to assemble and defend themselves, to kill, destroy and wipe out any armed group of any nation or province that might attack them and their women and children, and to seize their goods as spoil. This edict took effect throughout the provinces of King Ahasuerus on the thirteenth day of the twelfth month, Adar.
>
> (Esther 8:11–13)

The people rejoice and prepare to slaughter their enemies in every city of the province. No one resists them because now everyone is afraid of Mordecai, who has risen to such heights of power in the kingdom. "And the Jews struck down their enemies, killing them by the sword, doing as they pleased to those who hated them" (Esther 9:5). When Esther is again consulted by the king, she requests that Haman's ten sons be hanged. It is granted. And on the fifteenth day the Jews rest, making it a day of feasting and rejoicing (Esther 9:18).

Thus the feast of Purim's foundations were established

> to celebrate annually the fourteenth and fifteenth of the month of Adar, the days when the Jews rid themselves of their enemies, and as the month when their sorrow was turned into joy and their mourning into feasting. They were to observe these as days of festivity and rejoicing, days for giving food presents to one another and gifts to the poor. (Esther 9:20–22)

Esther's personal acts of civil disobedience result in the saving of her people, but they are also followed by a killing orgy that makes the opening scene of the book — the king's orgiastic banquet — pale. The feast of Purim — which celebrates in play, costumes, and feasting the death of Haman and his sons and all who were considered enemies of the Jews — unfortunately makes the initial scene of drunkenness and the flaunting of Vashti look almost civilized by comparison. The feast smacks of racism, genocide, and tyranny. Now it is Esther and Mordecai who reign, using the king for their abuse of power. It is just a reversal of who kills whom, with God on the side of the Jews. The villains become the victims, and the victims become worse villains. It is a terrible reversal of fortunes that escalates into the massacre of innocent women and children who had no part in the plots but are simply related to these perceived "enemies," who are numbered to be seventy-five thousand in the provinces.

Many Jewish scholars insist that the book originally ended at chapter 8, verse 17, with the promulgated edict and the celebrations as the people prepared to avenge their enemies: "It was a time of splendor and merriment, honor and triumph. . . . Many people of other nationalities were seized with fear of the Jews, and they embraced Judaism." These scholars thus argue that the actual frenzy of killing and disproportionate revenge was never practiced or encouraged, let alone used as the source of rejoicing, and that the text simply records the end of the threat to the Jews.

The background established, we can now return to the two women: Vashti and Esther. Let us start with Vashti. She is not Jewish. In fact, she was a zealous hater of the Jews and was, according to the rabbis, "the daughter of wicked King Belshazzar, Daniel's nemesis, and the granddaughter of Nebuchadrezzar [the hated king who destroyed the temple in Jerusalem and exiled the people to Babylon]."[5] She had insisted that Ahasuerus put an end to the rebuilding of the temple and had forced the Jewish women to strip off their clothes on every Sabbath and work.

Still, many contemporary women herald Vashti as the hero of the book, forgetting its setting of the threat of genocide to the Jewish people. They argue that Vashti is banished not because of her disobedience but because of the possible effects her action will have on other women without her power, who will follow her lead in standing up to their husbands:

> If Vashti were not punished, her decision could be the start of a major revolution. Other women might look to her as their model; her example would then empower them to rebel against the domination of their husbands. She was cast off because she was an enormous threat to the patriarchal status quo.[6]

One must wonder, however, whether Vashti thought of her defiance as an act that would inspire other women to similar behavior. Her actions indeed reveal the dignity of any person who resists being violated, even when the consequences are banishment from the system or death itself. But her story is not about resistance intended to inspire the lives of others.

Esther, too, is a product of her race, her culture, and, in this case, her historical experience of being a slave, as were all her people. She is sometimes accused of being complacent, subservient, and passive and of using her sexuality to get ahead. But her story is about survival of a nation in the face of history, a history that is tied to the people's faithless worship of other gods and of other nations' strength, rather than relying on their own God's protection with faithfulness and integrity. Esther belongs to a people who live in a precarious and dangerous situation, and any action of a member of that group can put individuals and the entire people in jeopardy of their lives.

An underlying issue is whom the women obey and whom they disobey. Vashti disobeys the king's command for personal reasons. She,

5. Darr, *Far More Precious Than Jewels*, 169.
6. Laffey, *Introduction to the Old Testament*, 214–15.

in a sense, shows obedience primarily to herself. Esther, in contrast, first obeys Mordecai and the traditions of fasting and prayer of her people before disobeying the king's order.

Esther, then, does nonviolent civil disobedience, backed up by her people. She uses her power, her place within a brutal society, for life, placing herself before God and relying on the power of God to turn the king's heart. And it all turns on that moment when the act of disobedience confronts the king and God changes the king's anger to gentleness. This is the story's meaning: how God intervenes to protect, defend, and succor his people in the midst of danger and despair, working with the people who have repented and are being faithful now in exile. It is about God's power in history and about how God's glory resides in his people who will be saved in spite of what history tries to do to them.

Esther is dependent not only on Mordecai but also on other slaves in the harem and those who serve the king as messengers, protectors, and teachers. She acts with her people, and she becomes a queen when she accepts the possibility of death on behalf of her people. She thus is obedient to God and to the demands that arise from the suffering of her people. Her story becomes problematic when she wins and Haman's plot is stopped and reversed. What are we to make of the killing orgy by the Jews? Is this justice? After all, once the crisis has passed for Esther and her people, they behave no differently than those who formerly enslaved and threatened them. Their behavior is not about liberation or freedom. It is tyranny, now sanctioned by religious decree. Even Scheherazade's story ends more humanly.

Judith Plaskow has written that she has experienced chapter 9 of the book of Esther as bloodthirsty and dreadful:

> This year, on the afternoon of Purim, I turned on my radio and heard that Baruch Goldstein had used the occasion of the holiday to mow down thirty Arabs praying in the mosque in Hebron. I realized the story as Purim Torah had not banished or addressed the layer of poisonous objectification of the Other contained in chapter nine.[7]

Chapter 9 is a hard text, one that many, if not the majority, no longer believe reveals the truth or expresses the values of the Jewish people.

---

7. Judith Plaskow, "Dealing with the Hard Stuff," *Tikkun* 9, no. 5: 57.

Plaskow puts it succinctly: "We learn from the Torah that there are whole groups of human beings who are so evil, or so other than we are, that marginalizing or destroying them is not only thinkable but divinely ordained."[8] She believes that you cannot explain away the text or relegate it to a past historical period. Instead the reading of these troubling passages can be used to turn them "into opportunities for communal conversation and learning." In this case, they can be used now to investigate the troubling attitudes of Jews toward Palestinians. The troubling texts should even be read in a manner — a chant — that emphasizes the disturbing nature of the texts themselves and the emotions and moral issues they bespeak. It's true, she says, that these texts have "helped a persecuted people survive." But they have other meaning as well:

> I also want to grapple in community with the dangers of the Purim story for a people with power, and with the criminal uses to which this text has been put, partly in my name. I continue to search for ways of dealing with a complex and contradictory heritage, and for ways of wresting life and justice from even its hardest places.[9]

An editorial in *Tikkun* published a couple of years after Plaskow's statement comments even more directly on what it means to grapple with a hard text. It reads in small part:

> So let's acknowledge during High Holy Days 5759 (September 20–30, 1998) that we Jews have a lot to atone for in Israel. For thirty-one years Israel has occupied close to 2 million people, denying them the right either to participate in Israeli elections or to create their own independent state. That occupation has been maintained through force and brutality, through documented human rights abuses (including continuing use of torture), and through the constant harassment and humiliation of the Palestinian people. . . .
>
> Future generations of Jews will ask how our generation could have gone along with so much depravity. . . .
>
> So in this High Holy Day season we commit ourselves anew to struggling for a very different kind of world, a world in which

---

8. Ibid., 58.
9. Ibid.

we can see God in each other, treat each other with kindness and gentleness, and rejoice in the beauty and wonder of the universe.[10]

On a more personal level, Esther can still serve as a model for hope and revolution for people in dangerous times. Leslie Marmon Silko, a Native American writer, once wrote: "The best thing you can have in life is to have someone tell you a story." And if that story is of hope, of resistance to evil, of nonviolent disobedience shared with others, of justice for all, and of the humanness of all, then that story is truly revolutionary and capable of saving one from death.

Another Esther, Etty (Esther) Hillesum, takes up some themes that throw light on the biblical Esther's actions and their consequences. In her autobiography, *An Interrupted Life,* Hillesum writes:

We shan't get anywhere with hatred. We have so much work to do on ourselves that we shouldn't be thinking of hating our so-called enemies. Every atom of hate that we add to this world makes it still more inhospitable.

Against every new outrage and every fresh horror we shall put up one more piece of love and goodness, drawing strength from within ourselves. We may suffer but we must not succumb.

That's when you said: "But that's nothing but Christianity."

And I retorted quite coolly, amused by your confusion: "Yes. Christianity. And why ever not?"[11]

This young Jewish women from Holland, who perished at Auschwitz, wrote in a situation more horrible and immediate than Esther's. Addressing God, she states: "Alas, there doesn't seem to be much You Yourself can do about our circumstances, about our lives. Neither do I hold You responsible. You cannot help us but we must help You and defend Your dwelling place inside us to the last."[12] And one of her last written phrases conveyed the essence of liberation and true resistance to all evil: "We should be willing to act as balm for all wounds."[13] This is the legacy of a more contemporary Esther, Etty (Esther) Hillesum, born January 15, 1914, murdered November 30, 1943.

---

10. Editorial in *Tikkun* 13, no. 5 (1998).
11. Etty Hillesum, *An Interrupted Life,* abr. ed. (New York: Penguin, 1991).
12. Ibid., 51.
13. Ibid., 196.

The stories of both Esthers are, in the end, about hope. Václav Havel says: "Hope is an orientation of the spirit, an orientation of the heart. It is not the conviction that something will turn out well, but the certainty that something makes sense, regardless of how it turns out."

And so we act; we obey and disobey; we resist and act for justice, not just for ourselves and our own, but for all, because of hope, because it is what is true, what is human, and what is the will of the Holy, what is the spark of the Divine in all of us. It is in times when hope is threatened, in Esther's times, in times such as ours, that her story — until it turns toward vengeance — is a story for all peoples. Like the storyteller Scheherazade, we need at least 1001 of these stories to stop the decree of death and slowly, ever so slowly, transform the hearts of all into hearts that are made of balm and gladness, in times worthy of celebration.

SEVEN

A JUDGE, A SLAVE GIRL, AND THREE WIDOWS

THERE IS A TALMUDIC STORY that appears in many other folk traditions. It is called "The Clever Carver," "A Woman of Some Wisdom," or "Wisdom Is in the Seeing." It is a good way to begin this chapter because of its insights and twists on seeing and using power for the benefit of others, though many may not understand why you exercise power in this particular way:

> Once upon a time there was a family that was visited unexpectedly by a prince. He had been traveling and lost his way. Coming upon this house off the beaten path he was given shelter and hospitality. They were poor, but as was the custom, they took the one source of meat they still had, the rooster, and prepared it for dinner. They gathered around the table, said the blessing prayers, and all waited hungrily for their portion. The eldest daughter was given the carving tools, and she set about dividing up the bird.
>
> Much to her parents' surprise she carved the bird and handed out the pieces strangely. The head went to her father, the body of the bird to her mother, all the available flesh to the children and herself, and the wings to the visiting prince. Nothing was said, but the parents looked at each other questioningly. The children, however, were delighted and attacked the rare treat on their plates. The prince, used to the lion's share of any meal, was stunned, but said nothing, just watched the girl closely for the rest of the meal.
>
> The children and the prince settled in for the night, and the father and mother at the first opportunity queried their daugh-

ter about the way she had carved the rooster. The girl was sure of her allotments and explained: "Father, you were served first, with the head of the bird, because you are the head of this family. And Mother, you were served next the main body of the bird, with its ribs, because you have borne each of us within you and still carry us like a ship on the perilous seas of life. And the children were given the meat of the bird because they are young, hungry, and the real heart of this family. And the prince — he will fly away tomorrow and never think of us again — so, he got the wings of the bird. If he went to bed hungry tonight, perhaps he will know that we go to bed hungry more often than not, and now we do not even have our rooster because of his unexpected visit." The parents were impressed with their daughter's common sense.

The prince was listening to the explanation and was fascinated by the girl's simple wisdom and deep understanding, blending the need to practice hospitality with the ongoing needs of her family and aware of others' behaviors and stations in life. In the morning he watched her with eyes open and receptive to her in a new way, and he was not surprised to find that he was in love with her.

Is she a clever girl or a young woman mature beyond her years because of poverty and experience? Does she possess a large dollop of common sense, or does she possess the desire for justice and the courage to act upon her convictions? These questions and some of the answers set the background for the historical epoch of the Judges in Israel.

After the death of Joshua, the Israelites were loose-knit tribes and clans attempting to settle in the land of Canaan, which was already occupied territory. They consulted together on occasion and made forays into the land, taking pieces of it, learning to live in sporadic times of peace with the inhabitants, and on other occasions fighting to retain their acquired territory. The Israelites were generally just surviving, at the mercy of roving nomads and fiercer tribes, subject to raids and plunder. Groups of them would gather around various leaders, who were common folk, but possessed of common sense and a focus that both remembered Israel's unique covenant with Yahweh at Mt. Sinai and saw the hand of God in their contemporary history. It was a savage time, and battles could result in starvation, destruction of harvests, and forced intermarriage. These leaders were primitive and yet wise, within their own historical frameworks. The introductory notes to the book of Judges in the Christian Community Bible remind us of what was meant by the designation "judge" in this context:

> These men [and notably one woman, Deborah] are known in history as the "Shofetim," a word that means both "chiefs" and "judges." We must remember that in Hebrew culture and even in the Gospel, the word "to judge" also means "to govern" (Mt. 19:28). For that reason those who have never been a member of a tribunal are called "judges." Perhaps we should understand the word "judges" in another way: these persons were the instruments of God's justice. The judges were not saints in the meaning we give this word. Nevertheless Israel saw in them the savior that God in his mercy was sending. To slay an enemy chief or kill the Philistines is no longer a religious act for us. But if we keep in mind their time and their milieu, these persons had faith and were courageous amidst so much cowardice. In awakening the passivity of their brothers and sisters, they were preparing for a new phase of their history.

And very early in the book of Judges we are told that

> the Israelites treated Yahweh badly; they forgot Yahweh, their God, and served the Baals and the Asheroths. Because of this, the anger of Yahweh burned against Israel and he left them in the hands of Cushanrishathaim, king of Aram, to whom they were subject for eight years. Then the Israelites cried to Yahweh, and he raised up from among them a liberator who saved them — Othniel the son of Kenaz, Caleb's younger brother. (Judg. 3:7–9)

This will be the pattern during this phase of the Israelites' history. They will know a period of relative stability, will begin to forget the covenant's demands and the necessity of clinging together as they worship the one God they belong to, and will slide into the worship of other gods. Then they will be left to the powers and whims of tribes and nations stronger than they until they begin to turn again toward Yahweh and cry out in their distress. Finally, they will be given a savior, someone to lead them through the hardest of the times, strengthening their resolve and pushing them to trust again in the power of the great protector Yahweh, who has always been their leader. And so we come to the story of Deborah, the woman judge in Israel.

Deborah

Now the Israelites have been oppressed for twenty years and held under oppression by the king of Canaan, whose army commander is Sisera. We are told that Deborah,

> a prophetess and wife of Lappidoth, became judge. She used to sit under what was called the Palm of Deborah, between Ramah and Bethel, in the land of Ephraim. There she resolved the complaints that the Israelites presented to her. And she sent and called for Barak, the son of Abinoam, who was from the town of Kedesh of Naphtali. She said to him, "This is the order of Yahweh: Go, gather the people on Mount Tabor and take with you ten thousand men from the tribes of Naphtali and Zebulun, for I am going to bring Sisera to you at the river Kishon with his chariots and men, and I will give him into your hands."
>
> (Judg. 4:4–7)

She is a prophetess, one who sees the hand of God in all events, relationships, and circumstances. As a woman with insight and foresight, she was honored and her words obeyed without question. She sat under a palm tree and held court. Dorothee Sölle, in a commentary on Deborah, writes:

> After the conquest, jurisdiction rests with the eldest who sat "at the gate" and gave advice, settled arguments and litigations, and decided on social problems. Deborah sat under a palm tree between Bethel and Ramah in this capacity. In this part of Palestine there are hardly any palms, and the palm tree named for Deborah, rising high at the edge of Mount Ephraim, was a rarity. Since the days of Paradise the palm tree has had mythical and symbolic significance; it is considered the tree of life, evergreen, symbol of eternal life, and a sign of hope and victory. The children of Israel came up to Deborah who sat under the palm tree looking for justice. Even Deborah's name, meaning "bee," is an

ancient symbol for royalty and for the beneficent mother; she nourishes her people with "honey."[1]

She orders Barak to assemble an army and be ready to go into battle, but Barak hesitates. He says something startling to her, given the times and the culture of the Israelites. He says: "If you will go, then I shall go, too; but if you do not go, I shall not go." Deborah answers: "I will go with you, but if you do it that way the honor of the victory will not be yours, for Sisera will be killed by a woman" (Judg. 4:8–9). Does he question her authority? Probably he is afraid and needs Deborah's presence with him and the soldiers as backup and security. For as prophetess and judge Deborah would have been admired, feared, and known as the mouthpiece of God's word, admonishing and summoning forth the power of God to be with them. She tells Barak: "Rise, for this is the day in which Yahweh shall give Sisera into your hands. Today, Yahweh goes before you" (Judg. 4:14).

The battle that ensues is furious and quickly turns in favor of the Israelites, with Sisera fleeing for his life, leaving his chariot behind. But the battle is not fought in a conventional military manner. We are told in Judg. 5:20 that "from the heavens the stars fought, from their orbits they fought against Sisera. The torrent Kishon dragged them away, the cold torrent, the torrent Kishon. March on without fear, my soul!" Sisera seeks refuge in the tents of an ally, Yael (Jael), the wife of Heber the Kenite.

But she is no friend or ally. She welcomes him, exhorting him to lay aside his fears, to come in and rest, feeding him milk. She gives him solace, and he sleeps. Then she moves with brutal efficiency, and with a hammer drives a tent peg through his head! Barak arrives and Deborah's words have come true. The victory is accomplished.

There are two notable turn-arounds. First, the battle is won by nature itself, heaven and earth obeying and siding with the Israelites, so that they do not even have to fight to defeat the enemy. Second, the general is betrayed by an ally, a woman who "acts like man," who kills cold-bloodedly and viciously, with no heart. Yael and Deborah are two ends of the spectrum of power, displaying the best and worst traits of humanity. In Deborah's victory song Yael will be called "blessed

---

1. Dorothee Sölle, *Great Women of the Bible in Art and Literature* (Grand Rapids, Mich.: Eerdmans, 1993), 118.

among women, . . . blessed may you be!" for her actions. And yet, jux-
taposed immediately after is the piteous plight of Sisera's mother, who
waits for her son to return:

> Sisera's mother looks out of the window, and she cries out be-
> hind the lattice: Why is his chariot late in coming? Why is his
> chariot delayed? The wisest of her women answers and says:
> Surely they are dividing the plunder — one captive, two cap-
> tives for each warrior; colored cloths for Sisera as booty, colored
> cloths twice adorned with raised embroidery for a scarf.
>
> (Judg. 5:28–30)

Sadly, we are not meant to feel compassion for Sisera's mother. She
is described as anticipating the plunder and booty, the capture of prisoners and women who will be made slaves and raped. Women and
children are always part of the spoils and the greater number of dead
and victims of any war. And yet the reality is there stark and unavoid-
able: murder and war are just that, murder and war. This is the usual
experience of not just women in war but everyone: they sit and wait
for the news and the names of the dead, their individual lives caught
in the tyranny of the army and the economic and political warring
factions. The brutal reality is: What of all the mothers, wives, sisters,
and children of those killed in battle or maimed, whether of Israel's
or Sisera's army? If you are a victim, does it really matter which side
won? Today, the religious belief is that these are atrocities, no matter
who commits them.

It was a brutal and barbaric time in the history of Israel. Deborah
sings of the might and the glory of God in her victory song, ending it
with the prayer: "So may all your enemies perish, O Yahweh, but may
your friends be like the brilliant sun!" And it appears that all goes
well afterward because we are told that "there was peace in the land
for forty years" (Judg. 5:31).

Deborah has thus brought about — at great cost in lives and suffering — a transformation in Israel. Her victory song announces early
on: "There were no leaders in Israel until I, Deborah, awoke and arose
as a mother in Israel" (Judg. 5:7). That line is crucial: there were no
leaders, no vision, no future, and no connection to the past. Deborah is
the connection to the past choice of poor nomadic tribes to be a people
who carry the torch of belief through dark periods of history. Deborah is a mother of Israel, a liberator of her people. In the beginning of

the Israelites' history when they first escaped slavery in Egypt, Moses and Miriam sang the praises of Yahweh and led the people. Now the song is in the mouths of Deborah and Barak, the gender roles reversed: Deborah has assumed Moses' role.

Male domination may have been woven into the texture of the daily life of the Israelites, but there are many stories, like that of Deborah, that contradict this monochromatic image. In every generation there are openings, fissures, in the texture of the dominant reality, and sometimes a light penetrates through one of these. Deborah is one of these lights. In fact this image of lights is connected to a midrash on our text and to Deborah's name. This is how the midrash reads:

> What was the special character of Deborah that qualified her to prophesy about Israel and to judge them? . . . In the school of Elijah it was taught: I call heaven and earth to witness that whether it be a heathen or a Jew, a man or a woman, a manservant or a maidservant, the holy spirit will suffuse any one of them in keeping with the deeds he or she performs.
>
> [What were Deborah's meritorious deeds?] It is said that Deborah's husband was unlettered [in Torah]. So his wife told him: "Come, I will make wicks for you; take them to the Holy Place in Shiloh. Your portion will then be with men of worth in Israel [who will be studying by the light of your wicks], and you will be worthy of life in the world-to-come." She took care to make the wicks thick, so that their light would be ample. He brought these wicks to the Holy Place [in Shiloh]. The Holy One, who examines the hearts and reins of mankind, said to her, "Deborah, since you took care to make the light for the study of my Torah ample, I will make the light of your prophecy ample in the presence of Israel's twelve tribes."[2]

It seems the spirit comes to rest on one not because of gender or even race or religion but because of one's deeds! Justice, compassion, and simple human kindnesses merit the outpouring of the spirit when it is needed in Israel and, it would follow, in the church and the world at large. God does great things for the people through the leadership of Deborah, who rises like a mother in Israel. This honorific title conveys

---

2. *Seder Eliyyahu Rabbah,* ed. Meir Friedmann (Vienna, 1902), 48; *Yalkut Shimoni, Judges* 42, in *The Book of Legends,* ed. Hayim Nahman Bialik and Yehoshua Hana Ravnitzky, trans. William G. Braude (New York: Schocken Books, 1992).

what she was chosen to be and to do for the people. She is a wise woman who will liberate her people from their oppression, provide protection, ensure their well-being, give them security and peace in the land, and teach them the way of the Word of God with authority.

Helen Graham, a Maryknoll sister, writes in a newsletter in the Philippines:

> To the question as to what might have been the source and scope of the authority of the wise woman in early Israel, the metaphor of the mother supplies a clue. An important indication of the mother's role is given in Proverbs where the mother's *tora* (or teaching) is placed in parallelism with the father's instruction (*musar;* Proverbs 1:8), and with his commandment (*miswa;* 6:20). The authority that the child-rearing function confers on women "is not qualified by the 'highest' authority of the father, but, rather, places a woman on exactly the same footing as her husband in at least one area of endeavor."[3]

The Jewish community in the first century honored Deborah as another Moses, her story paralleling his in every detail. Pseudo-Philo's collection *Biblical Antiquities* relates a scene at Deborah's deathbed that echoes another first-century Jewish text's depiction of the scene at Moses' deathbed. Cheryl Anne Brown quotes the latter text, in which a follower pleads with Moses:

> Now, Master, you are going away, and who will sustain this people? Or who will have compassion on them, and will be for them a leader on (their) way? Or who will pray for them, not omitting a single day, so that I may lead them into the land of their forefathers? How, therefore, can I be (guardian) of this people, as a father is to his only son, or as a mother is to her virgin daughter (who) is being prepared to be given to a husband; a mother who is disquieted, guarding (the daughter's) body from the sun and (seeing to it) that (the daughter's) feet are not without shoes? . . . Can I be responsible for food for them as they desire and drink according to their will?
>
> (*Assumption of Moses* 11:9–13)

---

3. From a newsletter for the National Consultation on Justice, Peace, and Human Rights, United Church of Christ in the Philippines; Graham is quoting *Catholic Biblical Quarterly* 43 (1981): 17.

Brown then comments on the text:

> Most of these roles — clothing, feeding, and giving drink —
> are characteristically feminine. According to the *Assumption
> of Moses,* Moses fills masculine and feminine roles on behalf
> of the people; according to *Biblical Antiquities,* Deborah fills
> many of the more traditionally masculine roles (leading, liber-
> ating, teaching Torah, shepherding) attributed to Moses, as well
> as more traditionally feminine roles. Again, we see that she is
> portrayed as Moses' counterpart.[4]

In the *Biblical Antiquities,* the account of Deborah's deathbed scene
is followed by a dirge that makes four statements about her. She is "a
mother in Israel." She is a holy one, a prophetess who works miracles
and intercedes for her people. She is a leader. And she has "firmed up
the fence around her generation." This last description may refer to the
historical reality of Deborah's time, when the people lived scattered
and without protection, without fences or walls around their encampments. Or the word "fence" (*torah*) may have a more metaphorical
meaning, referring to the law that held the people together and that
kept others out, kept others from defiling or destroying the tent or the
flock that belonged to Yahweh alone.

Deborah was worthy of remembrance by women and men in the
past and remains so today. Dorothee Sölle included a personal poem
in her commentary on Deborah that makes these connections:

> Bible-talk
> Something was missing in our beautiful evening
> There was our laughter
> at the custom of ordinary men
> to be always superior
> and Deborah planned liberation and led the campaign
> and Barak the general fought only when she came along
> There was our laughter
>
> Something was missing when we chatted
> There was our fear
> of winning but not being different

---

4. Cheryl Anne Brown, *No Longer Be Silent: First-Century Jewish Portraits of
Biblical Women* (Louisville: Westminster/John Knox Press, 1992), 68–69.

from the former victors
and Jael receives the unsuspecting guest
gives milk to him who asked for water
and murders the sleeping man
There was our fear

Something was missing, my sisters
There was our silence
will we be like Deborah and stand up
against the new holocaust and our fanatic
sons
will we be like Jael
against law and feelings
There was our silence

Something was missing
on the long way
to strength and weakness.[5]

The story of Yael and Deborah and this poem ask a question of women today: Is there something vital still missing from the exercise of authority, of leadership, and of prophecy in today's church and world? Perhaps the two stories that follow can reveal in more depth the qualities that are acutely needed in every nation and generation.

A Slave Girl

We begin with a maidservant, a young girl captured and enslaved by Aramean soldiers. The story is found in 2 Kings 5. The text is primarily about Naaman the leper, but we will look at events from the vantage point of the conquered one, the young woman. The story begins:

Naaman was the army commander of the king of Aram. This man was highly regarded and enjoyed the king's favor, for Yahweh had helped him lead the army of the Arameans to victory. But this valiant man was sick with leprosy.

One day some Aramean soldiers raided the land of Israel and took a young girl captive who became a servant to the wife of

---

5. Dorothee Sölle, "Verruckt nach Licht" (Crazy about light), in *Poems* (Berlin, 1984), 118; see Sölle, *Great Women of the Bible*.

Naaman. She said to her mistress, "If my master would only present himself to the prophet in Samaria, he would surely cure him of his leprosy."

Naaman went to tell the king what the young Israelite maid-servant had said. The king of Aram said to him, "Go to the prophet, and I shall also send a letter to the king of Israel."

(2 Kings 5:1–4)

It is remarkable what this one woman sets in motion! She is a captured slave, an indentured servant, dragged off in a raid, exiled now in enemy territory, far from her own people and religious sanctuaries. Yet she is bold enough to declare her belief in the prophet of her own people, whom she honors as holding the Word of the Lord, a power and a presence of the Holy unique among the other nations. Her suggestion passes from her mistress, the wife of Naaman, to the general of enemy forces, to the king, and then to the king in Israel, who sees it as ruse to start a war between the two groups.

But Elisha, a prophet in Israel, knows what Yahweh is planning. Elisha sends word to the king in Israel to send Naaman to him, so "that he will know that there is a prophet in the land of Israel." Naaman goes and Elisha tells him to go to the River Jordan, plunge into its waters seven times, and he will be cleansed, his flesh becoming as it was before. Naaman is furious. The order is stupid, without meaning for him. Why the River Jordan? Why not one of the rivers in his own land? He had expected to be touched, seared with power, dramatically healed, or at least Elisha should have cried out to his God and called on the power of his God's name: Yahweh. And again, it is the servants (other Israelite captives?) who reason with him, saying, "Father, if the prophet had ordered you to do something difficult, would you not have done it? But how much easier when he said: Take a bath and you will be cleansed." Is his wife's maidservant in that company, traveling with Naaman, as guide, encouraging him to obey?

Naaman is healed utterly, and he takes back to his own land sacks of earth from the land of Israel to build an altar so that he can worship the true God, Yahweh, even in his own country. He begs Elisha to pardon him because he must still accompany his king when the king goes to worship his god, and Elisha sends him home in peace. Naaman is gracious with his gifts and sure now in his praise of and belief in Israel's God, the only God.

What of the maidservant? She has known horror, fear, and loneliness in her young life, and most probably she has experienced physical
and sexual abuse, being subjected to the soldiers' humiliation and contempt. Yet eventually she is bought or brought to the household of a
prominent man. Her life would have improved immensely as a captive, although she is still a servant, an exile, and far from her own
people. But more than anything else she is a believer in the power and
presence of her God and knows that her God works in all lands, for
all people who obey his commands as they are expressed through the
prophet. She is an outcast and recognizes Naaman, for all his power
and prestige, as an outcast because of his leprosy. She has compassion
on those who own her. God works through her, and she is the source
of Naaman's being led to the prophet in Israel and to the experience
of healing and wholeness.

Was Naaman generous enough to release her from her servitude
and send her home? We know from Naaman's plea for forgiveness
that he had to go back to his world and that he and his household
would be alone now in their worship of Yahweh. But we do not know
if he freed the maidservant. The slave girl is never mentioned again.
We lose track of her, yet we know that she is a leader, a model for behavior under persecution and hardship. She is worthy of praise. True
authority does not only or primarily reside in the mighty of the land,
the leaders of armies or those respected among their own. True authority is more powerful, deeper, and truer than Deborah's, more hidden
yet more pervasive, crossing borders, healing and offering hope that
makes friends and equals out of conquerors and enemies. This servant
girl knows the power of the poor and the presence of God with those
who suffer and lives with dignity in spite of what she has experienced,
preaching the Word of God no matter her circumstances. She is in the
tradition neither of Deborah nor of Yael. She is, rather, in the tradition of Jesus, who commands the man born blind to go and wash in
the pool of Siloam and among those called blessed because they are
peacemakers, merciful, and see God everywhere.

Three Widows

There is another unnamed woman, a widow whom Jesus himself
points out to his disciples as worthy of imitation, who models behavior, belief, and worship for his community. She is contrasted to

the respected and honored leaders in Israel, who are in reality weak, unjust, and self-absorbed in their own importance, disregarding both God and other human beings. Jesus warns his followers at the very end of his public ministry, just before the conspiracy to capture and kill him is set in motion:

> As he was teaching, he also said to them, "Beware of those teachers of the law who enjoy walking around in long robes and being greeted in the marketplace and who like to occupy reserved seats in the synagogues and the first places at feasts. They even devour the widow's and the orphan's goods while making a show of long prayers. How severe a sentence they will receive!" (Mark 12:38–40)

Jesus is clear: these people — the rich and powerful — will be judged and sentenced most severely. They are not concerned with holiness, justice, or the honor of God, let alone care for the poor. They are concerned only with appearances, a good reputation, their standing in the community, and using their authority for their own gain and security. Those in the seats of judgment and in places of honor will be judged more critically than those without power or access to authority in Jesus' church and his Father's reign on earth. Jesus contrasts the behavior of these hypocrites with the true belief, pure worship, and heartfelt obedience of a woman no one would have noticed or thought to look at twice, an invisible person who stands out in God's memory and sight as worthy of being followed and as the one who has the wisdom of the Spirit:

> Jesus sat down opposite the temple treasury and watched the people dropping money into the treasury box; and many rich people put in large offerings. But a poor widow also came and dropped in two small coins.
> Then Jesus called his disciples and said to them, "Truly I say to you, this poor widow put in more than all those who gave offerings. For all of them gave from their plenty, but she gave from her poverty and put in everything she had, her very living." (Mark 12:41–44)

Other translations say that Jesus "observed" those dropping money into the collection box, just as he "observed" Simon and Andrew casting their nets into the sea in the first chapter of the gospel. After that first instance of observing, Jesus called Simon and Andrew to be his followers, calling them to leave their father, their livelihoods, their families, and their futures to cast their lot with his words and presence in the world (Mark 1:16–20). This word "observed" has connotations of obeying the law, of surrendering to the authority and power of another, of one who is worthy of being followed. Now, late in his ministry and teaching, Jesus has observed someone who is a follower, who is one of his disciples, a poor woman who practices her belief by giving everything she has, even her own means of livelihood and support. She lives, in her poverty, the life the disciples have been called to. She models behavior that is unassuming, hidden, and pure, as opposed to those who practice their religion for display, for the accolades of others, and from a prominent place in the community.

This woman without resources relies on God, worships God, and is ignored by those who should know better — the disciples, those who claim to be followers of the God of justice, mercy, and solidarity with those on the borders of society. In his description of her, Jesus is comparing her to himself, who gives all, even to the point of giving his own life as witness to and the last word on how to love, how to trust, and how to honor God in one's life. She alone gives God what God deserves: a complete sacrifice of herself. She alone worships and knows God. Her gift honors God more than all the others combined. Hers is the choice portion, the acceptable sacrifice that is pleasing. And she is also the accuser, the witness against those who worship yet treat others like herself unjustly, callously, living without integrity, relegating religion to outward pietistic practice. She, just by her presence in the community, judges them.

She is kin to the widows whose stories are told in the books of Kings, the one who helps Elijah even in her poverty and distress and the one who comes begging Elisha to help her with her dead husband's creditors, who seek to sell her children into slavery. In 1 Kings 17, we meet the widow of Zarephath, who meets Elijah as he enters the gates of the city and who obeys his blunt request for a bit of water and some bread. Even though she is starving, along with her young son, she goes to get him water and obeys his instruction to take the last of her flour and oil and feed him, sharing their meal with him. He tells her that in return for her obedience and generosity there will be enough for the three of them until the drought is over. Amazingly, she obeys though she is not an Israelite or a believer! She does, it seems, believe that God works outside the boundaries of her own religion and that Elijah's God must be obeyed even in the dire straits in which she finds herself.

Rebecca Asedillo speaks clearly of what this story says to us today:

> The eminent Asian theologian D. T. Niles once defined evangelism in the Asian context as one beggar telling another beggar where they both might find food. In our story, when the prophet, the traditional purveyor of comfort to the afflicted and affliction to the comfortable, and the traditionally-perceived "helpless" widow pooled their resources together, they were both fed. The prophet and the widow are companions in the struggle. They are inseparable.[6]

These poor, obedient, and generous widows are in every country, among every religious grouping. They are survivors, suffering under the calamities of historical events that put their very existence in peril. But almost no one makes economic, political, or social decisions on the basis of how they will affect these women and other poor women, children, and men. It seems only God watches them closely, using them as the benchmark, the indicator of right judgment and the coming of justice.

In an October 1, 1998, issue of the *National Catholic Reporter,* in an article entitled "Religion Battles High Finance," Dennis J. Coday highlighted the effects of the dominant patterns of decision making on the poor. The article focused especially upon the Asian financial collapse. Coday described a group meeting in Seoul that investigated the cause of the crisis and its effects in various countries. The explanation of the reasons for the collapse is fairly simple once one understands how multinational corporations operate. One of the devices is called "shorting the currency." Coday describes it:

> Shorting the currency is a strategy in currency speculation in which currency traders take out massive loans in a local currency and then start selling to buy dollars, causing the exchange rate to plummet. When the rate falls, they can repay the local currency loans for fewer dollars and pocket the difference. That happened in Thailand, South Korea, Indonesia and Malaysia.

---

6. Rebecca Asedillo, *Women of Faith: Bible Studies for Women's Groups* (Manila: Institute of Religion and Culture, 1996), 57.

As local currencies became worth less and less, Asian busi-
nesses could not repay the billions of dollars they had borrowed
from foreign sources. Real estate investment offered no returns,
and stock prices went through the floor. So the speculators and
the foreign lenders took their money out of the region.[7]

Of course this is a calculated and acceptable practice among in-
vestors, corporations, and countries that dominate world markets and
set the standards and limits on foreign loans. According to the article,
it is summed up in the phrase "cronyism and corruption." But, in
reality, there is more behind this situation than is apparent from the
technical description of what happened. Martin Khor, the director of
the Malaysia-based Third World Network, labeled the real cause —
he revealed a web that stretches back to deeper structures of sin. This
is what he says: "It's true that we have crony capitalism causing our
problems, but it is international crony capitalism of Wall Street controlling the U.S. Treasury [which is] controlling the IMF and the IMF
controlling the developing world. This is the crony capitalism."[8]

The first work of prophecy is to deplore existing sinful conditions
and expose the evil behind them, naming sin for what it is and naming
its source. And to do that, one must view the situation through the eyes
of the poor, the victims, and the numberless nameless people, giving
voice to those who are most severely affected by the structures that
destroy people's lives on a massive scale.

At the conference in Seoul, a number of women did precisely
this prophetic work. Susanna Yoon Soon-nyo, who chairs the Korean
Catholic Women's Community for a New World, spoke out on behalf of the few other women involved in the proceedings. Coday says
that she

> told the forum it was making a big mistake in not listening care-
> fully to what women were saying about the economic crisis.
> Yoon cited rising cases of unemployed men abandoning their
> families. "Women are given the task to take full responsibility
> for the family. This has always been the case in [Korean] history.
> In the wars and since, women have always sacrificed themselves
> to save the family," she said.

---

7. Dennis J. Coday, "Religion Battles High Finance," *National Catholic Reporter*,
October 1, 1998, 3.
8. Ibid., 4.

The conference's final statement incorporated these ideas: "Women, especially because of their suffering from the Asian economic crisis exacerbated by gender discrimination, need an official channel to express their needs and participate in dialogue for improvement." Coday comments, however, that "several women delegates were still disappointed, saying that tacking on women's concerns to the larger group's agenda still kept women marginalized."[9]

In God's account of history, both that of Israel and of Jesus of Nazareth, we are commanded to start with the marginalized and the borderline people when we look at economic and political crises; we are commanded to examine the structures of injustice and our own collusion with such sin, as church and as believers. Jesus in our story of a widow woman starts with her, with her situation, in contrast to most of us, who tend to tack on such a perspective at the end of our pronouncements and decisions.

Elijah, we should remember, moves in with the widow of Zarephath and her young son, living on the portion that God allots daily, and Jesus aligns himself with the widow who gives her very sustenance to God. This is where leadership must begin if it is to have integrity and validity in the community of those who believe in God.

A model for pragmatic responses to these situations is found in the story of the widow and Elisha in 2 Kings 4:1–7. The story is simple. A widow of a prophet who knew Elisha is hounded by her husband's creditors and she cannot pay. The creditors are ruthless, but operating under the law. They want to sell her two young sons into slavery for up to six years to pay the debt. This would not only add to her own misery but deprive her of her family, support, and love. Elisha asks her the simple question: "What can I do for you? Tell me what you have in your house" (1 Kings 4:2). Her response is telling. She has been reduced to having nothing but "a little oil for cleaning." But that is where Elisha starts, with whatever little pittance is at hand. He commands her to follow his instructions explicitly, and she does:

> Go and ask your neighbors for empty jars. Get as many as you can; then go into your house with yours sons and close the door. Pour oil into the vessels. And when they are filled, set them aside.

---

9. Ibid., 5

The woman went and locked herself in her house with her sons. They handed her the vessels and she filled them all. She said to one of her sons, "Bring me another vessel," and he answered, "There are no more." Then the oil stopped flowing.

As she went back to tell this to the man of God, he said to her, "Go and sell the oil to pay for your debts; you and your sons can live on the money that is left." (2 Kings 4:3–7)

The prophet, the leader, is seen as the one closest to the poor of the times, and the power of the leader is used for the poor, the desperate, and the despairing caught in the net of social indifference and injustice. The beginning of a solution to the widow's individual problem lies in an investment of what little she has, coupled with help from her neighbors, who contribute generously, sharing their resources and faith.

It seems the entire village contributed storage jars to help the woman. The amount of what she would receive was contingent upon the sharing of her neighbors, and together they overcame the economic system that was poised to prey upon the woman and her sons.

This miracle begins with connections. The widow approaches the prophet because her husband was known to be associated with him and knew him to be "God-fearing." We are bound to help and respond to the needs of those we are connected to in ministry, friendship, and the struggle for the truth and the coming of justice. This miracle begins with a network of people who are responsible for others when the need arises. The primary responsibility is economic stability that keeps families together when they are faced with death and the loss of a parent or their provider.

The miracle starts small, in households and small cooperatives that share basic human resources and goods that are necessary for survival. Oil is used for cooking, medications, healing, and heating. It is the base of many other products, like myrrh, nard, and bathing salts. And it is a staple in diets worldwide. This miracle, then, like Jesus' miracles with bread, begins with a staple. It grows because the community shapes an alternative economy — the sharing of the jars — in response to economic tyranny. The actions of the widow and her neighbors can serve as a model of how we and the church should approach issues of economic injustice. The heart of the method is the poor, the shunned, the "widow."

M. Cathleen Kaveny, an associate professor of law at Notre Dame Law School, has written about the early church's order of widows, an association that expressed the church's belief in Jesus' exhortation to care for the least among them (Matt. 25:35–40). The order also revealed the honor the church afforded widows because of their experience, authority in spiritual matters, and influence on the larger community of believers. Kaveny writes:

> To use the language of contemporary Catholic social teaching, by instituting the order of widows the early Christians exercised the virtue of solidarity in three ways. First, by providing the widows with food, shelter and basic care, the early Christians honored their equal dignity as human beings. Second, the members of the church did not content themselves with meeting those needs from a safe distance. By incorporating the widows into their ongoing communal life, the early Christians recognized that they all shared a common identity as brothers and sisters in Christ. And third, they were not satisfied merely to care for the widows (which had long been considered a meritorious act by the Israelites), nor even simply to count them as members of their community. Instead, they pushed beyond bare inclusion toward active participation by discerning ways in which the widows themselves could make an invaluable contribution to the common good. In so doing, the church forged an innovative form of social unity.[10]

This tradition within the church needs to be reactivated so that widows and those who find themselves in the category encompassed by the word *almanah* — which means "a once-married woman who has no means of support" — are given dignity, work that is a real service to the community, an honorable way to live, and a place in the community that cherishes them as beloved of God. In Jesus' ministry and life he singles out widows often as worthy of his intervention and saving power, as with the widow of Naim (Luke 7:11–17) and the widow who puts her pittance into the temple treasury.

We should also include the widow Anna, who praises the young child Jesus when Mary and Joseph bring him to be offered as firstborn

---

10. M. Cathleen Kaveny, "The Early Church's Order of Widows and the Virtue of Solidarity," *America*, September 12, 1998, 17.

sacrificed to the honor of God. Jesus cared for his mother, Mary, a widow, until he was thirty years old and then entrusted her care to John, the beloved disciple. And in the parable that Jesus tells of the widow and the unjust judge, the most startling reading declares that God himself is a widow with only one demand of all of us — that we acknowledge the power of God and obey the basic demands of the law and the covenant in regard to one another.

This has been a chapter on a woman judge named Deborah, a slave girl abducted and sold in a foreign country, and a number of widows identified only by the town or village where they resided. It has also been about power and authority and how true leadership is exercised, influencing the community for good. Leadership among believers in God witnesses first of all to the power of God in history, in disastrous situations, and in heart-rending experiences of suffering, war, slavery, and death. These stories have taught that one gesture, one decision, or one action taken in public can drastically alter history for the better if it begins in the reality of the oppressed or shunned and reaches toward God in hope. Such actions are the work of real prophets and prophetesses.

A friend, Peter Daino, a Marianist, told me a true story that happened in Rwanda. It was reported in the *Nation Kenya* newspaper. As recorded by Father Renato Kizito, it is a story of leadership, prophecy, and judgment; it is about believing in the midst of a world mad with violence, insanity, and the killing of the innocent. The story is stark, and the persons involved are, again, mostly nameless:

> On April 29, 22 people, mostly school-girls, were killed in an attack on a Catholic school in Muramba, Rwanda, in the Gisenyi region, near the Zaire (now Democratic Republic of Congo) border. According to Rwandan radio news-report, a group of armed men broke into the school, ordering the girls to divide into ethnic groups, Hutus on one side; Tutsis on the other. The girls refused and the men opened fire, killing 17 of them and wounding 14. A Belgian missionary nun, Sister Margarita Bosman, 62, who tried to stop the assassins, was also killed, and so were four other lay people.

Later in the article the reporter comments:

> The conciseness of the news agency report does not diminish the brave act of these teenagers. We can imagine their fear in

front of the gun, the threats from their tormentors, yet they chose to witness to their brotherhood [or common humanity], to die embrac[ing] each other rather than betray[ing] each other.

These little sisters...have passed a judgment to our world divided by the blind ferocity of ethnic hatred. It is a judgment delivered by the love and innocence that only the young ones know. They were adolescents, life opening up in front of them, yet standing together embraced and waiting for the bullets, they proclaimed that they were not interested in a society where a mere difference of tribal origin does not allow them to be friends, to be brothers and sisters.

Their story tells us that we must resist violence....We are called to oppose injustice in all its forms, including violence of the institutions and the government against their own citizens. When we oppose violence without resorting to violence, we are affirming the greatness of the human spirit.

And the article ends with a prayer:

Little sisters and brothers of Muramba and Buta [where a group of boys had been massacred], you who have refused to accept the madness of violence and racial hatred, forgive us, all of us who allow prejudice, division, hatred and violence to become so pervasive in our world.

These girls were prophetesses, examples of a nonviolent resistance to hatred that should penetrate to our very bones. Their examples — like those of all the women in our biblical stories — show that the works of the poor and the victims can rise above violence and hatred, greed and power. The message is clear: side with the victims, the poor, the nonviolent in every aspect of life. To refuse that is to side with those who bring death to the world. General Omar Bradley once said: "We have grasped the mystery of the atom and rejected the Sermon on the Mount. Ours is a world of nuclear giants and ethical infants. We know more about war than we know about peace, more about killing than we know about living." But we also have a choice, the freedom to chose otherwise. As Adrienne Rich writes: "I have to cast my lot with those who age after age, perversely, with no extraordinary power, reconstitute the world." This is the stuff true judges are made of, the basis of real leadership, and the core of freedom and love that ultimately is the only sacrifice our God demands from us.

Someone once gave me a Jewish midrash from a children's book called *Alexander's Lesson*. The only source referred to was Tamid 32b. It is a good story to end this chapter on women who model leadership and judgment and who are prophetesses calling us back to integrity as human beings while imaging for us what it means to be just and holy in the future:

Once upon a time Alexander the Great, who conquered many lands and cherished learning and the wisdom of other cultures and races, heard of the distant continent of Africa, and wanted to visit. He had heard rumors of vast wealth, diamonds, gold, expanses of fertile land, and fantastic animals and birds. He wanted to see this for himself as well as question the rulers on their justice and forms of judgment. But his advisers were against it. It was far off, and there would be many hardships and dangers along the way. But Alexander was intent on going and set out alone to search out wisdom and wealth in Africa.

After an arduous journey he arrived to find that Africa was a land populated and ruled primarily by women, and it was indeed a land of vast wealth, with a surplus of food and an incredible variety of strange creatures. A woman ruler had heard of Alexander and his kingdom. When he approached her, she questioned him: "Are you thinking of invading us or waging war on us? If you do attack and conquer us, what honor will you find? And if you happen to lose, what terrible dishonor for you, conquered by women!" Alexander was struck by her words and asserted that he was there on a peaceful visit and had no intentions of invasion.

It had been a hard journey and he asked for bread and something to drink. He was served an entire loaf of bread. When he picked it up, it weighed heavily in his hand, and he realized it was a solid gold loaf. Surprised, he asked, "Do all people here eat bread that is made of precious metals and jewels?" The woman's answer hit him hard: "No, but if you only wanted bread, why didn't you just stay at home in your own country? Surely you have more than enough food and drink to assuage your needs." Alexander was ashamed to be seen through so easily, and he replied that he had come to observe them, their court of laws, and to see how they rendered judgments. He was, he informed them, most interested in justice and wisdom and had heard fabulous tales about how justice was decreed and practiced in this land of Africa.

He was invited to sit and observe the courts when they met on a near daily basis. When the time came he was ushered into a room with a round table, comfortable chairs, books, and wide vistas of open space and light. The first case was presented. He could not believe what he was hearing. The first man approached and stated his side of the problem: "I bought a field from this man over a year ago. As I was plowing I found a large box that had been buried. Upon opening it, I realized it was full of treasure and immediately took it back to the man I bought the field from. After all, I am not a thief. I bought only the field and wanted to return his lawful property." The other man stated his version: "No, I cannot take the treasure that he found. I sold him the land and obviously everything that was in it, dirt, rocks, trees, and whatever he found underground. I am not a thief either and I do not own what he found."

The woman judge had listened carefully and with respect to both men who had traveled far to have their case decided by her wisdom. She looked at each in turn and then asked them if they had children. Both nodded yes — one had a son and the other a daughter. "Good," she said, smiling. "It is decided. They can be given to one another in marriage, and then both of you will benefit from the discovery of the unexpected treasure." The men were pleased with the judgment, but Alexander reacted rudely to her words. He spoke up, saying that in his kingdom there would have been an altogether different judgment. She asked him what he would have decided. "Simple. In my country we would have confiscated the treasure for the kingdom's coffers and killed the two men for their stubbornness and stupidity."

There was a strained and awkward silence in the courtroom. No one spoke for a long time, and Alexander realized he was being regarded with pity and concern, the way a distraught parent would regard a child who had committed a senseless act that harmed another. Finally the judge spoke directly to him and asked him a simple question. "In your country," she said, "does the sun shine on you and the rain fall on you?" He laughed and said, "Of course." "And do you have animals that provide for your needs: sheep, goats, cattle, birds, and wild beasts?" "Of course," he answered, "we are not that different from you and your country. But what does that have to do with anything?" She looked at him sternly and pronounced: "The sun shines and the rain falls in your country for the sake of the other creatures that dwell there. Certainly you and your people, as you describe them, do not deserve even air, sunlight, water, or life. You know nothing of justice or simple courtesy, and therefore you must know little or nothing of love and life."

Alexander was stunned and silent. The court continued to hear cases and he listened, slowly becoming shame-faced and humble in the face of what he heard and saw before him. People were treated with respect. The law served the best interests of all, including those not yet born. No one was allowed to be disrespectful or to shout and blame others or seek to provoke the taking of sides. There were long moments of silence and reflection, discussion with others, consultation with the books and earlier precedents. All left content that they had been listened to, that their concerns had been met, and that the decisions rendered had been careful of everyone, but especially of those who suffered or who were in extreme need. Cases overlapped, and ties were made between people who had previously not known one another. Justice became a large interlocking pattern where all were drawn closer together and harmony formed the backdrop of all lives.

Before Alexander returned to his land of Macedonia, he stopped at the gates of the city where he had witnessed the African justice. He wrote this for all to see on the gates of the city: "I Alexander of Macedonia was a fool before I visited this land where the women of Africa judge rightly and wisdom is the domain of all. I have learned the beginnings of wisdom and will remember their ways. This is the treasure I bring back to my own country."

If this was once a reality, or a memory, even just a hope, then today it can become a vision that creates places where women and men sit under palm trees and listen to the people's cry for justice, places where what is decreed is steeped in the promises of abiding peace born of justice for the poor and the truth of what it means to be human beings together on this earth. The art of judging rightly can be learned from sources most of us ignore, like the poor widow, the slave girl, and those on the edge of life and death.

EIGHT

WIVES AND WARRIORS

Rebekah, Zipporah,
the Wife of Isaiah the Prophet, and Judith

W HEN MRS. EINSTEIN was asked if she understood her husband's theory of relativity, she answered: "No, but I know my husband, and I know he can be trusted." While many may smile at this anecdote, others may not. Instead they may be annoyed and retort that the statement limits or devalues women and their abilities. In the recent past some women have criticized what they have interpreted as the tendency in the Bible and the church to remember and refer to women in the contexts of their primary relationships to others, especially the men of their lives. Thus contemporary women believe that to be known as someone's wife, mother, sister, grandmother, aunt, or even friend somehow disparages one's person. Women are, they say, to be seen as individuals, independent of their relationships to men. And yet if we are not remembered for our commitments, our loves, our bonds to one another, and our place in relation to others, what are we to be remembered for? It could be answered that we could be eulogized for what we accomplished, our work, our art, but if it is done primarily for our own benefit or self-expression, does that not reveal the narrowness and the limited boundaries of our world?

I was once sent a Valentine's Day card with the children's characters Winnie the Pooh and Piglet. I have kept it for its wisdom and deep understanding of love. It is a short conversation between the two:

> Piglet sidled up to Pooh from behind.
> "Pooh," he whispered.
> "Yes, Piglet?"

"Nothing," said Piglet, taking Pooh's paw, "I just wanted to be sure of you."

Perhaps in our deepest and truest moments we are seen and known by those who are sure of us and those we are sure of in our lives.

The Baal Shem Tov, a great Jewish storyteller, mystic, and prophet of the late Middle Ages, wrote of marriage, not the marriage of convenience or the marriage contracted for children, inheritance, or legalized sex, or even the marriage based on romantic love. He wrote of marriage as something intrinsic to each person's soul and ultimate meaning: "From every human being there rises a light that reaches straight to heaven, and when two souls that are destined to be together find each other, their streams of light flow together, and a single brighter light goes forth from their united being."

Another description of this reality was written by a seventeenth-century English woman who was pining for her husband after he died. She wrote:

> My love to my husband was not only a matrimonial love, as betwixt man and wife, but a natural love, as the love of brethren, parents and children, also a sympathetical love, as the love of friends, likewise a customary love, as the love of acquaintances, a loyal love, as the love of a subject, an obedient love, as the love to virtue, an uniting love, as the love of soul and body, a pious love, as the love to heaven, all which several loves did meet and intermix, making one mass of love.[1]

Antonio Machado, a Spanish poet, has also written of this remarkable tie:

> One summer night —
> my balcony door stood open
> and the front door also —
> death entered my house.
> He approached her bed —
> not even noticing me —
> and with very fine hands
> broke something delicate.

1. Quoted in Alan Macfarlane, "Marriage and Love in England: Modes of Reproduction 1300–1840," in *One Mass of Love* (London: Basil Blackwell).

> Death crossed the room, not
> looking at me, in silence,
> a second time. What did you do?
> He did not answer.
> I saw no change in her,
> but my heart felt heavy.
> I know what broke —
> a thread between us!

This connection, this sense of being one, beyond customary attachments, is a form of love that is honored in many of the stories of the patriarchs, the prophets, and their wives. It is a bonding born of faith, of enduring together, of knowing and experiencing the presence and power of the Holy in their lives together. In a sense, these relationships cannot be described using the categories and words available to us today. In the Bible, these intimate connections are often only hinted at in the public accounting of events, in the naming of a couple's children, or in asides apparently dropped randomly into the text.

Rebekah

We begin with Rebekah. She is first mentioned in a genealogy, which in itself is significant. In fact she is the first woman-child mentioned in a biblical genealogy. The genealogy is found immediately after the terrifying scene of Abraham's testing by God with the demand that he sacrifice his son as a burnt offering in a high place of Yahweh's choosing. Abraham passes the test. Isaac is released from the altar, and the blessing of God is given to Abraham, Isaac, and their descendants, who will be as numerous as the stars of the sky and the sands of the seashore (Genesis 22). Then follows a short genealogy that contains a short separate sentence that introduces Rebekah: "Bethuel became the father of Rebekah" (Gen. 22:23). Her grandparents are Milcah and Nahor, and so she is kin to Abraham, a participant in the covenantal relationship. With Isaac, she will be the way the blessings continue to enter the world. There is, at this point, no mention of her subsequent marriage to Isaac, but she is there already, part of the long-range hope of God for the people now chosen and bonded to him in covenant. Rebekah's name means "patience," and she will live out the meaning of her name many times over. She has the patience to water all ten of the servant's camels; she waits twenty years to bear children; and she waits double that many years to see her youngest son, Jacob, receive the blessing that she helps to secure from her husband, Isaac. And she will wait in vain for the return of her beloved son Jacob.

We are told that Sarah, Abraham's wife, lives to be one hundred and twenty-seven, and when she dies, Abraham buys a cave and buries her at Machpelah. Abraham is aging. A shadow of death falls on the text, and the focus is shifting to the next generation and how the blessings will continue. But Isaac is unmarried. It is the old man who arranges that a wife be found for his son. He entrusts his senior servant with the task of going back to his homeland, Haran, that he left so many years before to find a wife for his son. Abraham informs his servant: "He will send his angel before you, that you may find a wife for my son. But if the woman is unwilling to follow you, you will be free of this oath" (Gen. 24:7b–8). It seems that Rebekah will follow in the footsteps of Abraham and be asked to leave the land of her birth, to search out her future, staking her life on another's faith until she chooses that faith for herself.

And now it is the servant who in his prayer to God sets up a test: the first girl who offers him a drink and offers to provide water for all of his camels will be the one whom God intends for Isaac to marry. He doesn't even finish his prayers before Rebekah appears, carrying a pitcher on her shoulder. In two sentences we are told her lineage, her family ties, and that she is beautiful and a virgin of marriageable age. She immediately offers the servant a drink, and when he has finished, she tells him that she will water his camels until they have had enough. This is work, for he has ten camels!

In the Bible, this kind of meeting of a woman bound to the future often happens at a well. Later Jacob will meet Rachel at a well (Gen. 29:1–14), and Moses will meet Zipporah as she comes to water the sheep (Exod. 2:15–21). These people are nomads, and the location of water and of tents is one of the overarching realities of their lives. And then Rebekah offers the servant hospitality, inviting him to her family's tents. Later the servant explains his mission to Rebekah's father and her brother Laban. They are quick to reply: "This is God's doing. It is not for us to decide either way. Here is Rebekah, take her and go. Let her become the wife of your master's son as Yahweh has directed" (Gen. 24:50–51). Gifts are exchanged, but it is not until the next morning that Rebekah herself is asked if she agrees to the marriage proposal and if she will go. Her answer is simply put: "I will go." She goes with their blessing: "Sister of ours, may you increase to thousands upon thousands, may your descendants take possession of the cities of their enemies" (Gen. 24:60).

There is no account of the journey, although there are midrashic stories that tell of the servant trying to tell Rebekah that Isaac's father once tried to sacrifice him to his God. Then the other servants try to tell her, but they are hindered, and finally her own maidservant who has heard the stories tries to tell them — all to no avail. Rebekah arrives with no further information about her betrothed. Isaac is a man imprinted with a destiny, a story that sleeps in his flesh and memory, and yet there is nothing in the text that speaks of his reactions after the thwarted sacrifice. Now the story shifts to him. We are told he was in the custom of going out into the fields in the early evening to meditate. And during his prayer he looks up to see the caravan approaching. Rebekah veils herself, as was customary for a bride, and she is given to Isaac. This first meeting leaves the reader to wonder what transpired between them. All we are told is that "Isaac brought Rebekah into the tent of Sarah, his mother. He made her his wife, and he loved her; and Isaac was comforted after his mother's death" (Gen. 24:67).

Rebekah is a woman of courage, beautiful, hard-working. She now stands in the place of her mother-in-law, Sarah, as matriarch and a woman who decided upon her own destiny, leaving home and traveling to a distant place in response to hearing of the hopes and promise of Abraham and Isaac and their God. She has consented to being part of the covenant and the future of Israel. But what follows is a harsh reality for any marriage, especially in a community that depends on the next generation for survival. Rebekah is barren and bears no children for twenty years. Again the midrash tells stories of the contention between Isaac and Rebekah and of Rebekah's anguish and complaint. In the meantime, Isaac reveals to her in bits and pieces his own history and how his parents sought for an heir — how his mother's maidservant, Hagar, was given to Abraham, and Hagar bore Ishmael, Isaac's brother. Then follow the stories of the visit of the angels to Sarah's tent and her becoming pregnant in her old age. He tells Rebekah that waiting for twenty years is nothing. And then, finally, he tells the story of the testing of his and his father's faith, of the journey, and of his horror and fear when he realized what his father intended to do.

Finally, we are told that Rebekah, the wife, confidante and bearer of the promise of Yahweh, becomes the mother of twins and matriarch of the nation Israel:

> Isaac prayed to Yahweh for his wife, because she could not have children. Yahweh heard Isaac's prayer and Rebekah, his wife, conceived. As the children struggled together within her, she said, "If it is like this, why do I continue to live?" She went to consult Yahweh, and Yahweh said to her, "Two nations are in your womb, and two peoples will be born of you; one nation will be stronger than the other, and the elder shall serve the younger."
>
> When the time came for her to give birth, there were twins in her womb. The first to be born was red and his whole body was like a hairy garment, so they called him Esau. Then his brother was born and his hand had gripped Esau's heel so he was named Jacob. Isaac was sixty at the time of their birth. When the boys grew up, Esau became a skillful hunter, a man of the open country; Jacob was a quiet man living in tents. Isaac who had a liking for game loved Esau, but Rebekah loved Jacob. (Gen. 25:21–28)

We are told that Isaac loved Rebekah and prayed for her because it was her wish to have children. But now, pregnant, it is she who goes and consults Yahweh, seeking some respite from her pain and some understanding of what is happening to her. And to Rebekah alone is given an oracle, knowledge of God's intent and of the future. She knows from before the twins' birth that the younger is favored in Yahweh's eyes and the elder is destined to honor his younger brother. In an old midrash we are told:

> R. Levi taught that in the verse "The Lord said unto her: Two nations are in thy womb" (Gen. 25:23), the words unto her imply that the Lord said to Rebekah: "I shall reveal a mystery to thee: From thee shall [Israel], the foremost of the nations, come forth." Hence [of Isaac to whom this mystery was not revealed] Scripture says "Now Isaac loved Esau" (Gen. 25:28), whereas of Rebekah the verse goes on to say "Rebekah loved Jacob" (Gen. 25:28), because she knew what the Holy One, blessed be He, had revealed to her.[2]

---

2. "The Midrash on Psalm 9:7," in *The Midrash on Psalms,* trans. William G. Braude (New Haven: Yale University Press, 1959).

168   *Wives and Warriors*

Apparently the twins are named by Rebekah and probably the midwife who attended her. You can almost hear the conversation among
the women. As the first child emerges he is described as red and hairy
all over, and so he is named Esau, a play on the word *se'ar,* the Hebrew word for hair. He is followed by the second child, with his tiny
fist tightened around his older brother's heel, and he is named Jacob,
a play on the Hebrew word *aqueb,* which means heel. From the very
beginning in the book of Genesis, naming is a power that God shares
with human beings. What is remarkable in the First Testament is the
number of stories in which women — not men — name the children.
In fact, women name their children twenty-seven times in the First
Testament, while men do the naming only seventeen times. There are
eighteen speeches by mothers about the naming, while there are only
eight such speeches by men.

There is also a pattern of the mother choosing the younger son to
inherit the birthright over the father's usual choice of the firstborn son.
The matriarchs and queens in Israel have minds of their own, and their
prerogative in naming is also often exercised regarding who leads the
clan and nation into the future that God intends for the people. The
women work in tandem with God.

This choosing of one over another leads to contention. Within the
family the parents take sides, choosing one to favor: Rebekah because
of her feelings and information from the oracle and Isaac because of
his lack of knowledge. And there is more information. The maturing
young men are described as opposite, one in favorable terms, the other
in coarse language. Sharon Pace Jeansonne writes:

> Although the narrator does not explicitly state why Rebekah
> prefers Jacob to Esau (25:28), the use of epithets is most signifi-
> cant. Jacob is described as "a man of integrity (*is tam*), dwelling
> in tents" in contrast to his brother Esau, "a knowledgeable
> hunter, a man of the field" (25:27).[3]

This word *tam,* which is translated in the text as "quiet," has other
meanings. According to the *Hebrew and English Lexicon of the Old
Testament,* it can also be translated "of integrity, sound, wholesome."[4]

3. Sharon Pace Jeansonne, *The Women of Genesis: From Sarah to Potiphar's Wife*
(Minneapolis: Fortress Press, 1990), 63.
4. Brown, Driver, and Briggs, *Hebrew and English Lexicon of the Old Testament,*
1070–71.

It comes from the root word *tmm,* meaning "to be complete or finished." In light of what follows in the story of the stolen blessing, these meanings take on heightened intensity. We know there is strife and dissension between the two brothers from the beginning. Jacob one day cunningly gets a hungry Esau to sell his birthright over to him for some bread and lentil stew. The text comments that "Esau thought nothing of his right as the firstborn."

The stories of Isaac and Rebekah in many ways are written to parallel the stories of Abraham and Sarah. Now there is an interruption of the story of the twins. A famine develops, and Isaac and Rebekah go to Gerar, land of Abimelech, the king of the Philistines, as once Abraham and Sarah traveled to Egypt in search of food and grain. Isaac and Rebekah settle there for a time. Isaac, like his father before him, in fear or for protection, tries to pass his wife off as his sister. Isaac is afraid that other men will contest with him for Rebekah because of her beauty and will seek to kill him. We are given the sense of Isaac as frail, vulnerable, and not very courageous. He is a survivor but at great cost to himself and others. Abimelech discovers that Isaac has been lying to him. In her commentary on Rebekah's story, Sharon Pace Jeansonne adds an interesting piece of information that tells us much of Isaac's character:

> It is all the more arresting in this context, therefore, that Isaac is willing to place his wife in danger. Not only does he demonstrate poor judgment in placing Rebekah at risk, but Isaac appears foolish when he openly plays with or fondles Rebekah in such a way that Abimelech can readily discern that she is his wife (26:8). The text highlights this by the play on words between "Yishaq" (Isaac) and "mesaheq" (playing/fondling) because both words come from the Hebrew root "shq" (laugh). Isaac's fear, therefore, appears as a lack of trust in God.[5]

This pun could even suggest that Abimelech sees Isaac "isaacking" his wife. But what follows reveals the graciousness of Yahweh, for Isaac and Rebekah are now protected by the king's word, and they flourish and grow exceedingly rich in their sojourn. But because of their prosperity they are asked to leave. The wandering that once was the life of Abraham and Sarah is now that of Isaac and Rebekah.

---

5. Jeansonne, *Women of Genesis,* 64.

They settle in Gerar, but after a quarrel over water rights, they move on again. Eventually, though, peace is made between them and the Philistines, and they settle in Beersheba.

Then we are told as though in an aside that at the age of forty Esau marries Judith, a daughter of a Hittite, and Basemath, also a daughter of a Hittite, and "they made life bitter for Isaac and Rebekah" (Gen. 26:34–35). The dissension spreads through the family. Esau has betrayed the covenant agreement and married outside the promise. Isaac, however, is growing old, with "eyes so weak that he could no longer see" (Gen. 27:1) and he calls his firstborn, Esau, to him to pass the blessing onto him.

Again the stories of Sarah and Rebekah imitate each other. The most defining experience of Sarah's life is the announcement of and the birth of her son of the promise, Isaac. She first hears of it when she is listening at the tent flap, while the visitors tell Abraham of God's design. Now it is Rebekah who overhears Isaac telling Esau to go out hunting and bring him back some game so that he may give him his birthright blessing in the ritual manner. But Rebekah schemes to get Isaac to give his blessing to her beloved child instead of the firstborn. Her plan is both a plot carefully executed as well as the design of Yahweh that had been made known to her so long ago when both children were in her womb. Even trickery and deceit can serve the continued blessings of Israel. In fact, all things eventually serve a larger dream than any one person's agenda. Now is the decisive moment when Rebekah's ingenuity is brought to bear. She tells Jacob what Isaac intends and what she intends and that he must obey her commands explicitly. And he does.

She prepares food she knows Isaac likes. Meanwhile she takes some of Esau's clothes, covers Jacob's hands and his neck with goatskin, and sends him into his father before Esau can return. What transpires between the aging father and his youngest son is both comical and immensely sad. In response to his father's questioning, Jacob lies. His very appearance is a lie meant to confuse or dupe the old man into thinking it is the elder son. But in spite of the dissonance between the voice of Jacob and the feel and smell of Esau, Isaac imparts the birthright blessing to the youngest, as both Rebekah and, it seems, God had always intended. Like a scene in a tragedy, Jacob slips out just as Esau arrives to find out that he has been tricked out of both birthright and blessing. The conflict turns bitter. Esau be-

gins to comfort himself with the thought of killing Jacob as soon as
Isaac dies.

But the matriarch Rebekah, who knows everything that goes on in
the tents, hears of her older son's intent to murder Jacob. She realizes
she must send Jacob to safe-keeping until Esau's rage dies down. It is
her intention to send Jacob back to her kin, to the tents of her brother
Laban, and while there choose a wife for himself, since Isaac had commanded him not to marry a Canaanite woman. Jacob will leave, and
Rebekah will be left bereft of her beloved child, and uneasy in her
own place because of betraying her husband's confidence and choosing sides against Esau. And it seems Esau begins to realize how he
has disappointed his parents by marrying the Hittite women, and he
goes and marries again, this time to a daughter of Ishmael, within the
confines of the clan. We get a glimpse of Rebekah's feelings in regard
to her children and, now, her own life:

> "Now, my son, listen to me and flee to Laban, my brother, in
> Haran. You will stay with him for a time until your brother's
> fury has cooled; and when he has forgotten his anger and what
> you did to him, I will send someone to bring you back. Why
> should I lose both of you on the same day?"
>
> Rebekah said to Isaac, "I am weary of my life because of
> the Hittite women. If Jacob marries a woman from this land, a
> Hittite like these, what value is there left in life for me?"
>
> (Gen. 27:43–46)

This is the last we see of Rebekah. Her ruse has worked, and Jacob
has inherited the blessing. She sends him off to Haran to find his wife,
ostensibly to save him from Esau's murderous intent. Rebekah is a
believer in God and God's promises, and she knows now that Jacob
will continue the lineage, that he indeed has received his father's and
God's blessing. She has accomplished what she set out to do, in con-
junction with God's design. But she is a woman and mother who has
lost her beloved, the one whom she loved most. Like Abraham, who
was commanded to hand over his firstborn of the covenant, Rebekah
has had to let go of Jacob and see him leave her tents and her life.
Since she is not mentioned again, even when Jacob finally returns to
his own land to confront his brother, it is thought that Rebekah never
saw Jacob again and died before his return.

She must endure the presence in her tents of foreign women who do not share the dreams, beliefs, and hopes of her own people and her own heart. She and Isaac are once again alone together, as they were for the first twenty years of their marriage. We are told that she is buried with Isaac in the cave at Machpelah, with Abraham and Sarah, her ancestors in the faith and story of Israel (Gen. 35:27). But a contemporary midrash of Rebekah tells a story that speaks volumes of her own hopes and the reason for her actions. It is called "A Marriage Made in Heaven." The quote below is from the ending, as Rebekah reflects on being bound not only to husband or children but to Yahweh's indestructible dreams, a binding that began when she said, "I will go." This is how she ends the story that might be hidden under the text of Genesis:

In the same hour I bore Ishmael-like Esau and Isaac-like Jacob. They split between them again, like my husband and his brother, fear and trembling on one side, heartiness on the other. Right then I swore to alter balances, set heritance on hardihood, not nerves. Isaac, himself, poor self-despiser, hankered to swagger on in Esau's genes!

But from deep within the well between my thighs where destiny awaited ladling out, I chose the child that Isaac didn't (like it or not, a common marriage story), yet chose the child most like my spouse! Clapped bracelet-pelts on hairless Jacob's arm, and led him by that nose ring, mother love, to fool his father.

I'd told my sons what Isaac suffered at *his* father's hand. I don't believe in keeping things from children. "It's quite all right to act this way," I said. "Not only is your father blind, he's also had to turn deaf ears to God for fear of what God's voice might say. He just can't hear the choice of heir God urged him toward. It's up to us to make interpretations. I always wanted you to share, to get along. Remember everyone gets something, more or less. I hope you'll make me proud and be good sports about it. Since we're clearly actors in God's play, let's make the best of all our roles. If it's to weep, we'll do so; if to exult, we must with all our might. Above all [let's] not draw back from what's ordained."

And so I fooled blind, dying Isaac into glory, which consists, at least in part, of getting yourself written into the right story. Then, cradling my old husband in my arms, I lulled his way to rest with our old made-in-heaven song. The well, the tent, the twins, the blessing, I sang.

"Look," I urged into his white-blind eyes, "look at the lengths to which the Holy One goes, for — like it not or like it — us."[6]

The midrash may seem too modern in spots, untenable in others, fanciful or even playful or too heavily slanted toward a fated destiny. But it reveals a woman who could make decisions and act on them, grow to love her husband and understand his own relationship with God while still having her own relationship of revelation with this demanding divinity. She prays and is listened to, and the text of Genesis reveals clearly that women sometimes know better than the men what God is about and that they could work in tandem with God for the future of their people. And one must imagine that Isaac more than suspected what she was up to in the blessing tale and afterwards admired her for her courage and choices. They were separate in their persons but were bound in their love, their marriage, their children, and their relationship with Yahweh. They were both, first of all, children of the promise, and together they passed on their heritage to the future, so that we, thousands of years later, may inherit it from them. Blessed be God forever!

Zipporah

Now we turn to look at Zipporah, the wife of the prophet Moses. We meet her, with Moses, at a well. Moses has killed an Egyptian in his rage, and he has been exiled from Egypt by the Pharaoh. We are told that he "went to live in the land of Midian. There he sat down by a well." The encounter is recorded:

> A priest of Midian had seven daughters. They came to draw water and fill the troughs to water their father's sheep. Some shepherds came and drove them away; but Moses went to their help and watered the sheep.
>
> When the girls returned to their father Reuel, he asked them, "Why have you come back so early today?" They said, "An Egyptian protected us from the shepherds, and even drew water

---

6. In Norma Rosen, *Biblical Women Unbound: Counter-Tales* (Philadelphia: Jewish Publication Society, 1996), 76–77.

for us and watered the sheep." The man said, "Where is he? Why
did you leave him there? Call him and offer him a meal."

Moses agreed to stay with the man and he gave Moses his
daughter Zipporah in marriage. She had a child and named him
Gershom, to recall that he had been a guest in a strange land.

(Exod. 2:16–22)

Already roles are reversing. As once Rebekah offered water and
watered the herd of camels for Abraham's servant, now it is Moses,
the foreigner running from execution in Egypt, who waters the
women's sheep, drawing the water from the well. The components
of the ritual meeting of husband and wife who will together bear
their own children and the children of the nation into the future are
all present: the well, the drawing of water, the stranger, the woman,
hospitality, and the invitation to return to the tents for a meal together.
This image of meeting at the waters has become a metaphor in spiritual treatises not only for the marriage bond that is forged in heaven
but also, in Origen's words, for "the whole of scripture [that] is concerned with the marriage of human beings to God's word." Origen
continues:

> All these things which are written are mysteries. Christ wishes
> to espouse you also to himself, for he speaks to you through the
> prophets saying: "I will espouse you to me forever and I will
> espouse you to me in faith and in mercy, and you shall know the
> Lord" (Hosea 2:21f).
>
> The innermost core of scripture and true religion is the unity
> of human beings and the Word. The servant who mediates the
> encounter is the prophetic word of the Old Testament. Christ
> sent this word in advance to prepare his advent. But, like Re-
> becca, one needs patience and practice to draw water from the
> well's depths, and to draw it even for camels who are an image
> for irrational and perverse people.[7]

Origen reveals what the Spirit might want to say to communities
reading the texts many generations later. Later in the commentary,
Origen writes: "Observe how many things take place at waters, so
that you too may be invited to come daily to the waters of the Word of

---

7. Quoted in Theresia Heither, "Origen's Exegesis and Genesis 24," *Theology Digest*
40, no. 2 (summer 1993): 141–42.

God."[8] When the text is viewed as inspired, then no story is to be seen, heard, or read as a historical account. Every story hides knowledge of the mystery of God's ways of relating to us. Somehow these marriages are not just binding the two individuals together, or two clans or tribes. They are binding people together in the context of God's word, with the Spirit of God, with the testament of the law, in this earlier covenant.

After the incident at the well, we meet Zipporah in a line in which we are told that her father, Reuel, gives her in marriage. We are told that he is a priest of Midian. We know also that Moses is of the tribe of Levi, a priestly family. Both husband and wife are priests in the ancient understanding. Her child is named, this time by Moses, Gershom. His name means sojourner, and, like his father, he is only visiting for a time in this place and will return with his father and mother to Egypt. Their second child is named Eliezer, which translates as "my father's God is my helper; he has rescued me from Pharaoh's sword." Both children tell the story of their father for future generations.

Zipporah's clan are shepherds. The notes in the Christian Community Bible tell us:

> As a shepherd in the desert, Moses learns the raw life, poor and free, like that of Abraham. He lives among the Midianites, who are more or less descendants of the father of the believers (Gen. 25:2). Thus, then, Moses receives from his father-in-law, Reuel, also called Jethro (3:1), the traditions about Abraham and his faith in the one and only God.

This is Moses' time of apprenticeship, of learning the faith and history of God with his people and the art of being a shepherd, not only of sheep, but of people and clans. One thinks of Zipporah teaching him her knowledge of water, grazing places, and dangers from other nomadic tribes, bandits, wild animals, drought. She would have also introduced him to long periods of solitude, to the isolation of tending the sheep, and to the songs and prayers of her people. The desert, his wife, and the Spirit of God are his teachers.

Moses pastures the sheep of his father-in-law, Jethro, as he will one day pasture the sheep that belong to Yahweh. One day he leads the

---

8. Ibid., 143.

sheep to the far side of the desert at the base of Horeb, the mountain of God. Moses has settled down and has begun a family with Zipporah, but his people are still enslaved in Egypt, crying out to God as their oppression worsens. On Mount Horeb, Moses meets God and is commanded to leave, to go down into Egypt, and to bring his people out, leading them to a land flowing with milk and honey (Exod. 3:16–17). Moses obeys:

> Then Moses went back to Jethro, his father-in-law, and said to him, "I am going back to my brothers in Egypt to see if they are still alive." Jethro said to Moses, "Go in peace!" . . .
>
> Moses took with him his wife and his sons. He put them on a donkey and set off for Egypt, holding in his hand the staff of God. . . .
>
> At a lodging place on the way, the Angel of Yahweh approached Moses and tried to kill him. But Zipporah took a flint stone and cut her son's foreskin and, with it, she touched the feet of Moses, saying, "You are now my husband by blood!" And the Angel left him. Zipporah said "husband by blood" because of the circumcision. (Exod. 4:18, 20, 24–26)

Moses returns with his family to become the liberator of Israel, the greatest prophet of the nation, and the one most honored and loved by God in Israel's history. But as he seeks to obey God, he encounters an angel of God who intends to kill him. The tradition in the Jewish community is that Moses was raised in Pharaoh's household as an Egyptian and was never circumcised. He thus would have had no part in the covenant with God. He is still cut off from the people and so from Yahweh. All men who belong to the covenant bear the mark, the sign of that belonging, in their flesh. And in Judah's tradition one must bear this sign of circumcision in order to participate in the liturgy of Passover. Abraham is given this rite by Yahweh (Gen. 17:9–14), and afterward, every male child is circumcised on the eighth day, as sign of belonging to this covenant with God. Moses is to be the leader of these people, but he is cut off from the covenant without this ritual. The practice of circumcision was common in most of the ancient desert tribes, either as an initiation into adulthood or as preparation for marriage. In Israel alone is it the binding tie among believers in the one true God.

And so it is Zipporah who saves Moses' life from the avenging angel. Moses' own life is indeed saved any number of times by the women in his life. First by the midwives, then by his mother and sister, then again by Pharaoh's daughter. Now, as a grown man, his wife saves him with a religious ritual. In all the history of Israel's faith there is no other story where a woman circumcises either her own son or her husband.

Irene Nowell has summed up who this woman Zipporah is for Moses and for the people of Israel:

> Zipporah's action is unique and redemptive. Ordinarily circumcision is performed by the father; there is no other biblical story of a woman circumcising anyone. By her action, Zipporah saves Moses' life. She delivers Moses from death, as Moses will deliver the Israelites. Stands between Moses and an angry God. God gives her the moment and she becomes a mediator, just as Moses does when God threatens to destroy the people because of the golden calf (Exod. 32:1–14).[9]

Quick-witted Zipporah acts first as priest and believer in relation to her husband and child. She is mentor *and* equal to Moses, the only difference being that she acts within a private realm and he in the public domain. Although Moses is described often in the story of Exodus as one who walked with God, it seems he first walks with Zipporah, his wife and savior.

These two people were as one, though each is also a person in his or her own right. This model of marriage and of the covenant becomes a rare blessing for all those who believe and who marry in the tradition of Israel. The Baal Shem Tov was revered as a teacher, storyteller, and holy man. One of his followers writes of what he did when his wife died:

> When the Baal Shem Tov's wife died, it was obvious that he was suffering very greatly from the loss. It was not the way of the Baal Shem Tov to be concerned with worldly things, and the members of his household asked the reason for his anguish.
>
> The Baal Shem replied that he [was] suffering because his mentality would have [to be buried and] lie in the ground. He

---

9. Irene Nowell, *Women in the Old Testament* (Collegeville, Minn.: Liturgical Press, 1997), 57.

said, "I was looking forward to rising in a flame. But now [without my wife], I am but half a body, and it is impossible. It is for this reason that I suffer so."[10]

These relationships between fierce believers and servants of God cannot easily be dismissed or criticized by contemporary standards. Their experience and their stories must be read through the veil of faith to be appreciated and understood.

There is a tale told in the city of Weinsberg, Germany. When you visit the city on a tour, you climb high above the town to a fortress that is more than half a millennium old. There, overlooking the city, the guide tells you what happened here back in the fifteenth century:

Once upon a time the city was under siege, being starved out. No one entered and no one left, except to be buried. Sickness and near-starvation were rife in the city. Finally the commander of the enemy troops decided to launch an all-out attack and destroy the entire city. But he was advised by his counselors to have some pity before attacking and allow all the women and children to leave. After all, what glory was gained from slaughtering the helpless? Word was sent down to the city. There were negotiations back and forth. But before the city would agree to let all the women and children go free and unharmed through the soldiers' lines into safety, they bargained for one more thing. Each women would be allowed to carry with her one personal possession, whatever she deemed most valuable. The bargain was struck.

The soldiers stepped back and the gates of the city were thrown open. First came all the children tightly holding whatever was their prized possession, a doll, toy, basket, blanket, or picture, whatever they could carry with them. And behind them came the women. The commander and all the troops waiting to attack watched while every woman carried her one possession: her husband slung over her shoulder like a potato sack!

They say, when they tell the story, that the enemy commander kept his word and retreated, but not until he met with the woman who set up the negotiations in the city, engineering the "battle" from behind the scenes. Some people claim he married her since

---

10. Dov Baer of Linitz, translated by Aryeh Kaplan.

she was widowed. Others say, no — that's not really part of that story!

Like Zipporah, the women saved their husbands.

The Wife of Isaiah the Prophet

In chapter 8 of Isaiah we are introduced to Isaiah's wife, who has no name:

> I went to my wife; she conceived and gave birth to a son. Then Yahweh said to me, "Call him 'Quick to plunder — Booty is Close,' for this is Yahweh's word: Before the child knows how to say 'father' or 'mother,' the wealth of Damascus and the booty of Samaria will be carried off by the King of Assyria."
>
> (Isa. 8:3–4)

In the Hebrew translations, she is not described as wife, but as the prophetess, for the word used, *nebiah,* indicates a prophetess. But what about this woman, the prophetess who is wife to Isaiah, the towering prophet and suffering servant of Yahweh, the voice of the poor and those in distress because of others' sin? Who is she and who was she to Isaiah and to God? She is effaced behind the overwhelming presence of her husband and only surfaces in the shadows of her children's names. They reveal an ongoing relationship bound intimately to the fate of Israel as well as to God in the covenant bond. This bond and relationship are experiencing trauma, struggle, and a time pregnant with both the peace of the one promised to come and the wars and torture of a world that refuses the healing rivers and gently flowing waters of Shiloah (Isa. 8:5). Isaiah will go on to say: "So I will wait for Yahweh who hides his face from the people of Jacob. I will hope in him. Here am I and the children he has given me. We are signs and portents in Israel from Yahweh Sabaoth, who dwells on Mount Zion" (Isa. 8:17–18). Yahweh hides his face from his people, and Isaiah's wife hides her face as well, an apt image of the loving, faithful, ever-present, tending God they both serve. One serves by speaking, and the other serves by being silent and hidden, like the pauses and rests in-between words and notes of a musical score. Both are essential to the message and the music that are made.

Isaiah will endure terrible sufferings, walking for three years, naked and barefoot, and though once he was of noble birth he will accompany Israel through some of its darkest hours. His end is unknown, except that it is thought to be a horrible one, torturous and bloody, as the songs of the suffering servant attest. And this woman who loved him suffered and prayed with him on behalf of the stubborn people.

The Jewish midrash *Ta'anit* 23a–b contains a story about a rabbi and his wife who pray together. It is in the tradition that speaks of Rebekah and Isaac praying together:

> Rabbi Hilkiyah was a grandson of Honi the Circle-Drawer, and whenever the world was in need of rain the Rabbis sent a message to him and he prayed and rain fell. . . . He said to his wife, I know the scholars have come on account of rain; let us go up to the roof and pray, perhaps the Holy One, Blessed Be He, will have mercy and rain will fall. . . . They went up to the roof; he stood in one corner and she in another; at first the clouds appeared over the corner where his wife stood. . . . [The scholars asked him,] Why, Sir, did the clouds appear first in the corner where your wife stood and then in your corner? [He replied:] Because a wife stays at home and gives bread to the poor which they can at once enjoy whilst I give them money which they cannot at once enjoy. Or perhaps it may have to do with certain robbers in our neighborhood; I prayed that they might die, but she prayed that they might repent.[11]

The wife's prayers take precedence because of their closer connection to the poor, to forgiveness and mercy, and to deeds and a life of compassion. Within the Jewish community, women have told me that they do not want others to know the effect of their prayers or to be witness to their power. They quote what they say are Solomon's words: "The honor of God lies in hidden things." They would prefer to honor God and be known and honored by God rather than by their neighbors or strangers. Some things, especially things that have to do with the Holy, are not necessarily for the eyes of all, even for the edification of others.

Years later the prophet Joel will write, echoing other prophets' words:

> After this, I will pour out my Spirit upon all flesh.
> Your sons and daughters will prophesy,

---

11. Leila Leah Bronner, *From Eve to Esther: Rabbinic Reconstructions of Biblical Women* (Louisville: Westminster/John Knox Press, 1994), 102–3.

> your old men will dream dreams,
> your young men will see visions.
> Even upon my servants and maidens,
> I will pour out my Spirit on that day.
>
> (Joel 3:1–2)

The essence of the prophet or prophetess is sacrifice, pain that comes from conscience and seeks to dent the hardness of others' consciences, and it is never bitter or self-serving. Its anger is always on behalf of others, and those who speak also accept pain as an inevitable reaction to their words — pain inflicted heartlessly by those who resist hearing the truth. Prophecy is about displacement from culture, nation, and the norm, wherever it is found, because it invariably leads to the destruction of those who do not "make it as things are constructed." These people are called out of any normal life and consecrated to defying the majority and the mainstream while siding with those who by their very presence shout at our deaf ears that we are not honest, not holy, and not living with integrity. There are many hidden prophets among us who are the backbone of those who stand up front. Like the young woman Thérèse of Lisieux, who died at age twenty-four in a cloistered convent in France and is now a doctor of the church, we must learn that there is another order besides the dominant one or the contemporary one. She wrote: "Each small task of everyday life is part of the total harmony of the universe."

Isaiah's wife was a prophetess. The prophetess or prophet is about giving bread and word to the poor. They are about reminding us of what it means to be human beings, made in the image and likeness of God. Whatever this essence is, it is beyond description in terms of masculine or feminine. It is more basic than being a woman or a man. Archbishop Desmond Tutu tries to speak of it from his culture:

> Africans believe in something that is difficult to render in English. We call it *ubuntu otho*. It means the essence of being human. You know when it is there and when it is absent. It speaks about humanness, gentleness, hospitality, putting yourself out on the behalf of others, being vulnerable. It recognizes that my humanity is bound up with yours, for we can only be human together.[12]

---

12. Quoted from an Amnesty International calendar.

Perhaps the prophets and prophetesses could express this essence and call people to it because they had known it first in their own flesh and together known it in their own marriage relationships, and with God.

Judith

The book and the character of Judith do not appear in the Jewish canon, although the story is considered edifying, even a constructed narrative that fostered national resistance around the time of the Maccabean revolt. The book is, however, included in the Christian canon. Once thought to be historical, the story is now considered a composed work that was written to help the Jewish people deal with outside threats to their life and faith. The book and the heroine Judith, whose name means simply "the Jewess," seek to encourage and give heart to a people terrified in the face of historical events. Judith's God is described and prayed to as "God of the lowly, helper of the oppressed, upholder of the weak, protector of the forsaken, savior of those without hope" (Judith 9:11).[13]

An image that appears strongly in the book is that of "the hand of Yahweh." An instance that is used liturgically during the Easter Vigil readings is from Miriam's song, when she cries out: "Your right hand, O Lord, glorious in power, your right hand, O Lord, shattered the enemy" (Exod. 15:8). Helen Graham says that this metaphor of the hand has a special twist in the book of Judith:

> Here the hand of Judith becomes Yahweh's agent for the salvation of the Jewish people. In her Victory Song, which is the culmination of the celebration of her victory over Holofernes [the enemy general], Judith proclaims that "the Lord Almighty has foiled them by the hand of a woman" (Judith 16:5).[14]

Exegetes believe that the character of Judith is a mixture of other biblical women's attributes: such as Yael, Deborah, and Miriam. She, like Yael, kills a general: Judith severs Holofernes's head with his own

---

13. Unless otherwise noted, all translations from the book of Judith come from Helen Graham, M.M., "Hand of Yahweh: Hand of a Woman: A Study of the Song of Judith (Judith 16:1b–17)," dissertation, Loyola School of Theology, Quezon City, Philippines, 1995.

14. Ibid., 75.

sword, and blessings are heaped upon her, as Yael and Deborah are blessed for their deeds on behalf of Israel. Like Deborah and Miriam, she sings her victory song. The historical period of the events in the book covers about five centuries during which Israel was constantly threatened by war, siege, and invasion by more powerful nations. It was probably written sometime in the second century before Christ, around the time of the Maccabean revolt (187 B.C.E.). In fact, Judith looks and acts a lot like the leader of that revolt, Judas Maccabeus. Their names are even similar. They both pray before they act. And just as Judas cuts off Nicanor's head and his right hand after defeating his army and displays them on the city's walls (1 Macc. 7:47), so Judith cuts off Holofernes's head and hangs it on the city wall (Judith 14:1, 11).

The gruesome story is about primitive peoples and the reality of war, murder, assassination, and deceit while at the same time extolling Judith as the model of faithfulness, trust in God under impossibly difficult circumstances, and belief in God's care of his chosen people. Holofernes is the epitome of a vicious enemy ravaging the land and people with an immense and brutal army. He kills, destroys, and leaves nothing standing, including the shrines and places of worship, declaring that the only god to be worshiped hereafter is King Nebuchadrezzar.

The people have heard the horror stories about Holofernes, and he is on the way to attack them. They pray, fast in a frenzy of fear, covering themselves in sackcloth and ashes, begging and screaming for God to come and save them. Judith appears in answer to their prayers. She is described as a young, incredibly beautiful, pious, and wealthy widow, an oddity in Israelite society:

> As a widow, Judith remained in her house for three years and four months. She had built a room on the rooftop of the house where she lived. She covered herself in sackcloth, put on widow's garments, and fasted all the days of her widowhood with the exception of the eves of the Sabbath, the Sabbath.... She was exceedingly beautiful and very pleasing to look at. Manasseh, her husband, had left her gold, silver, servants, cattle and fields, and she remained the owner of all this estate. No one could say anything evil of her because she greatly feared God. (Judith 8:4–8)

In a word, the woman is perfect. She hears of the doings in the city, the anguish of the people and what the leaders are planning to do — surrender in five days if God does not intervene. They are testing the God of Israel as their ancestors did. This lack of faith on the part of the leaders and the people is a betrayal of the covenant. Once again the people sin and must be rescued by God's mercy and power at work among them in one chosen to be God's presence with them. Judith is chosen and sent. She confronts the elders harshly, accusing them of wrongdoing in regard to God. Her words sting:

> Who are you to put God to the test and take God's place when you answered the people? That is not the way to call for his mercy, but rather, one that leads to his wrath. For if you cannot probe the depths of the human heart nor know what a man is thinking, how can you understand the God who has made all things? Do you know his mind or understand his thoughts? No, my brothers, do not annoy the Lord our God. For if he does not wish to come to our help within these five days, he has the power to protect us for as many days as he wishes or else to annihilate us in front of our enemies....
>
> Let us beg him to come to our help. He will listen to our plea, if it pleases him....
>
> Now, my brothers, let us show our fellow countrymen that their lives depend on ours, that the safety of the Sanctuary, the Temple and the Altar rests with us. Much more, let us thank the Lord our God who is putting us to the test as he did our fathers.... Is not God making us pass through fire as he did the others to prove their hearts? The Lord is not punishing us, but he scourges those who draw near to him in order to admonish them. (Judith 8:12–15, 17, 24, 27)

First she admonishes, then teaches the leaders how to pray, how to stand before God, and how to stand together so that the people will take heart from their actions and words. She is now the leader, and all will praise her, beginning with Uzziah, the leader who speaks of her wisdom, her intelligence, and her natural goodness of heart. Then he asks her to pray for rain — the people are desperate in their need. But she informs them she is going to do something else entirely:

Judith said to them, "Listen to me, I will do something that will be handed down from generation to generation of the children of our race. Tonight you will stand at the gate of the town and I will go out with my maidservant and, by the time which has been fixed for you to hand over the town to our enemies, the Lord will visit Israel through my hand. But do not try to find out what I shall do for I will not tell you, until I have fulfilled what I will do."

Then Uzziah and the leaders said to her, "Go in peace and may the Lord our God go before you so that you may take vengeance upon our enemies." (Judith 8:32–35)

And then Judith prays, "at precisely the same moment as incense was being offered in the House of God at Jerusalem" (Judith 9:1). Her prayer encompasses the whole chapter. It begins vehemently and with bloodthirsty intent, recounting another time when battle was engaged in and the Israelites were victorious in spite of their being ineffectual as an army or nation, but dependent solely on God's power to win the war. It is a brutal recapitulation in detail of rape, murder, and blood. She puts the prospect of this battle in the context of an affront against the God of Israel and says that God will be the one fighting with them, for them, on behalf of his honor, for it is "you, Lord, [who] decide the outcome of wars" (Judith 9:8). And then her prayer becomes very personal and very strange in its request:

Consider their pride, let your anger fall on their heads and give to my hands, the hands of a widow, the strength necessary for what I have decided. By my lying lips punish the slave with his master and the master with his servant; put an end to their arrogance by the hand of a woman.

Truly your strength is not in number nor your power in strong men, for you are a God of the humble, the defender of the little ones, the support of the weak, the protector of the abandoned, the savior of those in despair.

Yes, God of my fathers and God of the heritage of Israel, Ruler of the heavens and the earth, Creator of the waters, King of all creation, listen to my prayer.

Give me tempting words to wound and kill those who have conceived cruel designs against your Covenant, your consecrated House, Mount Zion and the House which belongs to your sons.

Make the nation and all the tribes know that you are God, all-powerful and strong, and that, apart from you, there is no other protector for the people of Israel. (Judith 9:11–14)

She has decided upon this plan alone, without consultation with the elders or anyone else, and it will be a one-woman show of power and strength, cunning and killing, all for the honor and glory of God.

She rises from her prayer and attends to her toilet, systematically preparing her weapons for battle, as would any warrior about to go into battle. "She made herself extremely beautiful in order to attract the attention of the men who would see her" (10:4b). Her servant is given a bag with provisions — an oil jar, flour made from barley, small cakes made from dried figs and fine flour, all carefully wrapped. They set off together. Judith may be the one who does the deceiving and the actual killing of Holofernes, but her unnamed maidservant accompanies her and is in it with her from beginning to end. Off they go, escorted out of the city by their leaders and young men who open the gates for them. An Assyrian patrol meets them and escorts them to the tent of Holofernes. She parades herself before the soldiers, letting them ogle and eye her, but regal and aloof: "They were captivated by her beauty, and on seeing her, they praised the sons of Israel and said to one another, 'Who can look down on the people who have such women? It would be a mistake to leave one man alive; they would be able to deceive the whole world' " (10:19). That statement is ironic, more true than they know at the moment.

She prostrates herself before Holofernes and is raised up by the servants. The intrigue is in full swing. She is assured of Holofernes's protection. She replies, in the voice and terms of a servant to a master, that she will "not lie to my lord tonight. And if you follow the advice of your servant, everything will be accomplished by the hand of God and my lord will not fail in his undertakings" (11:5b–6). She flatters him, praises him to the skies, and then says that her nation will never be conquered, except if her people disobey their God and sin, which they now intend to do, to her horror, and so she has fled from them, to him because of the great things that will come to pass now. She describes herself as a pious woman, who will stay with him, leaving only at night to go out toward the ravine with her servant to pray. She will know precisely when her people have sinned and will report it to him, so that he can launch the offensive at just the right moment. He responds that power is in his hands and she has done well to come to him because "destruction is the fate of those who despised my lord [the King Nebuchadrezzar]" (11:22). The trap is sprung; the bait is set; and in due time — the deadline is five days more — he will literally lose his head that is already spinning.

She moves into his tent, but won't eat for fear of sin, having brought her own food with her. He's concerned that her food supply will run out, but she assures him that "your servant will not have finished what I have brought with me before the Lord will have carried out by my hand what he has decided to do" (12:4). And so for three days she stays in the camp, and every night she and her maid go out to the ravine to pray. On the fourth day, Holofernes can wait no longer and prepares a dinner party, but without inviting any of his officers. This is to be for Judith and himself alone. When the invitation comes, Judith is all butter and cream, accepting and fawning once again. At the dinner, Holofernes eats and drinks heavily, while Judith and her servant eat the last of what they brought with them. "Holofernes was bewitched by her, and he drank a great quantity of wine, much more than he had ever drunk on any single day since his birth" (12:20). The tale reads like something from an Arabian or Indian harem story, with the cobra mesmerizing the one it will strike with one deadly blow.

And she does. Everyone is sent off so they can have a bit of privacy, and Judith sends her servant to the door, as watch woman. Judith stands over his bed — he's besotted — and prays. She takes down his sword, which hangs on the bedpost. Then "she seized the hair of his head saying, 'O Lord God of Israel, give me strength, this very moment!'" (13:7). She strikes him twice, severing his head. She rolls his body in the bedclothes, puts the head in her food satchel, and goes out to her servant, heading off to the ravine as is her nightly custom, entrusting the bag to the servant's hand. Together they circle around and return to the city. The deed is done. Once inside the city, she proclaims: "Praise God, praise him! Praise God who has not withheld his mercy from the House of Israel. This very night he has crushed our enemies by my hand" (13:14). And she lifts high the head and triumphantly proclaims what she has done, with help from the Lord: "The Lord has struck him down by the hand of a woman. As truly as the Lord lives, it was my face that seduced him to his undoing, but the

Lord has protected me. This man could not sin with me to disgrace or dishonor me" (13:16). And the rejoicing and the battle hymns begin!

Judith is blessed by Uzziah in wild terms: "My daughter, may the Most High God bless you more than all women on earth" (13:18), and all the people join in the praise: "Amen! Amen!" She orders them to hang the head on the battlements of the city. In the morning, the Israelite warriors will assemble while their enemies will go to rouse Holofernes and find him dead. Then the Israelites can attack the Assyrians, who will be thrown into confusion and despair, shamed by one Hebrew woman. The enemies flee. They are followed and slaughtered, their encampments pillaged. Judith herself gets Holofernes's tent and everything in it. The women from the city form a choir around her. She supplies them with olive branches to plait wreaths, and they come into the city singing, with Judith leading them in a victory dance. Then Judith intones her song.

She blesses God for what he has done through her hand, singing of what has happened in her own voice. She exalts: "Her sandals delighted his eyes, her beauty captivated his soul, and the scimitar cut through his neck" (16:9). This is the first part of the song. The second shifts the focus to God, who is invincible, wonderfully strong, glorious, and shows mercy to those who fear him (16:13, 15). When she and those with her arrive in Jerusalem, she offers as sacrifice all the loot that she has been awarded from Holofernes's tent and stays for three months rejoicing in the saved sanctuary. She returns to her house in Bethulia and dies at the age of 105. Before she dies, "she set her maidservant free" (16:23). The story ends with the words: "No one again threatened the people of Israel while Judith lived, nor for a very long time after her death" (16:25).

So this is Judith, revered for her devotion to the sanctuary, her piety in remaining a widow, her observance of *kashrut* (dietary laws), her great fasting and prayer, her nationalism and courage, as well as her steadfast confidence in God alone. But many people have trouble with her, considering her somewhat less than pious: an assassin, a liar, a seducer, flaunting her beauty, someone with no respect for the dead, arrogant and proud, acting on her own without support or knowledge of the community, even assuming that her plan is God's plan. The book and Judith's own victory song fluctuate: her hand, God's hand; her glory, God's glory. It is she who has "foiled" the enemy (16:5), but it is God who "crushes wars" (16:2). In some ways she resembles

Delilah (Judges 18) because they both use their sexuality to seduce
with intent to kill. The only difference is God is on Judith's side while
God is not with Delilah. Judith is meant to have our sympathies while
Delilah, who grabs Samson's hair and cuts it, stealing his strength, is
a villainess. Judith is definitely an ambiguous figure.

A startling phrase appears both in the song and in Judith's prayer.
It is a phrase that may be able to lead us to a fruitful appropriation of
elements of the story of this ambiguous figure. The phrase occurs in
verse 9:7 in Judith's prayer and 16:2 in the song. It reads: "The Lord is
a God who crushes wars." The translation in the Christian Community
Bible reads: "You, Lord, decide the outcome of wars." However, the
phrase is also found in Isa. 42:13: "The Lord God of hosts shall go
forth and crush war; he shall stir up jealousy, and shall shout mightily
against his enemies." Helen Graham adds:

> A similar phrase also appears in Hosea 2:20, where it reads as
> follows:

> > I will make for you [Hebrew "them"] a covenant on that
> > day with the wild animals, the birds of the air, and the
> > creeping things of the ground; and I will abolish [literally
> > "break"] the bow, the sword, and war from the land; and I
> > will make you lie down in safety.[15]

Helen Graham and other theologians are interested in appropriating
meaning from the Judith narrative that can be used with integrity now,
thousands of years later, when any war has such destructive capabili-
ties that war can no longer be seen as a viable — let alone laudatory —
option. Judith is no longer a heroine to be imitated in behavior, but
does her song contain kernels of truth that now are meant to be drawn
forth and planted everywhere? Graham writes of the passages that
contain the startling repeated line, "Yahweh makes wars to cease" or
"Yahweh who crushes wars":

> Both passages are connected and are suggestive that the entire
> book might be read as literature critical of war and the war-
> machines of the world's powerful nations. In other words, the
> Judith narrative might be read not only as a defeat of the Assyr-

---

15. Ibid., 74.

ian king Nebuchadnessar and his general Holofernes, but as a defeat of war itself.[16]

The image of God as the divine warrior has often been used to validate killing, deceit, and military attacks on enemies — all in God's name, for God's glory. The image dominates much of Israelite religion in the First Testament and has dominated most of Christian history in the two millennia since the advent of Jesus, who exhorted his followers to "love unto death" all men and women as friends, as God loves all the peoples of the earth. This "love unto death" was to be practiced in loving one's enemies and in refusing to retaliate against or in any other way harm others. The militaristic image has been appropriated by any number of fundamentalist groups to ensure religious blessing on war, high- and low-intensity conflicts, murder, even terrorist acts. But what if this metaphor for militarism and overt violence is set within texts that speak of a persistent hope, prayer, and fervent desire to end all war?

The startling phrase repeated in Judith's song and prayer is connected to many other passages in the First Testament that speak of a desire for peace, resistance to war, and the hope that there will be a time when war is abolished and the real victory will be over war. Graham lists a number of such passages, and there are many more. Some of the most obvious are these:

> For with us is the Lord of hosts, the God of Jacob, our refuge.
> Come, see the works of the Lord — the marvelous things he has
>   done in the world.
> He has put an end to wars,
> broken the bows and splintered the spears,
> set the shields and chariots afire.
> Be still, know that I am God. (Ps. 46:8–11a)

> Blessed be the Lord, God our savior, who daily bears our
>   burdens!
> Ours is a God who saves; our Lord lets us escape from death . . . ,
> scatter[s] the nations who delight in war. (Ps. 68:20, 21, 31b)

Psalm 68 covers a multitude of the mighty works of God. This God is the power behind all of creation and the forces of the universe, but

---

16. Ibid., 243.

is also the father of orphans and protector of widows, a giver of shelter to the homeless, one who sets the prisoners free and provides for the needy. He is also engaged in battle, trampling the bloodthirsty underfoot in their own blood. But what is also there in the text and of utmost importance to us is God's desire to save and to scatter the nations that delight in war. In the visions of Isaiah there are the dreams of shattering the implements of war, turning spears into pruning hooks and swords into plowshares:

> He will rule over the nations and settle disputes for many peoples. They will beat their swords into plowshares and their spears into pruning hooks. Nation will not raise sword against nation; neither will they train for war any more. But each one will sit in peace and freedom under a fig tree or a vine of his own, for the mouth of Yahweh of hosts has spoken.
>
> (Mic. 4:3–4; and Isa. 2:4)

Perhaps when we read the book of Judith we are meant not to admire Judith's religiously grounded use of her femininity to assassinate the enemy but to look at the book with the eye of the Spirit of Peace and see that war is being mocked and ridiculed. If one lone woman can take down an entire empire, then what is the use of expending huge amounts of money on developing weapons and plotting for war? War is seen to be ludicrous, useless, a dead-end, shaming all those who in their power make war on the poor, the humble, and those who cannot protect themselves. War is seen as being in direct opposition to God's intent when the earth and the heavens were created, an affront to all birds, beasts, fish, trees, and land, since war destroys all in its path. War is seen as revealing inhumanity, as human beings breaking faith with God and other human beings, a blind stumbling in rage that is senseless and self-destructive. It is the ultimate injustice and sin against God and his creation.

Perhaps the real heroines and heroes of our time are those who search for a glimmer of hope, of peace, and of human dignity for all peoples. Theologians like Helen Graham do this, as do victims of war around the world who endeavor to abolish war, using all the means at their disposal, not the least being the texts and interpretations of scripture and tradition. With them as our examples, each of us must grow into a way of life that abhors war and violence, a way that is nonviolent, tolerant of others, and open to all women and men as human

beings who love and cherish life as we do. In his book *Arctic Dreams,*
Barry Lopez writes:

> How [is one] to live a moral and compassionate existence when
> one is fully aware of the blood, the horror inherent in all life,
> when one finds darkness not only in one's culture but within
> oneself? If there is a stage at which an individual's life becomes
> truly adult, it must be when one grasps the irony in its unfolding
> and accepts responsibility for a life lived in the midst of such
> paradox. One must live in the middle of contradiction because
> if all contradiction were eliminated at once life would collapse.
> There are simply no answers to some of the great pressing ques-
> tions. You continue to live them out, making your life a worthy
> expression of leaning into the light.[17]

And in the meantime we can tell each other the following Yiddish
folktale. It is called "Skotsl's Here!" "Skotsl kumt" is a Yiddish greeting from one woman to another when they meet, and especially when
they visit in each other's houses:

> Once upon a time the women started complaining: everything
> that's any good belongs to the men or only the men are allowed
> to have fun. It's not fair. It's the men who read from the Torah
> and dance with it on festivals, hugging it to their hearts. It is
> men who are required to pray; women don't have to. It is men
> who are exhorted to do good deeds, to store up merit. It's not
> fair. Women are supposed to have the children, take care of the
> children (and the men), and provide food, shelter, clothes for
> them. It's not fair.
>
> So one day a delegation of the women got together and de-
> cided it was high time things changed. After all, as far as they
> could tell, in reading the texts, didn't the Holy One, Blessed Be
> His Name, make men and women equal, in his likeness? So it
> was time to send someone to the Holy One to get him to set
> things right here on earth. Things had gotten too far out of hand,
> for far too long. All the women agreed. But how were they going
> to get their delegate up to heaven to negotiate with God?
>
> It was going to take some work, a lot of work and physical
> strength, but they could do it together. They chose the woman

---

17. Barry Lopez, *Arctic Dreams* (New York: Macmillan, 1986).

who was most skillful with words. After all she had to present the case and the situation as it had developed on earth, and she had to converse with the Holy One, who loved words. Witness the Torah! So Skotsl was chosen. It was unanimous. Then came the hard part. How to get her up there?

They'd watched the men, even children, building things with blocks. They would do the same, but they would use their bodies, one on top of the other. First they dug a pit, and the strongest woman knelt down on all fours in it, bracing herself against its sides. Then one after another, first in fours and threes, then in twos, they stacked themselves up, and up and up, with each new woman climbing higher and higher and kneeling so the next woman could follow. The pyramid of women grew and grew. The ones on the bottom were shaking under the weight, but everyone tried breathing together, humming so that their strength would hold. They were all thinking about giving birth, not to their babies this time, but to a new world, a new order of things where all would be equal, where men and women would be equal the way it was really meant in the beginning.

Finally they were almost to the heavens, and it was Skotsl's turn. Up and up she climbed, carefully over the bodies of all the other women. She encouraged them to hold fast as she slowly inched her way upward. At the top she stood and reached into heaven. She was there! But just then, a poor woman who was bent from all her long years of work just couldn't hold up any longer, and she sagged under the weight. In an instant they collapsed into confusion, bruises, and pain. And when they finally pulled themselves out of the heap they had fallen in, Skotsl was gone! They could find no trace of her. Obviously, she'd made it into the presence of the Holy One. It wasn't a total loss after all!

Should they try it again? Were there enough of them? While they discussed these questions, things stayed the same. The women were still not considered as good as the men, and the men kept claim to all the best things: like the Torah and scriptures, study, prayer, and dancing in the religious rituals. It wasn't fair. But not to lose hope! All the women knew: Skotsl got into God's presence. They were sure of that, and they knew Skotsl well. She would return. She'd come back and things would change, oh, would things change!

And so, whenever the women visit each other's homes, when the door is flung open, they cry out: "Skotsl kumt!" ("Skotsl's here!"). And who knows, one day, some day, she will be!

[Who knows? Maybe she's already here, and the word is getting around — that is my addition to the story and my heartfelt hope.]

The wives and warriors we've examined in this chapter were like Skotsl — straining toward the Holy One, offering courage and hope.

NINE

SISTERS

Leah and Rachel, Martha and Mary

S ISTERS. I have five of them: an older sister, who died in her mid-forties, and all the rest younger, some by as many as fifteen years. Some I know well because I'm a godmother of their children or because they are closer to me in age. Some I hardly know, having left home when they were very small. Events and circumstances change whatever the relationships were and are: the death of my parents and my older sister, marriages, jobs, geographical moves, divorces, suicides, illness, and the passing of time. Whenever I ask women what changes this relationship most, the answer is invariably, "Men!" And then they mention age, vocation, and whether or not they have children, especially if one has them and the other does not. It is the case with all sisters. In stores when you go to look for greeting cards between sisters, most of them concentrate on when we were young, growing up, memories and imagined childhoods of bliss, carefree times together, play and a magical world, which, of course, rarely existed.

Leah and Rachel

Rachel, the younger sister, and Leah, the older, share many of these still-contemporary realities in their lives, even though they lived as Israelites thousands of years ago in Bedouin society, which was matriarchal. The outward structures of this society were patriarchal, but the inner life of the family and relationships were controlled by the women. One was Jewish through one's mother, and status within the community was intimately bound to children. And status was tightly bound to the future of the tribe, security within the clan, one's identity, and survival as a group. Women and men did not marry for love; they married for children, for the life and future of the tribe, for inheritance and for the Israelites, to pass on the promise of Yahweh given in the covenant. It is in this context that we meet first Rachel and then her sister Leah.

Jacob, running from his brother Esau's rage at being cheated out of his birthright and blessing as firstborn, is sent by his mother to her clan, headed by her brother Laban, to find a wife. Jacob's story, his identity, and his future were conceived in deceit and self-interest, aided and abetted by his mother's love. This theme of deceit, trickery, and betrayal will continue as a strong undercurrent throughout the story.

So Jacob sets out toward his mother's homeland. At a well, he speaks with some shepherds and finds out the sheep they are tending belong to Laban. A woman approaches the well, and he is told she is Rachel, one of Laban's daughters. The meeting has all the characteristics of a betrothal scene: "[While] he was still speaking with them [i.e., the shepherds], Rachel arrived with her father's flock, for she looked after them. As soon as Jacob saw Rachel he went forward and rolled the stone from the mouth of the well and then watered Laban's flock. Then Jacob kissed Rachel and wept aloud" (Gen. 29:9–11).

They meet. This time though it is Jacob who waters the sheep and does the work, introduces himself as kinsman, and is welcomed into Laban's household. This is a story of love at first sight. He stays a month and begins to work for Laban, but Laban insists that Jacob be paid for his work. Then we are introduced to the two sisters, Leah and Rachel:

> Now Laban had two daughters; the name of the older one was Leah and the name of the younger was Rachel. Leah's eyes were weak, but Rachel had a lovely figure and was beautiful. Jacob had fallen in love with Rachel and he said, "I will work for you for seven years in return for your younger daughter, Rachel." Laban said, "It is better for me to give her to you than to any other man; stay with me." (Gen. 29:16–19)

This text reveals much. It tells us that Jacob is used to breaking traditions and codes. He acts on his own wants and initiatives. At that time it would have been unseemly for a man to ask for a younger daughter if the elder was not married, but Jacob is passionate about Rachel and is aggressively pursuing his own future now. Her bride-price of seven years' work reveals how highly he considered her. We are told: "To win Rachel, Jacob worked for seven years which seemed to him only a few days, because he loved her so much."

The one-line descriptions of the sisters speak reams about their lives in the clan. Leah has weak eyes (she is described by a weakness, a lack), and Rachel is described as beautiful, with a lovely figure (a feast for the eyes). This sets up a tension between them regarding their worth and usefulness.

Still, contemporary midrashic traditions tell stories of a tenderness between the two. There is a play on words — "weak" eyes can also mean tender or "soft-hearted" eyes. The stories tell of Rachel leading her sister when she has trouble seeing her way, of protecting her, and of her being almost like a beloved daughter-child to her elder sister. But deceit enters the story.

We are given to believe that it is Laban who deceives Jacob. The text reads: "But when night came [Laban] took his daughter Leah and gave her to Jacob and he lay with her" (Gen. 29:23). Jacob is shocked when he wakes up: when morning came, there was Leah! Now Jacob — who had earlier deceived Esau — is the one who is deceived.

By now it is obvious that Laban is rich and manipulative. From the beginning he realized that Jacob, in wearing his heart on his sleeve, was giving him grounds for making sure both his daughters are married, while he continues to have Jacob work for him. And Jacob is not in any position to argue. He is a sojourner in the land, and it seems he has no gifts, flocks, or money. He has only his own service and work as barter.

We ask, however, how did he pass an entire night with Leah without knowing who she was? After all, he'd worked for Laban for seven years and had had contact with both sisters on a daily basis. How could he have been so unaware? This obviously has been a sticking point even among the rabbis from very early on, and there is a poignant, sad, and tender midrash that explains how it happened. The midrash is developed in relation to a historical event that occurred much later in Israel's existence, when the temple in Jerusalem was destroyed as punishment for the people's unfaithfulness and sin. Even God is weeping and tells the prophet Jeremiah to go and get the patriarchs Abraham,

Isaac, Jacob, and Moses from their tombs so that they can all lament and mourn together. Rachel interrupts God and speaks at this moment:

> At that moment, the matriarch Rachel broke forth into speech before the Holy One, blessed be He, and said, "Sovereign of the Universe, it is revealed before Thee that Thy servant Jacob loved me exceedingly and toiled for my father on my behalf seven years. When those seven years were completed and the time arrived for my marriage with my husband, my father planned to substitute another for me to wed my husband for the sake of my sister. It was very hard for me because the plot was known to me and I disclosed it to my husband; and I gave him a sign whereby he could distinguish between me and my sister, so that my father should not be able to make the substitution. After that I relented, suppressed my desire, and had pity upon my sister that she should not be exposed to shame. In the evening they substituted my sister for me with my husband, and I delivered over to my sister all the signs which I had arranged with my husband so he should think that she was Rachel. More than that, I went beneath the bed upon which he lay with my sister; and when he spoke to her she remained silent, and I made all the replies in order that he should not recognize my sister's voice. I did her a kindness, was not jealous of her, and did not expose her to shame. And if I, a creature of flesh and blood, formed of dust and ashes, was not envious of my rival and did not expose her to shame and contempt, why shouldst Thou, a King Who liveth eternally and art merciful, be jealous of idolatry in which there is no reality, and exile my children and let them be slain by the sword, and their enemies have done with them as they have wished?"
>
> Forthwith, the mercy of the Holy One, blessed be He, was stirred, and He said, "Thus saith the Lord: A voice is heard in Ramah, Lamentations and bitter weeping, Rachel weeping for her children; she refuseth to be comforted for her children, because they are not (Jer. 31:5).[1]

This story reveals a bond between the sisters that is stronger than the marriage arrangement. Even though Rachel loves Jacob, she loves her

---

1. "Lamentations Rabbah, Proem 24," in *The Midrash,* ed. and trans. H. Freedman and Maurice Simon et al. (London: Soncino Press, 1951).

sister longer and differently, caring that she not be humiliated by her husband to be.

The biblical text reminds Jacob — and us — subtly of deceit in the family, for in response to Jacob's indignant questioning, Laban says: "It is not our custom to give the younger daughter before the first-born" (Gen. 29:26). The word "firstborn" is the same that has been used to describe Esau and the birthright/blessing that Jacob stole from his brother. To placate Jacob, after the bridal week, Rachel is given to Jacob as a wife, and during the next seven years he works again for her. Laban gives Rachel a maidservant, Bilhah, who will also bear children to Jacob. And Laban gives Leah a maid, Zilpah, who will also bear children by Jacob. The family is now in place. The relationship between the sisters will be complicated by children as well as Jacob's distinctive affections toward them. The text says it straight out: "He loved Rachel more than Leah" (Gen. 29:30). And it is worse still. We are told in the very next line: "As Yahweh saw that Leah was not loved, he let her have children; but Rachel was barren" (Gen. 29:31).

Suddenly Yahweh appears in the story as another party to all these arrangements. It's almost as surprising as Jacob finding Leah in his bed. The translation in the Jewish Bible is much more revealing of what is happening and what will take place now that God is a more active participant in the proceedings. It reads: "Now when the Lord saw that Leah was hated, he opened her womb." The text suggests that Leah was hated by Jacob, Laban (who has conveniently married her off), and even Rachel, who apparently comes to be resentful of what little her sister is given.

Leah has four children in quick succession. The names of the children reveal much of what is transpiring between Rachel and Leah in their relationship with Jacob as well as their relationship in the larger clan, even in their relationship with Yahweh as individual women. We read:

> Leah gave birth to a child and named him Reuben, for she said, "Because the Lord has seen my affliction; my husband is sure to love me now." She gave birth to another son and said, "Yahweh saw that I was neglected and has given me this son as well"; and she called him Simeon. Again she gave birth to a son and said, "This time my husband will be united to me because I have

borne him three sons." That is why he was called Levi. She again gave birth to a son and said, "This time I will praise Yahweh [alone]." That is why she named him Judah. After that she had no more children. (Gen. 29:32–35)

At least now, in the community, Leah has honor and status, as well as the love of her children, even though her marriage is loveless. The love is between Rachel and Jacob. The experience of bearing children changes Leah's understanding of herself, as well as her relationship to both Rachel and Jacob. The names she gives her children reveal the growth of her own sense of self and what is important. In many ways this story is not only about children and how God's power operates in families and societies but also about how an unloved woman comes to a sense of her own worth and a realization of her connection to God. Through her lacks — the lack of love around her, her frustrations, loneliness, and despair — she grows up and matures as a woman who knows God, on her own terms, not in relation to her sister or her husband. These first four children speak about her. First, in Reuben, "God sees her humiliation." Then, in Simeon, "God hears." In Levi, "Jacob will be attached." And in Judah, there is a phenomenal shift of focus: "I will praise Yahweh [alone]." By the time her fourth child is born, Leah is being weaned from the need for her husband to give her validity. She is honoring God's place and power in her life, not Jacob's. In a sense, Yahweh is Leah's midwife, her companion and friend, giving her equality in her community and a growing sense of self-awareness and strength. She knows God's compassion in her very flesh and routine of domestic chores and wifely duties, as well as in the joys and hardships of raising children and accommodating others' needs on a daily basis. Leah is learning who she is.

Now Rachel begins to have trouble with her relationship with Jacob, with her sister, and with Yahweh. We read:

When Rachel saw that she bore Jacob no children, she became jealous of her sister, and so she said to Jacob, "Give me sons or I shall die." Jacob became angry and said to her, "Is it my fault that God has deprived you of children?" She then said, "Here is my servant Bilhah; sleep with her so that she may give birth on my knees; so the child will be mine." And she gave Bilhah her servant as wife to Jacob. She became pregnant and bore him a son. Rachel then said, "God has done me justice! He has heard

my prayer and given me a son." That is why she named him
Dan. Bilhah, Rachel's servant, bore a second son to Jacob. And
Rachel said, "I have had a mighty struggle with my sister and I
have won!" And so she named her son Naphtali. (Gen. 30:1–8)

Rachel grows desperate. In her culture, she has no power without
children, and as time goes by Jacob's passion and love are not enough
to sustain her personal life or her place in the community. Her line
is demanding, desperate, pitiful: "Give me sons or I shall die." Jacob's reaction reveals that, in some sense, Rachel had made Jacob her
god, expecting him to fulfill all her needs, rather than looking to herself and to God for what only God can give: children and the kind
of profound relationship that can reveal one's meaning and place in
the world.

And then, like Sarah, who had found herself in the same position,
she takes the matter into her own hands and gives her maidservant,
Bilhah, to Jacob. With her, he has two children, who are, technically,
according to tribal custom, Rachel's children. They are named Dan
("He has given me justice") and Naphtali ("I have struggled mightily"). The first son gives her some legal leverage in her clan, and with
the second child she reveals that her relationship with Leah has long
been adversarial, over power within her community. She now sees
herself as having a foothold and a place to stand.

Next it is Leah's time to have no more children. She follows
Rachel's suit and gives her maidservant, Zilpah, to Jacob, and she
has two children with him. "Leah said, 'How fortunate!' and named
him Gad. Leah's servant bore a second son to Jacob. Leah said, 'How
happy I am! Women will call me happy.' So she named him Asher"
(Gen. 30:9–13).

The struggle continues, revealing a hateful daily struggle between
the two sisters. Reuben, Leah's first son, collects mandrakes, an herb
thought to promote conception, and Rachel asks for some. Leah re-
torts: "Isn't it enough for you to have taken my husband? Now you
want to take my son's mandrakes as well!" Their relationship has de-
teriorated and is fraught with pettiness and rancor. Rachel makes a
deal with Leah: in exchange for the mandrakes, Leah can sleep with
Jacob that night. Now, in echo of another story, Rachel sells the access
to her husband's bed for a pile of mandrakes, much as Esau sold his
birthright to Jacob for a pot of porridge and lentils.

That night Leah again conceives and names the child Issachar ("He made a wager"), and the next child, a sixth son, is called Zebulun ("He has given me a beautiful gift"). Her seventh child is her only daughter, Dinah, whose story is painful and short-lived because of the violence and deceit of her brothers.

After Leah has had eleven children, the focus shifts again to Rachel, as it had in the beginning of the story: "Then Yahweh remembered Rachel and let her have a child. She became pregnant and gave birth to a son. 'Yahweh has taken away my shame,' she said. And she called the child Joseph saying, 'May Yahweh give me another son'" (Gen. 30:22–24).

Rachel, like Leah, has now known shame and confusion, as well as hope and delight. She has her own child, Joseph, who will become the one who will carry the hopes of the people forward, in spite of his own siblings' hatred and jealousy. It seems that she and Jacob lavished their affection and personal choice on Joseph as publicly as Rebekah had once done with Jacob. It will be the cause of dissension in the family as well as the trigger for events and choices that will take Joseph from his family many years later. Joseph is both vindication for his mother's long barrenness (like his grandmother's) and the impetus for a wish, a prayer for another child, who will be the last, the twelfth son, Benjamin ("The son of my right" or "The son of my pain").

The question now is: Will Rachel and Leah learn compassion for each other as God has had compassion on both of them, each in her own time? The Hebrew words for compassion and womb share the same root. Both of the women are in the throes of having their compassion enlarged, their hearts widened, and their awareness stretched through their lives and relationships with Jacob, with each other, with their surrogate mothers, and with their children.

Renita Weems has written about the children and the legacy they bear into their own future lives:

> [Leah had] been through sadness. (Reuben, "Affliction," fell from leadership and blamed himself.) She'd been through self-blame. (Simeon, the pitiful baby brother, was taken hostage by Joseph and made to carry the blame of what the other brothers had done.) She'd been through anger. (Levi, the impulsive, impetuous brother, mercilessly slaughtered Shechem for the rape of Dinah.)

But as many of us already know, it takes time to shake off old memories and old patterns of thinking. It takes a great letting go of things.[2]

Somewhere along the line, Leah met God in all the mess of raising kids and working hard, cooking, cleaning, taking care of sick servants and children, fetching water, and running a nomadic household, listening to rumors and back-biting. With Judah, she says in effect: "I can't keep blaming everyone else (Laban, Jacob, Rachel, God) for my unhappiness. I must take measures to change my situation."[3] She starts seeing, with her weak eyes, the tenderness of what God is trying to do with her and in her life and person. She stops expecting others to be her gods. She will continue to have children, but their names reveal that she is now esteemed by other women and is not in competition per se with Rachel.

What does Rachel learn? We are told that Rachel begins to be jealous of her sister and her power to have children. The word used is "envied," the same that will be used to describe Joseph's brothers' feelings about him. Her distraught cry to Jacob has hidden within it a terrible irony. She beseeches him, "Give me sons or I shall die." And she will die, in giving birth to the youngest, Benjamin. She is like many of the matriarchs and women of Israel who cry out in their lack, their helplessness, and their being exiled to the fringes of their society by what they have no power over. But unlike Rebekah, or later Hannah, she does not turn to God. She turns to her husband, her lover, Jacob, who is put in the untenable position of being god. His reply is understandable. What can he do? He loves Rachel, and he has children by Leah. He has the best of both worlds. And Rachel perhaps shifts her focus and changes her mind and heart at this point, because she decides rationally, not passionately, to give her maidservant to Jacob to obtain what she wants and needs now, what he cannot give to her. Her world will no longer depend entirely on him, though we have the sense that she still loves him. Her ache for her own children is not dissipated, but her standing in the community is now rectified.

Rachel becomes very pragmatic after she has her first two children. She wants the mandrakes that Leah's son collects and is willing to buy

2. Renita Weems, "Leah's Epiphany," *The Other Side* (May–June 1996): 44–45.
3. Ibid., 45.

them in exchange for an "unscheduled" night with her husband. Mandrakes have long been seen in primitive societies as a fertility drug, or considered an aphrodisiac. This whole scene, which may appear petty or inconsequential, tells us some very important information. Sharon Pace Jeansonne writes:

> Leah's response belies the depth of her anger and exasperation. In a forceful statement she cries, "Is it a small matter that you took my husband? Must you even take my son's mandrakes?" (Gen. 30:15). This statement indicates that as the second but more beloved wife, Rachel has usurped Leah's position of privilege as first wife and firstborn. It also indicates that at some point in the marriage Rachel has obtained sexual monopoly of Jacob. By revealing this fact in Leah's outburst to Rachel, the narrator leaves open the possibility that Leah was ignored by Jacob's choice rather than by Rachel's conspiracy.[4]

Whether or not Jacob is aware of it, his sexual activity is controlled and manipulated by the two women and used as leverage or as sledge hammer in their struggle for position in the family. But, in the end, it is God alone who controls life and death, children and the future. Leah's later children and their naming confirm that she has learned about God's power in her life. Rachel, however, in spite of her attempts to become pregnant using the mandrakes, does not become pregnant for more than another three years. Rachel is learning through long suffering that it is not within her power to have children. That is reserved to Yahweh.

The structure of the text suggests that the source of Rachel's fertility was God's listening to her. Did Rachel, likewise, finally listen to her sister's pain and humiliation and see that they both were suffering and that she was aggravating her sister's pain? We are left wondering, for now the two sisters have to deal with their father's cheating ways and with Jacob's cleverness in becoming wealthy in flocks and herds and the animosity that is developing between the two men.

Jacob declares that it is God who gave him an increase in lambs, ewes, and goats. Jacob then meets Yahweh and is told to return to his own land. The women prepare to leave with Jacob, and they are in

---

4. Sharon Pace Jeansonne, *The Women of Genesis: From Sarah to Potiphar's Wife* (Minneapolis: Fortress Press, 1990), 77.

agreement on their past and their future and on leaving their father. We read:

> Then Rachel and Leah replied, "Have we still any share in the inheritance of our father's estate? Haven't we been regarded by him as foreigners since he has sold us, and well and truly used up our money? Surely all the fortune that God has taken from our father belongs to us and to our children. So do then all that God has told you." (Gen. 31:14–16)

In spite of any of their personal troubles, their loyalties are shared. And Jacob consults his wives before leaving for his own homeland. This will mark a new era in their relationships. As Jacob gets ready to go, Rachel "took advantage of Laban. While he was shearing his sheep she stole her father's family gods" (Gen. 31:19). In stealing the gods, Rachel acts on her own. Then she and Jacob, with obvious help from Leah, together trick Laban, and they flee with as much as they can take with them. Three days later, Laban realizes what has happened. He catches up with them. When he comes into Rachel's tent to look for his gods, she hides them under the trappings of her camel seat and promptly seats herself there, excusing her lack of courtesy in rising to greet her father with the statement, "I am having my period" (31:35).

The anger and hurt that have built up between father and daughters is clear enough. They have been wronged and treated unjustly by their father and now Yahweh is with them. They have both been betrayed by their father from the beginning and treated with disrespect, as little more than livestock. Now they will act independently of him and assure their own future with Jacob. They are getting even, righting the scales. The story of Rachel stealing what was most important to her father — his idols — and outwitting him with her words is not the only story where one of the matriarchs acts so cunningly and singularly. Obviously women could and did use their power whenever the opportunity arose. In this case Rachel's behavior is applauded because Laban's gods are not hers or Jacob's. And she sits on them! Whether or not she really was ritually unclean at the time or just deceiving her father, she reveals her disdain for his gods, his behavior, and his values. She has sided with Jacob's God, Yahweh, and will not be deterred.

Jacob, his wives, and the children journey on toward Jacob's homeland, where he plans a long-overdue reconciliation with his brother

Esau. Before meeting his brother, he separates his children, leaving them with their specific mothers, and he takes them all to safety. But Jacob's preferences are still in effect. Rachel and her children are put at the back of the camp, farthest away from Esau's soldiers. Leah and her children are placed next closest to the rear, and Zilpah and Bilhah and their children are placed in front.

After Jacob's encounter with Esau, the group moves on, to Bethel and then toward Ephrath. On the road Rachel goes into labor, and the birth is painful and deadly. She dies. The scene is sketched briefly and poignantly:

> Rachel gave birth and the delivery was very difficult. When she was in great pain, the midwife said to her, "Courage! For now you will have another son." And as she breathed her last — for she was dying — she called him Benoni (which means: son of my pain), but his father named him Benjamin. So Rachel died and was buried on the way to Ephrath — that is Bethlehem — and Jacob placed a pillar over her tomb which marks the place of the tomb to this day. (Gen. 35:16–20)

Both women, in the end, deal with human conflicts and issues that every woman must face and contend with: being loved and chosen and being unloved and rejected; the estimation of others and a source of personal identity that comes from within; dependence, independence, and interdependence; and the choice of which God to worship and where primary loyalties will lie, as well as how to use one's sexuality rightly.

Dorothee Sölle writes of the two women's connections to women today:

> Motherhood is not idealized in the text, but observed realistically as a matter of life and death. Rachel, after all, shares the fate of millions of women in the pre-industrial world and the great majority of the poor who today still have to get along without obstetrics or adequate health care. She died during the very painful birth of her second child, Benjamin.
>
> There is probably nothing that distinguishes the contemporary world more from the world of the Bible than our relative lack of preoccupation with motherhood. In our affluent world we have learned over time to separate motherhood and sexuality

and to consider sexual happiness as an indispensable part of life while motherhood is optional. According to the biblical account, from the outset of human history children, and the continuity of life through them, were of the utmost importance: for us it is not procreation but sexual intimacy in relationship that becomes the focus. Our biblical predecessors did not view life as the property of individuals, out of which as much as possible has to be "made," but as a loan from God, connecting us with those before us and those who will follow us.[5]

The women struggled mightily with their father, with Jacob, with one another, and with Yahweh.

Is it possible, we wonder, that Rachel and Leah ever reconciled, becoming friends? Just because it is not recorded doesn't mean that it didn't happen. And there are many midrashic stories in the Jewish community of the women conspiring to help each other, the stories based on hints and pieces of the text itself. A story told in Orthodox communities explains that Leah, like her mother-in-law, Rebekah, had a dream and knew that Jacob was to have twelve sons. And when she stops having children, it is she who decides Jacob needs more wives, so as to have more children. She then sends in her maidservant to him, and Rachel follows suit. In these stories, all four of the wives — the women who are the daughters of Laban and their maidservants — work together to ensure that Jacob has the requisite number of children for the tribes of Israel (the tribes are referred to as the twelve tribes of Rachel). Later all four women pray together that Rachel will become pregnant, and their prayers are answered.

Leah has the last mention in the story of Jacob and his wives, the two sisters. In Gen. 49:28–33, we are told that Jacob gives instructions to be buried in the cave at Machpelah with Leah, where Abraham and Sarah and Rebekah and Isaac were buried. Leah rests with Jacob, while Rachel lies alone, in a place that has become a place of pilgrimage for those in exile, needing mercy.

Rachel's and Leah's lives are even more intertwined than Esau's and Jacob's. The men struggle and lie and are reconciled, and the women struggle and weep and are reconciled, if not in the text, then in the futures of their children and the silence of the stories not told.

5. Dorothee Sölle, *Great Women of the Bible in Art and Literature* (Grand Rapids, Mich.: Eerdmans, 1993), 79.

Perhaps it is in these stories not specifically told that we are to find the
directions for the ways of the Spirit today: in the necessity for women
to be reconciled to their own worth and bound first of all not to men,
other women, or their children, but to their God. In that primary relationship with God, each and all learn compassion, community, and
long-range visions and dreams for all their children and all peoples.
Even the matriarchs' maidservants — slaves who gave birth to one-
third of the tribes of Israel — need to be noticed and given their place
in the tradition. Just before the telling of Rachel's death in childbirth,
there is a one-line mention of another maidservant: "At that time Rebekah's nurse, Deborah, died and was buried below Bethel near the
oak. That is why it was called the Oak of Tears" (Gen. 35:8).

She is named! Her name is Deborah, and if she went with Rebekah
when Rebekah went to meet Isaac, then she has lived with and been
a companion to Rebekah for sixty-five or seventy years. Or, since it
seems that she dies when Jacob and his wives and children are returning finally to his parents' home, did Rebekah send her to help with the
children of her daughters-in-law? At any rate, she has a tree planted in
her memory, and it is named also. It is "Oak of Weeping." Did Jacob,
Rachel, Leah, their maidservants, and all of Rebekah's grandchildren
weep for the loss of their grandmotherly nurse? It appears that trees
and women are bound together in the traditions. For another Deborah
in the book of Judges will sit under her tree, a palm tree, and share her
wisdom with the tribe (Judg. 4:4–5). It seems that in this people that
belongs to God, all will one day be one, equal and drawn together in
ties that are stronger than passionate or romantic love, progeny, family, caste, or sociological levels, stronger than sin, evil, or personal
weaknesses.

Rachel and Leah have no angelic visitors, no nightly encounters
with the Holy. Their places of revelation are more mundane: child care
and among servants, slaves, shepherdesses, nurses, and midwives. In
their tedious labors that must have been back-breaking, monotonous,
and plain dirty, they lived out their understandings of God and the
covenant and grew out of their self-absorption and rivalries. Somehow these matriarchs remind us that keeping a household, raising
children, and surviving with one another is sacred work and that it
can be nurturing for those who give the care as well as receive it.
This tradition of caring for the elderly, the sick, the unwanted, the
unloved, the children, and the weak is the work of the community and

the people that never ends and is the usual place where God teaches us self-knowledge, wisdom, and community-living skills as well as who God might be to us and with us. This is where the women's epiphanies happened. This life, all of our lives, is grist and ground for revelation. All people of the covenant must learn to forgo society's rules and values, to forbear in the midst of distress, being unloved, in distressing and strained relationships, to forget rivalries and past slights and injustices. But it takes time, a lifetime.

And many, many lifetimes later, Rachel and Leah come together. In the story of Ruth, at its end, we hear a remarkable blessing from the elders: "We witness. May Yahweh make the woman coming into your house like Rachel and Leah, who together built up the house of Israel. May you prosper in Ephrathah and be of good standing in Bethlehem" (Ruth 4:11). They are mothers in Israel together, sisters and friends at last.

An Asian story called "A Ton of Rice" highlights many of these issues in Rachel's and Leah's lives and what they must learn, what we all must learn:

Once upon a time there was a woman who wanted wisdom, peace, understanding, and knowledge. She was a simple woman, a wife, a mother, a householder with all the chores and work that are a part of that life for so many. But she was determined to get what she wanted out of life and not let her lifestyle and status interfere with her deepest longings.

And so she went to the sage Zang Zhu and did him honor, asking to be one of his students, but telling him bluntly that she had to learn fast because she just didn't have a lot of time on her hands. If she could attain to enlightenment quickly, then she could return to her husband and children, her servants and responsibilities calmly, peaccably, and with great power that all could benefit from. She told the master that she'd do anything he told her to and obey his words explicitly.

The master looked at her kindly and blessed her saying, "Your intention and devotion are good. In fact this desire is the first requisite. I will give you some specific practices and instruction in prayer, silence, and meditation so that in time you will be at peace, wise in all your dealings, and full of light." He instructed her to do these beginning exercises and to report back to him at intervals, and in these short times together he would slowly bring her to holiness and strength. But she was impatient.

"No," she insisted, "I don't have time. Isn't there something I can do right now, over a couple of months' time, even a year or two, and attain to enlightenment? Then I could return and my life and relationships would be more harmonious and freeing."

He looked at her and, blessing her again, said: "This intensity of desire is good, but you also need infinite amounts of patience with yourself, with others, and with life itself. He then asked her, "Do you have children?" "Yes," she said, "four." "Ah! Good! They eat rice daily, yes?" "Yes," she said, "they love it. But what does that have to do with anything?" He explained: "In all your children's lifetimes they will probably eat a ton of rice! What would happen if one of them, or all of them, tried eating it all at once?" She was stunned to silence. "Yes," he echoed her thoughts, "they would be sick. They would come quickly to hate rice and refuse to eat, and they would come to great harm. That's the way it is with wisdom, self-knowledge, and enlightenment. It cannot be done all at once, but step by step, day by day, all your life. You need great impassioned desire, but you must also have great abiding patience. Remember: great desire and no hurry!"

Rachel and Leah, sisters sharing the same husband, raising their children together, and struggling with one another, with life, and with Yahweh, had to learn great desire and no hurry! And we must all do the same, learning to contemplate and observe the daily occurrences of our lives in all their details because this is the mother lode of revelation, the source of our maturity, and the place where we all learn compassion and wisdom.

Martha and Mary

Now we jump ahead to Luke's gospel and his portrait of another set of sisters, Martha and Mary, whose brother is Lazarus. Unlike Leah and Rachel, neither Martha nor Mary is married, but their encounter with wisdom in the person of Jesus is just as subtle, seemingly competitive, and fraught with contention as the dealings of their ancestors in faith. Their short story follows upon Jesus' encounter with a teacher of the law who comes to Jesus inquiring, "What shall I do to receive eternal life?" Jesus counters with his own question, "What is written in the scripture?" and the teacher answers correctly with the core of the law of the covenant:

> "It is written: You shall love the Lord your God with all your heart, with all your soul, with all your strength and with all your mind. And you shall love your neighbor as yourself." Jesus replied, "What a good answer! Do this and you shall live."
>
> The man wanted to keep up appearances, so he replied, "Who is my neighbor?" (Luke 10:27–29)

Apparently the man has no problem with loving God entirely and completely, just with loving people. He wants Jesus to be specific — so that he is required to do only the bare minimum or bare essentials in regard to others.

In reply to the teacher of the law's second question, Jesus tells the parable of the Good Samaritan. Jesus, good teacher that he is, sets up the story so that the teacher himself must answer who of the three characters — the priest, the Levite, or the Samaritan — had "made himself neighbor to the one who had fallen into the hands of the robbers" (Luke 10:36). The Samaritans as a group were detested by the Jews, and Jesus' point is that one must make oneself a neighbor to all, even one's enemies and those made inhuman by one's own social or religious group. The teacher has to acknowledge that the essential moral operating principle is compassion or mercy toward others, especially those in dire situations, like the man who "fell into the hands of the robbers [who] stripped him, beat him and went off leaving him half dead" (Luke 10:30). Jesus has the last word, and it is a command, a clear law if one wants to experience eternal life: "Go then and do the same." This last line could be an exact replica of Jesus' earlier line to him: "Do this and you shall live" (Luke 10:28).

It is in this context that Jesus, like the man who fell in among the robbers, is traveling on his way and enters a village where the encounter with Martha and Mary takes place. The previous parable was a story of an encounter between Jesus and a teacher of the law, who was outside Jesus' community. Now we move inside Jesus' community of disciples and friends, into a household where Jesus — like the unfortunate victim the Samaritan took to an inn — will be offered hospitality, companionship, and human warmth. We read the story in this light:

As Jesus and his disciples were on their way, he entered a village and a woman called Martha welcomed him to her house. She had a sister named Mary who sat down at the Lord's feet to listen to his words. Martha, meanwhile, was busy with all the serving and finally she said, "Lord, don't you care that my sister has left me to do all the serving?"

But the Lord answered, "Martha, Martha, you worry and are troubled about many things, whereas only one thing is needed. Mary has chosen the better part, and it will not be taken away from her." (Luke 10:38–42)

The story is short, but it has a long history of misinterpretation. These interpretations are usually simplistic and out of context with the rest of the chapter as outlined. They give us either/or dichotomies, where one sister is held up as model and the other sister finds herself supplanted and pushed into the shadows.

Jesus is still the teacher, but now the teacher being honored in a household with attention both to his words and to his human needs of food, drink, and a place to lay his head for a while. A saying in the Talmud is instructive here: "Hospitality is a form of worship." The act — and art — of feeding others is as much a form of reverence and love as it is a service rendered. It is as much an experience of intimacy as a conversation can be.

In the history of the church, especially in the Middle Ages, this passage was interpreted to validate the act or vocation of contemplation over against that of action on behalf of others in the world. In this light, contemplation was seen to be the "better part" of the Christian life.

However, it is important to note that in Jesus' own life there is no such opposition or distinction. Jesus prays intimately and for long periods of time, mostly at night and alone with his Father, and then spends his days in the midst of and besieged by crowds of needy people. He even seems to interrupt or discontinue his prayers when anyone needs his ministrations, comforting, or forgiveness. When he goes off to be alone upon hearing the news of John the Baptizer's murder, the crowd pulls him back. His compassion surfaces at the sight and sound of their overwhelming distress and their need for direction and the care of a shepherd.

Rachel and Leah struggled over securing attention and love from Jacob, their community, and their children. Now Martha and Mary seem to be in competition for Jesus' attention and favor, apparently offering two ways of relating to him.

This has been the generally accepted reading of the text, though there are occasions where radically different insights have been gleaned and taught. Dorothee Sölle sheds some light on these other ways of digging into the text:

> This spiritualizing and anti-Jewish tradition of interpretation in favor of Mary and against Martha was counteracted not by the Reformation but by an entirely different movement: that of the mystics. Meister Eckhart (ca. 1260–1328), in a radically novel interpretation (Sermon 28), moved the still immature Mary to the initial stage of spiritual life, but regarded the mature and experienced Martha as having closer proximity to what is needed. "Martha was afraid that her sister would get stuck in sweetness and well-being," he observes. Martha wishes Mary to be like herself. And Eckhart continues his inspired Christian but non-clerical reinterpretation, one which reflects the spirit of the flourishing women's movement in the late Middle Ages: "Therefore Christ said and meant: 'Be calm, Martha, she, too, has chosen the good part. This part will get lost from her, but the highest good will be bestowed upon her. She will be blessed like you.' "[6]

Unorthodox? Surely, but this reading is from someone schooled and experienced in the mystical tradition of contemplation. Now it is not a question of either/or and the pressure to choose between the two sisters and the two traditions of the spiritual life, but more a matter of stages, with Mary being younger and less experienced and Martha being, surprisingly, equal to Jesus as a teacher in her own right.

Another mystic, Teresa of Ávila, follows in this tradition, adding to Eckhart's thought. Sölle quotes her:

> Believe me, Martha and Mary must be together to accommodate the Lord and keep him with them forever, otherwise he will be served poorly and remain without food. How could Mary who always sat at his feet have offered him food if her sister had not jumped in? And his food is our gathering souls, that they may be saved and praise him in eternity.

---

6. Ibid., 272.

Sölle adds her own comment to Teresa's words:

> Only both sisters together can "accommodate" Christ to give
> him a place in the world.
> In our affluent world there exists a great longing for spir-
> ituality, absorption, contemplation, and mysticism. Mary may
> become the symbol of this incomplete, immature spirituality.[7]

Those in our history who have been publicly recognized for the
depth of their spirituality, their prayer, and their sense of God both in
their own souls and in the world turn the more acceptable and widely
used interpretation upside-down. But what is Jesus attempting to teach
Mary, Martha, and his disciples who are present? What is he trying to
teach all of us?

Neither of the previous interpretations takes into consideration the
first thirty-seven lines of the chapter. Prior to the encounter with the
teacher of the law who attempts to test him, Jesus has sent his disciples
out two by two as workers in the harvest. He speaks of the homes they
are to enter and stay in, eating and drinking and accepting hospitality
in exchange for sharing the good news. Some towns and villages will
welcome them, and others will reject them. Jesus says to them: "Whoever listens to you listens to me, and whoever rejects you rejects me;
and he who rejects me, rejects the one who sent me" (Luke 10:1–16).

And then when the seventy-two disciples return, rejoicing in their
power over demons when they use Jesus' name, he teaches them what
their priorities should be. He says:

> "Nevertheless, don't rejoice because the evil spirits submit to
> you; rejoice rather that your names are written in heaven."
> At that time, Jesus was filled with the joy of the Holy Spirit
> and said, "I praise you, Father, Lord of heaven and earth, for
> you have hidden these things from the wise and learned, and
> made them known to little children. Yes, Father, such has been
> your gracious will. I have been given all things by my Father, so
> that no one knows the Son except the Father, and no one knows
> the Father except the Son and he to whom the Son chooses to
> reveal him."
> Then Jesus turned to his disciples and said to them privately,
> "Fortunate are you to see what you see, for I tell you that many

---

7. Ibid.

prophets and kings would have liked to see what you see but did not, and to hear what you hear but did not hear it."

(Luke 10:20–24)

The entire chapter is a teaching about joy — on knowing God as Father, as Son, and as Holy Spirit — and about those to whom this knowledge is given. It is about those who are chosen to know God, those to whom Jesus chooses to reveal the Father, the little children. The phrase "little children" is problematic in our contemporary society because of how we read the text — with the eyes and ears of psychology and a culture that is child-centered and child-focused. In Jesus' milieu, "little children" were those without any rights, those ignored by adults; but the phrase had wider meaning — encompassing large groups in society who were deemed unworthy, heretical, and ignorant. Slaves, servants, Samaritans, and women would have thus been seen as "little children."

Then Jesus tells the story of the teacher of the law — someone wise in the ways of the law, the dominant society, religious culture, and power, one who knows the answers but whose love is shallow. The teacher looks down upon the Samaritan, the very person Jesus declares not only loves his neighbor but loves God with all his mind, soul, and strength because he practices this love, using all his resources and without stopping to question who the person in need might be, or whether he is worthy of care and life. This Samaritan knows the Father.

Then we encounter Jesus with two women who are hospitable, welcoming, and caring for his needs. Martha throws open her house to him and his disciples, feeding them and giving them a place of rest and solace. Mary listens to him, caught up in his words, watching him without thought of anything else. She is fulfilling Jesus' earlier words to his disciples. She is fortunate. She is blessed to see and hear what kings and prophets wanted to see and hear and did not. Jesus is choosing to reveal himself to these two women, who may not be wise and learned but who are in the honored group of "little children."

Martha would have been listening with one ear, seeing with one eye, the other on her tasks, her cooking, and her guests' needs. Mary was listening to Jesus' words, but she was not yet doing the work of attending to the needs of others, of healing, of feeding the hungry. Earlier Jesus tells the seventy-two disciples he has sent out:

Whatever house you enter, first bless them saying: "Peace to this house." If a peaceful person lives there, the peace shall rest upon him. But if not, the blessing will return to you. Stay in that house eating and drinking at their table, for the worker deserves his wages. Do not move from house to house. (Luke 10:5–7)

Jesus' presence — his blessing, his teaching — brings peace. It rests upon those who accept him, his words, his person, and the gift that he seeks to give: knowledge of his Father. And he stays with them. Martha and Mary are both learning, like the other disciples, what their priorities should now be. Both of them are learning Jesus' interpretation of what it means to love God with all your heart, soul, mind, strength, and resources, and to love one's neighbor as oneself. They are learning eternal life and its effects in the here and now.

Martha's question reveals her lack of peace: "Lord, don't you care that my sister has left me to do all the serving?" In Jesus' pattern of teaching, he doesn't answer her question. It's the wrong one! Jesus' very presence in the world, in her house upsets the usual order of things. He introduces a new way of "serving." Serving food is necessary, but thoughtful listening is necessary also. Martha, like all human beings, is flawed, but she is learning. Mary has unwittingly stumbled into the new relationship that Jesus is offering to anyone who will accept it, while forgetting to serve Jesus and attend to his human needs. She's learning too.

In the *Philippine Bible Study Guide,* Rebecca Asedillo writes:

Someone has to plant the grain, water the seedling, harvest the rice, dry it, mill it, cook it and serve it. Indeed it would hardly be consistent with Jesus' character for him to be suggesting a hierarchy of roles and functions within his movement. While most earthly institutions, including the church, would have some form of hierarchy, Jesus himself has said that the greatest in God's kingdom are those who serve (cf. Mark 9:35; 10:43). In the words of Leonardo Boff, if there be a hierarchy in the church at all, it must always be "a hierarchy of service."[8]

In another vein, some women scholars say that this story reflects developments in the structures of church in the first century in the area

---

8. Rebecca Asedillo, *Women of Faith: Bible Studies for Women's Groups* (Manila: Institute of Religion and Culture, 1996), 90.

of *diakonia*. This word included serving at table, including the table of the Eucharist, the proclamation of the word, preaching, and ecclesial leadership in the house churches. In this story, the functions — service at table, and the study, teaching, and preaching of the word — are split, although the story portrays both women in positive roles. Jesus is teaching the inner core of his disciples, and both Martha and Mary are participating in these activities, bound to both breaking the word and breaking the bread.

The real sticking point is Jesus' reference to the "better part." What is it? Have the disciples earlier in the chapter chosen the better part in going out to preach the good news and bring in the harvest that Jesus sowed in his word and deeds? Has the Samaritan chosen the better part in going down into the ditch to save the man who fell in among the robbers and then taking him to an inn where he cares for his needs? Does Jesus himself choose the better part by choosing to reveal his Father to those who are left out, ignored, and disdained by others, including those who would consider themselves practicing religious people?

Are Jesus' words in our story focused not on Martha's or Mary's roles or lifestyles or place in the community but on this moment and his need? Does Martha need to "overhear" more of Jesus' heart? Does Mary need at some point to get up and do something, to express her understanding, to seek to not only listen to the words but obey them? The questions, important as they may be, are misdirected. We have in the recent past focused all the attention on the two women, while the heart of the story is not them, but Jesus — just as Jesus has been the real focus of the preceding texts.

Jesus is God in human flesh bending down to us, and soon he will be hung on a cross, publicly humiliated, and executed for his words of truth, his deeds of compassion, and his subversive image of God and what constitutes love of God and so love for others. Is Mary silently sitting at the foot of the cross while Martha is still at a distance? Barry Lopez, in one of his children's stories called "Crow and Weasel," says that people sometimes need stories more than they need food to survive. Does Jesus, at this moment, need someone to listen to him more than he needs food? Is Jesus seeking intimacy, acceptance, and love from all present? What if the point of the story is to focus not on Martha or Mary but on Jesus and what Jesus is trying to share with them of his knowledge of God the Father, of his own life and impending death, and of love?

There is an ancient Celtic image of a knot that interlaces two or more strands or threads to form one whole. The knots tend to be endless, intricately fashioned, and almost impossible to follow as the design becomes like a maze. But its very intricacy is what makes it such a work of art and beauty. One of the many symbolic meanings of these knots is the long, tortuous, and overlapping interconnections of humans on their journey to spiritual maturity. The knot also suggests a restless spirit that changes, backtracks, loops around, and is transformed in the process, yet is always one. A profound communion is revealed in the binding of the two or more interlocking pieces.

Perhaps Martha and Mary are like the two strands, and Jesus' point is that the two women's ways merge yet remain separate. Together there is an energy, a life, that cannot be experienced alone. Perhaps this is Jesus' teaching, with a hint of the mystery, about knowledge of God and about the expressions that love can take in his household, when God is more than guest — when God is friend.

St. Ambrose wrote: "Does it not happen when we are pondering something in the scriptures and cannot find the explanation, that in our questioning, in our very seeking, suddenly the highest mysteries appear to us?"

If we truly believe that the scriptures are inspired of God, then we must struggle with the text as mightily as Jacob and Esau, or Rachel and Leah, or Mary and Martha struggled to understand their own lives and what God was saying to them and their communities. Like Mary, we are apprentices at Jesus' feet seeking knowledge of the Holy. Like Martha, we are servants seeking support and affirmation. Like the other disciples, we are watching and listening and not understanding. Like the teacher of the law, we are seeking to justify ourselves. Like the returning seventy-two disciples, we are rejoicing over the power of God let loose in our lives. But our priorities are still out of whack.

Perhaps the "better part" changes as we are transformed into little ones who come to know God the Father as Jesus reveals this mystery to us. Perhaps the "better part" in this story concerns not the word or the ritual service within the community but the choice of associating more closely with the crucified, the victim of the robbers, and the one stripped, beaten, and left for dead.

There is an Indian story that might shed some light on this story, on the reality of struggle as intricately bound up with our lives together and with God:

Once upon a time a young man sought out an old wise woman, whom some said was a saint. The hut was almost empty, with only simple necessities and a cherished possession or two. As they sat together peace soothed the visitor. They spent time in silence together and then he asked the burning question of his heart: "Do you know where I can find God?" She looked at him with interest and didn't answer for a moment. Then she said, "That's not an easy question. I need to think on it so I can answer you clearly. Can you come back tomorrow after I've prayed?" Immediately the young man nodded his assent. And then the old woman added, "Would you bring me a glass of milk when you come?"

The night could not pass quickly enough for the young man, and he was back at the hut, with his glass of milk as requested, right on time. He was welcomed in, and they sat together in silence again. As he waited, not really with any patience, the old woman poured the milk into her begging bowl. Then she stirred it with her fingers, swirling it around and around, lifting it with her fingers. Of course, the milk ran through her fingers, and she frowned as it fell back into the bowl. She did this over and over and over again, never looking up at him.

He was impatient and wanted his answer. He watched, wondering what in the world she was doing with the milk. But she kept at stirring the milk, lifting it and looking at her hand after it had run down her fingers and back into the bowl. Finally the young man couldn't stand it anymore and blurted out, "Please, what are you doing? What are you looking for?"

She looked up at him and said, "I had heard that there was butter in milk. I'm looking for the butter, but I can't seem to find it." The young man almost burst out laughing. He was quick to correct her, saying, "No, no. It's not like that at all. You don't understand. The butter isn't in the milk. It's not separate from it. You have to convert it. You have to make it into yogurt and then churn it to make the butter come out."

She beamed at him. "Very good! You do understand. And you have the answer to your question." He looked at her dumbly, uncomprehending. And she drank the milk in her begging bowl. "I believe," she said, "it is time for you to go home. Go and churn the milk of your life, of your heart and soul and your relationships, and you will find God! Remember — keep stirring, lifting, swirling, converting, and transforming. God's there, hidden in your life, not separate from it, or from you."

I have told this story only once aloud, and as I told it I realized: ah, it's all in the gift we give to another, in a gift that another drinks from her begging bowl. That is where wisdom and knowledge are revealed, where we are saved. It's all in the churning, in the struggle, and in moments when our lives collide with others' lives. And there is no one answer, there are as many answers as there are people. But all the answers are bound to compassion and suffering intricately woven into the knotted and tied gift of life. That is the better part.

TEN

ANCESTRAL GRANDMOTHERS

Eve and Mary

ALL STORIES BEGIN with some version of the metaphor "in the beginning" or "once upon a time," in the tradition of what has gone before them. Even creation stories begin this way, as they seek to give multivariant readings of how things came to be, who was the Maker of all things, and why things are the way they are in the world: both good and not good. The foundational stories that concern us are primarily in the book of Genesis, though others are scattered throughout the entire text of the First Testament. With the incarnation, there is another beginning altogether, one that is fully perceived only in light of the accounts of the resurrection. That story changes all the other stories that follow, and in retrospect we read all the earlier stories differently. The stories of creation and the incarnation thus illumine each other. To see this clearly, let us go to the first of the creation stories.

Eve

The first account is familiar, so familiar as to be daunting in the depth of its description and consequences. Here is the finalé of that account:

> God said, "Let us make man in our image, to our likeness. Let them rule over the fish of the sea, over the birds of the air, over the cattle, over the wild animals, and over all creeping things that crawl along the ground." So God created man in his image; in the image of God he created him; male and female he created them. God blessed them and said to them, "Be fruitful and increase in number, fill the earth and subdue it, rule over the fish

of the sea and the birds of the sky, over every living creature that
moves on the ground."

God said, "I have given you every seed-bearing plant which
is on the face of the all the earth, and every tree that bears fruit
with seed. It will be for your food. To every wild animal, to
every bird of the sky, to everything that creeps along the ground,
to everything that has the breath of life, I give every green plant
for food." So it was.

God saw all that he had made, and it was very good.

(Gen. 1:29–31)

And so it was. The story sings with exaltation, with life, with possibilities. This is the overture of the making of human beings and their
place in the universe along with God. In fact, they carry the imprint
of God in their very form and the substance of their being. And I say
"being" because this is the generic creation of human beings, not yet
separated out into male and female. This is what constitutes humankind, all of a kind, not singular or individual yet. Mary Phil Korsak
explains:

> On the sixth day, *Elohim* makes a human, *adam,* different from
> other living creatures: it is specifically described as being in *Elo-
> him*'s "image" and "likeness." The sexual nature of *ha-adam,*
> "the human," is explicitly mentioned: "the human" is *zachar
> u nequva,* "male and female." Male and female are potentially
> fertile but at this stage they do not appear to be separated. Re-
> ferring to the human couple, the text switches from "them" to
> "it" and back to "them" again. Some, commentators conclude
> that *ha-adam* is androgynous. The human, male and female, is,
> are instructed to be fruitful, to subdue the earth, to govern other
> creatures and to enjoy a vegetarian diet. Here is a first glimpse
> of a future Eve. She is the female side of *ha-adam.*[1]

The word Korsak uses to translate this *ha-adam* into English is
"groundling." It isn't until three chapters later that this groundling receives a name — Adam; at that point, the groundling is no longer
referred to as "it" in the text, but becomes "him." And it is only in the
second chapter, in the second telling of the creation story, that there is

---

1. Mary Phil Korsak, "Eve, Malignant or Maligned?" *Cross Currents* (winter 1994–
95): 455.

differentiation or separation of the two beings; there they become not just groundlings, but a male and a female, a man and a woman. Now there is another story, altogether different than the first. I use Korsak's translation.

> YHWH Elohim made a swoon fall upon the groundling
> it slept
> He took one of its sides
> and closed up the flesh in its place
> YHWH Elohim built the side
> he had taken from the groundling into woman
> He brought her to the groundling
> The groundling said
>
> > This one this time
> > is bone from my bone
> > flesh from my flesh
> > This one shall be called wo-man
> > for from man
> > she has been taken this one. (Gen. 2:21–23)

In the first story, they are created with one another. In the second story, one is created from the other while the first one is asleep, or swooning, unconscious of itself or what is happening to it. In the first story, things are created in shared substances and then are separated out, as the light was separated from the darkness and the waters below were separated from those above. There is movement, but it has to do more with a rearrangement of powers and energies than with divisions. This applies also to the second account of our beginnings as human beings. Korsak explains:

> Like the separated couples of chapter 1, *ish* and *ishah*, man and woman, are similar and dissimilar. Like them, they are close to one another and, at the same time, they strain apart in a state of tension that is characteristic of life in general and of the human couple in particular.
>
> At the level of language, the sameness of the couple is expressed in the common syllable *ish*, found in *ish* and *ishah*, "man" and "wo-man." The odd syllable in *ish-ah*, "*wo*-man," expresses their difference. "Woman" is also said to be *negdo*, "the counterpart" of *ha-adam* (Gen. 2:18, 20). The root *neged*

expresses proximity and opposition. Here, in the differentiated form of a "woman" confronting her partner, "man" is a second glimpse of Eve. Thanks to her appearance, *ish* recognizes his own identity. Although tradition has often taught otherwise, there is no mention of "man" as a potentially independent human being before this point in the text.[2]

This second story is not just another creation account; it is a story that builds upon the version that comes before, adding more information about humans and their meaning, their essence. And that essence has to do with oneness: the humans now exist together; they are naked (without covering); and they are not ashamed (Gen. 2:25). They have been created for each other.

The third story, which comes in Genesis 3, is not so much about the essence of human beings but about how things got to be the way they are in the world today. We are introduced to the serpent, who is described in the first line as "the most crafty of all the wild creatures that Yahweh God had made." The serpent initiates the conversation with the wo-man, beginning with a deliberate altering of the command Yahweh had earlier given ("You may eat of every tree in the garden, but of the tree of the Knowledge of Good and Evil, you will not eat, for on the day you eat of it, you will die" [Gen. 2:16]). The woman begins by correcting him, repeating the command accurately. The wo-man now begins to have a uniqueness that is "like God's," for she speaks, sees, takes, eats, and shares the fruit — she makes decisions. And when she does that, myriad changes are set in motion that neither wo-man nor man could have imagined or foreseen. After all, there is no story before them. This is where it all begins, in seedling form, with the groundling and his wo-man. And as soon as this action is completed there is, in effect, another world than the garden world:

> They heard the voice of YHWH Elohim
> walking in the garden in the breeze of the day
> The groundling and his woman hid from YHWH Elohim
> in the middle of the tree of the garden. (Gen. 3:8)[3]

Now their world contains choices, self-consciousness, a perception of difference, and the sensations of vulnerability, insecurity, and fear.

2. Ibid., 457.
3. Ibid., 458.

They have become more than groundlings. They have become flesh and blood, mortal as opposed to ever-living. And they both hide from the Other that they resemble but are now separated from as well. Then comes the judgment on their choices and decision making. All three characters are altered. The serpent loses its ability to speak and becomes apparently just another species of wild thing on the earth. Both human beings enter a new pattern of living and dying, with *adam*-man knowing work and toil to survive and eat and the wo-man knowing another form of pain in child-bearing. It is only at this point that the wo-man is finally given a name: Eve. She sets in motion the story here on earth, and she, as her name attests, is associated foremost with the "living":

> The main point of verse 3:20 is Eve's connection with Life. Only secondarily, but very suitably, can she be considered the mother of humankind.
>
> In fact, the appellations, *Hawwa,* mother of *hay,* connect Eve with the symbolic world of the garden, in which the central reality is the tree grown by YHWH Elohim among "all the trees attractive to see and good for eating." The tree is first presented as *ets ha-hayim,* the "tree of life":
>
>> YHWH Elohim made sprout from the ground
>> all trees attractive to see and good for eating
>> the tree of life in the middle of the garden
>> and the tree of the knowing of good and bad.
>> (Gen. 2:9)
>
> *Hawwa, hay, ha-hayim:* the assonance of these words point to the women-life-tree-of-life relationship.[4]

In a sense there are three levels of the story of the making of humankind, and more specifically the making of Eve. The first is that of human beings in the universal pattern; the second is about the separating out of woman and man; and the third is about the becoming of the woman, Eve. She initiates the human being into life, all of life — goodness, badness, knowledge, decision making, and giving life to other human beings who will also die. The story now moves out of

---

4. Ibid., 459.

the realm of myth into the reality of life itself as we all know and experience it, with good and evil, life and death, suffering and delicious delight. And only now does the real story of Eve, a human being and a woman, begin with any individuality, personality, and singularity.

Her story is full of tragedy, wonder, life and death, and something altogether new and unknown before: murder, a particular kind of murder called fratricide, an intimate form of killing. Poor Eve is the one who knows the consequences of this kind of murder, though she does not do this new thing called murder. Her firstborn does: Cain. It is amazing how we concentrate on Eve's decision to eat of the tree of life and almost completely ignore the real sin and horror of the Genesis story: the murder of one human being by another, his brother. Eve's real story is one of giving life, suffering, and delight, a story that culminates in the knowing of grief, separation, and horror. She is mother and then with time the grandmother of all that lives and so dies.

And so it's time to look again at Eve without blame, without scapegoating, without conveniently saying that she's where it all started, and without associating all women with Eve's "guilt." Her story is more about "what in the world happened." It is meant to evoke wonder, questions, meaning, delight, and freedom. It is meant to make us see more deeply into the nature of our choices and into the relation between death, birth, and life. Joseph Campbell says that a myth is a story that never happened — because it is still happening now. Eve's story is about what all human beings experience in relation to their being in the universe — separate from others but with others; in relation to God but separate from God; capable of choosing good and of choosing evil; capable of telling the truth and of lying; knowing joy and knowing pain and death.

This story is not so much about the first sin as about the first choice, the first confrontation with something that opposes human beings — this opposition appearing in the form of the serpent. The word "sin" comes from a root meaning that can be translated as "missing the mark." It entails a lack; it entails reaching for something but not grasping it. This is what it means to be a human being, and the story tells all of us some things about what it means to find ourselves outside the garden and struggling with knowledge, choices, life, suffering, and death. It posits that everything that is created is separated from everything else, but it also says all things once had an original harmony, including men and women, and including all human beings and God. The whole rest of the story is up to us, to all human beings.

The story contains both terrifying and delightful suggestions. It is up to us now to risk finding them and drawing them back into relationship and bringing life and breath into everything. As the Jewish storytellers say: re-creation involves finding all the scattered sparks of God, blowing on them gently, and drawing them into one flame. When all the sparks are one, the Promised One will come again. The core of the story is about the Maker who set us in the garden and pushed us out, but the garden is still there, still here. Life is about obeying the command: to be fruitful, increase, subdue the earth, and once again make it the garden as it was in the beginning, but now with our knowledge, struggle, choices, and relationships, and our God.

There are elements of this "making" of the world and all that is within it in many other traditions. The Cochiti Pueblo Indians of New Mexico have a story they call "The Scattering of the Stars":

Once upon a time things fell apart. But then there was a great rain and flood that came and cleaned the world. Everything began to live again: trees, plants and wildflowers, grasses, beans, corn, squash. The four-legged and things that crawl and fly came out of their hiding places and the Cochiti came out too. They came southward from the cold harsh north.

They were led by their Mother as they went back home and she would tell them stories of what it was before the great waters washed over everything and why the waters came. The people forgot. They forgot that all were brothers and sisters: the birds and beasts, the two- and four-leggeds, the earth and all that it gave in each season, the waters and the sky. And they forgot and treated things cruelly, as though they weren't all one, but scattered and unknown. They walked toward the south and reminded one another that it was not to be that way now.

They traveled together. But they didn't notice when they left one little girl behind. She was struggling to keep up, but her little legs wouldn't go as fast as the others. It was the Mother who noticed and came back to her. She called her by name, Kotci-manyako, and gave her a plain white cotton bag tied tightly. "Here," she said, "keep this. No matter what happens, don't open the bag. It will keep you safe." The girl asked, "What's in it?"

"It doesn't matter," said the Mother. "What you must remember is that it will keep you safe and you must not open it." She promised she'd obey the Mother and they caught up with the others.

But Kotcimanyako was curious and kept wondering what was in the little bag that the Mother had entrusted just to her. She felt it and smelled it, shook it and listened to it, put her tongue on the outside of the bag but could not tell what was inside. She slipped and fell behind again. But she remembered the Mother's words. The bag would keep her safe. Don't open it. She watched the trail, looking for footprints, and smelled the trees and plants all around her. And she loved the colors of the sky and the haze over the mountains. She was not afraid, but she did wonder what was in the bag.

Night came and she was tired. She slept a little and when she awoke it was colder and so dark, so black and she felt so alone. She held on to her bag, remembering that it would keep her safe, but oh, she so wanted to know what was in the bag. Finally she decided. She would open the bag. She wouldn't touch anything in it, or take it out. She'd just look and tie it back up tight again. She carefully untied the string and many, many knots. When she got the last knot the bag was bulging, moving, stretching like it was alive! And little sparks and specks of light were getting loose. They flew around her like tiny birds. They made her smile. She held the bag tight in her hands. They were lovely, but more and more were getting out. They were flying farther away and higher up. She was losing a lot of them.

She tried to catch them and put them back in the bag. But it was impossible. There were so many now, and when she would stuff one back in, the bag would open more and others would get loose. Then she dropped the bag and it seemed to explode and all the sparks and specks were free. There were thousands and thousands of them, more than she could ever count. She was frightened. What had she done?

But she watched entranced too. They flew up and up and scattered everywhere she looked in the heavens. The dark was not so cold or black now. It was studded with blinking lights, bits and specks of white fire. It was beautiful, much better than it was before. She wasn't so frightened now and remembered that the

Mother had said that what was in the bag would keep her safe. And she still had a few of the lights. Oh, she didn't have many, only a couple of handfuls. But she made sure they were tightly tied and caught in the bag.

She got up and started to walk by the light of her lights and after awhile she caught up with her people. The Mother had left to do other things and the people were learning how to live in their new home. Kotcimanyako told them about the lights, and one night when it was very very cold she let all the others go free because that's what the others wanted her to do. She took them out and one by one threw them up into the heavens, scattering them with intent. You see these are the stars we know about and have names for and stories of what they are and how they got there. But all the others — we don't know their names, and, sadly, we don't know their stories either. We have all the stars and their lights, but what we lost when Kotcimanyako let them out was all their stories. The Mother said they would keep us safe and they do. But the stories, ah, they would have kept us safe and taught us so much more. So that's why some of the stars in the sky make pictures that remind us of our stories, and some — lots of them — have no names and we have no stories to go by.

Becoming human entails choosing and losing as well as being gifted and learning how to be safe and how to live, suffer, and die together. All of us have sought to make meaning out of our lives and the hardness and darkness, the loneliness and the unknowns. This is the myth — the meaning of the Genesis stories for all human beings. And then, only then, comes the story of Eve, first mother and so grandmother of all the living: those who know both delight and pain, pleasure and suffering, life and death. Her story begins in these words: "And the groundling knew his woman Eve (Gen. 4:1)."[5]

The consequences of this knowing is that Eve becomes pregnant, and the first child is born. "She named him Cain, for she said, 'I have got a man with help from Yahweh' " (Gen. 4:1b). Eve now has her own name, but not her husband, who is still simply *ha-adam*. It isn't until the end of the chapter that the roles are reversed — then the groundling will have a name and Eve will become "his woman." (Gen. 4:25 reads:

5. Ibid., 461.

"Adam knew his woman again.") Eve's story, Eve as a woman and a person in her own right, is found here in the fourth chapter of Genesis, the fourth piece of the creation account. Her story is thoroughly human, containing pathos, tragedy, hope, life and death, murder, exile, pleasure, pain, loneliness, sorrow, and prayer braided through the everyday toil of work, eating, tilling the fields, raising flocks, and offering sacrifice. She is, however, only mentioned at the beginning and the end of the chapter.

She names her first child Cain, whose name is oftentimes rendered as meaning "acquisition," and she sees the birth as having come with help from God. And then "she later gave birth to Abel, his brother. Abel was a shepherd and kept flocks and Cain tilled the soil" (Gen. 4:2). This is life and time passes. The story then turns toward the children and how they live, and they make choices. Abel brings the first and the finest to Yahweh as his offering, and Cain, the elder brother, brings fruits of the soil, but no mention of the firstfruits. And God is pleased with one offering and not with the other. We do not know how Yahweh manifested his pleasure and displeasure with the offerings. But God is depicted as knowing Cain, and Cain talks with God. Their conversation is very important:

> Then Yahweh said to Cain, "Why are you angry and downcast? If you do right, why do you not look up? But if you are not doing what is right, sin is lurking at your door. It is striving to get you, but you must control it."
>
> Cain said to his brother Abel, "Let's go to the fields." Once there, Cain turned on his brother Abel and killed him. Yahweh said to Cain, "Where is your brother, Abel?" He answered, "I don't know; am I my brother's keeper?" (Gen. 4:6–9)

It seems that although Adam and Eve are exiled from the garden, they are not exiled from the presence of, the knowledge of, or communication with God.

In this conversation between Cain and God, the word "sin" is used for the first time. Cain will commit the first sin. He will do what is not right, and he will do it consciously — he knows that sin is "lurking at [his] door." God tells him that sin is striving to get him, but Cain does not control it. Cain's answer to God is telling as well. He says: "I don't know." He lies about the murder. God's judgment will be to separate him from the ground because Abel's blood now cries out from the ground and Cain will no longer have a connection to the earth or any place. He will be exiled from other human beings because he has chosen death; he has committed the first sin: murder. We are told that he "went from Yahweh's presence and settled in the land of Nod, to the east of Eden" (Gen. 4:16). Cain is condemned, but Yahweh, the God of life, will have no part in death. He marks Cain out so that no one will kill him. It seems from the very beginning that God has an aversion to capital punishment, no matter how heinous the crime.

But what of poor Eve? She has known intimacy with Adam, pleasure, the pain of bearing two children, and the joys and sorrows of daily living. But now she knows death intimately, many kinds of death. She knows murder, hate, and the exile of her murderous son. She knows the consequences of freedom.

She must have been the first one to wail, to keen and weep, to mourn for another, and to let it out in a lament, a cry of pain and loss that echoed and bounced off the stars and stayed in the air. This was something unheard of, unknown, unimagined, rude, and horrible. Most probably her laments were mixed with tears, choking sobs, and horror. And her laments with time grew quieter, deeper, seeping into her bones and mind and taking root there.

Together she and Adam are learning what it means now to be not like God — to be something other. And this other is human beings' own making. There are consequences to every choice and action. How is life reconfigured in the face of death, murder, and exile? Eve creates in her living the form of mourning and hoping we call lamenting. How many other things did Eve, first woman, first wife, first mother, and first grandmother, create? She knows God now as she never knew God in the garden. This is her work — learning to live with grace and with life in the face of suffering and death.

The only other mention of Eve in all of the First Testament comes at the end of Genesis 4:

> Adam again had intercourse with his wife and she gave birth to a son and named him Seth; for she said, "Yahweh has given me another child in place of Abel since Cain killed him." To Seth also a son was born and he called him Enosh. At that time people began to call on the name of Yahweh. (Gen. 4:25–26)

Again, in the child's name we find the shifting awareness and self-knowledge of the woman who names. Now God has gifted her with another child, a child she is to love as she learned to love Abel. Now she does not "get a man-child with the help of God"; instead she is the one to receive life at the hands of a compassionate God who sees, knows, and has pity on her aloneness, her emptiness, and her ache. This God listens to her sobs, her cries, and her anguish and gives her another life to mother, to nurture, and to fill her days. She becomes a grandmother, with her first grandchild named Enosh. Things are settling down into new patterns, and the people begin to call on the name of Yahweh aloud. This calling on the name of God seems to have been born of the new, everyday patterns of living and dying.

The portrait of Eve is sketchy, but it outlines a shape that can be filled in with other stories and with midrashim. The rabbis told stories of Eve, many of which were full of affection, kindness, and even gratitude, aware of her as gift both to Adam and to all the living. There are the stories of God walking with Eve in the garden before Yahweh gives her to Adam in marriage, stories of God standing behind Eve and gently and firmly braiding her hair in long plaits so that she will know how to become even more attractive. These gestures of intimacy pull Yahweh down into the garden and make this Yahweh tender and careful of what has been made lovingly in his own image.

There are stories of condemnation and blame, but they are all too well known, so we won't repeat them. But there are others less known, like this from the Babylonian Talmud, Sanhedrin 39a, the Book of Legends:

> A Caesar once said to Rabban Gamliel: "Your God is a thief, for it is written, 'And the Lord God caused a deep sleep to fall upon Adam, and he took one of his ribs' " (Genesis 2:21). Rabban Gamliel's daughter said, "Leave him to me and I will answer him." [Turning to Caesar], she said, "Send me a police officer." "Why do you need one?" he asked. She replied, "Thieves came to us during the night and took a silver pitcher from us, leaving one of gold in its place." "Would that such a thief came to us everyday," he exclaimed. "Ah!" said she, "was it not Adam's gain that he was deprived of a rib and given a wife to serve him?"[6]

---

6. Quoted in Naomi M. Hyman, *Biblical Women in the Midrash: A Sourcebook* (Northvale, N.J.: Jason Aronson, 1997); Hyman is quoting *Hayim nahmn Bialik and Yehoshua Hana Ravnitzky,* trans. William G. Braude (New York: Schocken Books, 1992).

The text of Genesis and what underlies it can be read in as many ways as there are readers. The text forces an active reading, filling in the gaps, generating new stories.

A simple story that echoes the story in Genesis is told by Carlos Vallejo. It is called "Of These Trees Ye Shall Not Eat":

Once upon a time a master decided to test his favorite disciple and took him into his library. There were shelves of books, wall to wall. And he instructed him to dust each and every one of the books daily and that he was free to look through and read any of the books that he so desired, except for the books in this one section of the bookcase. He carefully pointed it out and said, "Don't even dust here or touch a book. Don't even dust a shelf." And the disciple promised.

He did his task with great attention, dusting every book and staying away from the forbidden section. Week after week the master would come in and check and see that no book in the special section was touched. He smiled and praised the student-disciple. In fact the master secretly observed him while he dusted and knew that he didn't touch anything. Then one day he announced that he was going away for a month and would return to inspect everything. The rules stood as they had been articulated.

The master went off and returned on the day appointed. And looked carefully through the library. Not a book had been touched. Not a speck of dust had been bothered. The master stood before the forbidden books and reflected long and hard.

The next day he called all the students together and had his favorite disciple stand in front of all of them and he angrily accused the disciple of failing him utterly. "You obeyed, but you obeyed thoughtlessly, mindlessly. I was sure that you would take one of the books and look through it and learn something incredible. But even more importantly, I had planned something even better! I could then have taken you before all the group and insulted you and berated you for disobeying and you would have learned compassion for others and humility on your part in your future dealings with others. You would have become finally a leader that is both human and wise. But all that is lost now. Because of your lack of desire to know, because of your

slavish obedience and self-righteousness in doing only and precisely what was asked, you have foiled all my hopes and plans
and you are still without human compassion or flexibility or a
true desire for knowledge and wisdom. Be gone! I don't want to
see you ever again!"

He added the query, "What would have happened if Adam
and Eve had not eaten the apple?"[7]

In our interpretation of our stories we are rigid, unimaginative,
and self-righteous. We are content to blame others rather than to look
around at the world and realize a story is happening now. Our story
is open because it is about choosing, about freedom. Our all-knowing
God loves us enough to set us free, giving us the choice on whether we
will love back or love at all. Who knows what Wisdom intended from
the beginning? In our Easter Vigil liturgies we proclaim "O happy
fault" in regard to this "sin" of our forbears, proclaiming that since the
beginning God has been not only about making but about redeeming.
Again, in the traditions there are stories about whether God should
have created us in the first place and dialogues with the angels who
went both ways until God said, "It's a moot discussion. I already did
it. They are created."

And there are stories about God's knowledge of the incarnation,
about God becoming human as part of the original story and keeping that knowledge even from the angels and using it as the test case
with them: with some failing and others passing gloriously when commanded to fall before the image of the first human beings and to
serve them because God would become like them, a human being
born of a woman and subject even to death. It would be a death that
was brutal, chosen, and inflicted on another because of anger, fear,
and self-righteousness. And so we meet another character in the long
story, Mary, sometimes called Ave, as the reversal of the first woman's
name, Eve.

Mary

Mary's story has suffered almost as drastically from lack of imagination as has Eve's story. Most interpretations have simply cast Mary

7. Carlos Vallejo, "Of These Trees Ye Shall Eat," in *Tales of the City of God* (Anand,
India: Gujarat Sahitzn Prakash, 1992), 104–8.

as the antithesis of everything Eve was seen to be or not to be. Yet we know little specifically about Mary. We are given geographical locations, an isolated village in a back-water region of an occupied territory, and we are given her place in a genealogy that purports to go back to the very beginnings (Matthew 1). She is remembered as being in the line of kings through her husband, Joseph, and she is remembered as the mother of the long-awaited one. The text reads: "Jacob was the father of Joseph, the husband of Mary, and from her came Jesus who is called the Christ — the Anointed" (Matt. 1:16).

Mary's and Eve's stories seem all about how they conceive and why and who their children will be for the people. But the how is a bit different: "She has conceived by the Holy Spirit, and will bear a son, whom you are to call 'Jesus' for he will free his people from their sins" (Matt. 1:20b). This all happens to fulfill prophecies made eight to nine hundred years earlier. The information is relayed in a dream, and there is no "knowing" between husband and wife. The knowing is between God and a woman. In this rendering of the story in Matthew, that's about all we know. When this woman appears in the text, she never speaks a word. She does not do the naming, as was the custom. She is always described as being seen with the child and being Mary, the mother.

Then the child and the mother are in mortal danger from Herod, a man who has made choices that make him more and more inhuman. His choice, like Cain's, is murder. He is afraid of this child's life, of stories that reek of hope and the promise of freedom. So he chooses to kill the child. An angel tells Joseph, the father, of Herod's intention, and the family flees. In response Herod "gave orders to kill all the boys in Bethlehem and its neighborhood who were two years old or under" (Matt. 2:16). In response, "a cry is heard in Ramah, wailing and loud lamentation: Rachel weeps for her children. She refuses to be comforted, for they are no more" (Matt. 2:18). The threads woven between Eve, Rachel, and Mary are plaited with blood and cries for comfort, justice, and life. When the immediate threat of Herod is over, because of his death, Joseph takes the child and his mother home to Israel. And that's one of Mary's stories.

We know the end of her child's story. He is killed, murdered by others in cold-blood. She knows suffering, injustice, helplessness in the face of others' choices, loss that cannot ever be replaced, although in another story she is given, like Eve, another child, another son to take as her own. As her firstborn dies, he gives her into the care of a younger brother, John, and with another mother named Mary they become a new kind of family, a family born of a relationship of word, life, hope, suffering, and death.

There is another story full of angels, told from her point of view, at least vicariously through Luke's inspiration. It has more personality, more emotion, and a sense of awareness that grows and knowledge that is learned. There are an annunciation and an acceptance, a word of submission and obedience. Mary says, "Yes, let it be. Let it come true. Let the words take on flesh and the story be told. Let it change, and let there be new knowledge loosed and freed in the world." This time she is asked; she is needed by God because the story has gotten much larger and more complicated. It has layer upon layer of meaning and dead ends. The story is still interwoven with those of other women, like Elizabeth and Zachariah, who have children, but the pattern has taken unexpected turns. Now children are not born of knowing in the usual ways. They are born out of time, born of virgins, and born without men knowing their wives. They are born of Spirit and of God's Word, and they are God become human beings, become man, become vulnerable to death. And all because of love.

Like Eve, Mary chooses, takes risks, and walks into the unknown. She's young, but then Eve certainly was too. Unlike Eve, Mary has another woman, a friend, to go to in her need and questions. She greets Elizabeth and the air is full of Spirit, children dancing inside wombs, and freedom aborning. There are recognition and singing of the praise of God. The old, the barren, the unborn, the virgin, the women, the children, and two men who will not know women in the usual ways are writing a new story altogether with the Spirit of God. And it's worth singing about. So the song, the story, tells of souls and spirits that seize hold of flesh that exalts. It says that servants and the lowly and the ones blamed in the past are now blessed and looked upon with great delight by the eye of God. And this God has been hiding and trying to get into the story at every juncture since the beginning, and always it was mercy that was trying to gain entrance into those who lived in his presence (unlike Cain, who departed from Yahweh's presence).

And there's more. The proud, the mighty, the knowledgeable, and the sure are going to be put down. Those who were rich, who had more than the others, who hoarded, who acquired and did not give the best or share will know emptiness, and those who were hungry and in want, aching in emptiness, will know good things. What a reversal in the story as it's been told so far! Of course there were always other stories, hidden and in bits and remnants scattered in the other one, but now that's the story that is rising and being remembered, coming true. It is mercy's story, a story trying to be told from the beginning.

Mary stays with her woman-friend who understands and shares some of her wonder for awhile and then goes home to live apparently as everyone else does, until it's time for the story to be born as a human being. The child is born, away from home, with strangers who provide shelter and with angels singing and dancing like stars in the sky. And we are told the woman listens to the story of the shepherds when they come to see, the story they have heard from the skies. Now it is a tale about Mary and Joseph with the baby lying in the manger (Luke 2:16). It's an astonishing story. We are told: "As for Mary, she treasured all these messages and continually pondered over them" (Luke 2:19).

Then she and Joseph take the child to offer him to God, in obedience to the laws of old, and they meet ancient ones with stories of what will be because of this child and how his choices will have consequences for her especially but also for all who come into his presence. He will be the cause of many people's rise or downfall, a sign of opposition and contradiction to what has become acceptable and known. She will know something else as well: "A sword will pierce her heart and soul so that the secret thoughts of everyone will be brought to light" (Luke 2:34–35).

Later they will go home, and the years will go by, and they will live together with nothing all that unusual happening, until a dozen years later. It is then that she and Joseph leave Jerusalem unknowingly without the child, and when they go back to get him, they learn that they have never known him. He is not what they have come to know. He says to his mother: "Why were you looking for me? Do you not know that I must be in my Father's house?" The text then says: "But they did not understand this answer.... As for his mother, she kept all these things in her heart" (Luke 2:50, 51).

In all the gospels except John's, this is the last we see of her. The Acts of the Apostles mentions her once, when she was with Jesus' followers after his death and the Spirit came again. The text says: "All of these together gave themselves to constant prayer. With them were

some women and also Mary, the mother of Jesus, and his brothers"
(Acts 1:14). Wherever she appears in the larger story of the good news
about her child Jesus, Mary is found with the Spirit. She knows the
Spirit of God in her heart and in her flesh.

And she appears again in the gospel of John. It is a heart-wrenching
and all-too-human story. She stands witness at a public execution:

> Near the cross of Jesus stood his mother, his mother's sister
> Mary, who was the wife of Cleophas, and Mary of Magdala.
> When Jesus saw the Mother, and the disciple, he said to the
> Mother, "Woman, this is your son." Then he said to the disci-
> ple, "There is your mother." And from that moment the disciple
> took her to his own home. (John 19:25–27)

This is the last will and testament of a man in agony, making sure
that what he loves has intimacy and care after death. It is a new form
of genealogy, of giving birth so that life is passed on and given to
the future. It is not based on blood ties, birth, or marriage, but on
a shared relationship between people who know each other in love,
in this person Jesus' flesh and spirit, and in the Father's will. Mary
is first described in the text as Jesus' mother, standing with her sister
and another woman friend of his, Mary of Magdala. Then she becomes
"the Mother" when Jesus sees her there with the disciple. She stands
in Jesus' presence, knowing he will die, but he still has work to do. In
the midst of his pain, he separates himself out from her as mother/child
and makes her mother to all the disciples. She is to be the mother to all
those who stand with him in death, and they are to take her home as
their mother. She has become the mother of all those who live because
of this human being, this man's life, his death, and his soon-to-be
resurrection. She's become the mother and the grandmother of life
that cannot be indelibly harmed by suffering or even by death.

Her silent lament has been heard as clearly as Eve's wail of pain at
the reality of death chosen by one human being for another: murder.
And the compassion of God has answered again by giving new relationships and new life, stronger than death, stronger than biological
generation or old kinship ties. There is another family now, another
possibility to the story, another choice with freedom and imagination
and life never dreamed of, even throughout the times of the old stories. Suffering and death are as intimate with life as are delight and
joy. Perhaps it was meant to be from the very beginning. But both

these women have so much in common: they are both the mother of the living. They are both the mother of all sorrows. They are both the mother of all those who make choices, both terrible ones and ones that are good and holy. They both sing and lament, know living and dying within their own bodies and spirits, know God, and know love and intimacies as well as isolation and loneliness, emptiness, and mystery.

The only difference is that Eve had no stories to go by in her life. She made them up as she lived and others lived and died around her. Mary had so many stories, songs, poems, lamentations, and memories to go on as she lived. Both knew the dark night and bright dawn, just reversed in time: Eve knew these in the beginning of her life, Mary at the end of hers. We know both their stories as our own, and because of them our lives are bright darkness and life that knows both death and resurrection. But neither of them is the whole story; not even together do they begin to tell it all. We do have an intimation of the story's end. It's found in the book of Revelation:

> A loud voice came from the throne, "Here is the dwelling of God among men [human beings]: He will pitch his tent among them and they will be his people. God will be with them and wipe every tear from their eyes. There shall be no more death or mourning, crying out or pain, for the world that was has passed away." (Rev. 21:3–4)

Until then, suffering and death will constitute an essential part of our lives. Eve was confronted by the serpent and chose. Mary was confronted by the angel Gabriel and chose. Each of us is confronted by the serpent and by the Holy. Each of us must choose. As with Eve, Mary, and Jesus, suffering and death are the contexts for choices that can lead to new life and understanding. Thomas Merton in one of his journal notes put it this way:

> When suffering comes to put the question: "Who are you?" We must be able to answer distinctly, and give our own name. By that I mean we must express the very depths of what we are, what we have desired to be, what we have become. . . . And if we have become what we are supposed to become, the interrogation of suffering will call forth from us both our own name and the name of Jesus.

   The story that encompasses Eve and Mary is about changes in the most profound aspects of human existence: life and death. To either demonize Eve, the mother of all the living, or divinize the mother of Jesus serves only to obscure the depth of the story's meaning and to kill imagination, which is essential if we are to live and die as human beings with grace. The person of Jesus, born of woman and the Spirit, broke all the old sensibilities, thinking, reasons, and patterns. To keep interpreting the ancient stories as though God in Jesus did not become human, live, chose to die with us, and be raised by the will of the Father and the favor of the Spirit is to betray our humanity far worse than anything ascribed to the first woman and man. We all have to make the choice and learn to take responsibility for the knowing that is consequence of all life. Not to honor all the stories in light of the Word become flesh, born of the first woman, Eve, the mother of all the living, and of her great-great-great-granddaughter, Mary, is to refuse to believe in the One who spoke and brought all things into being. It is to belie the wondrous possibilities that the Holy One may still have in store for us, for all who choose life and what is good, but who also know in their flesh the consequences of choosing what is not good, what is not human and divine.

   There is a story that perhaps tells these stories of Eve and Mary together so that they become our story as well. This version of it is in Richard McLean's collection *Zen Fables for Today:*

   Once upon a time there was a princess, the youngest child of a great and mighty Lord. She was traveling one day, being carried by her attendants and accompanied by an entourage that obeyed her every whim. As they passed by the gates of a city she noticed an old woman curled up by the side of the road. She was ragged, sick, hungry, and near death from the cold, slow starvation, and being left alone. Without thinking the princess gave orders for the woman to be picked up and put in her litter and taken to her house, where she was nursed back to strength. The princess would come to visit her daily and see how she was doing, feed-ing her, singing songs to her, telling her stories, and making sure that she was treated with great dignity and respect because of her many years. She recovered and the princess was delighted. When it was time for them to part, the princess gave her a warm shawl that had been a gift from her own mother, coins for food, and a bag for her few belongings, all the gifts she had been given during her stay in the princess's rooms.

The poor woman was grateful and so she too gave a gift. It was wrapped with care in one of her old rags, now washed clean but thin and mended. The princess opened it to find a mirror, a plain one set in old polished wood. The old woman explained, "This was my mother's, and before that her mother's. It has been in our family for many generations. It's not just any mirror. It is full of mystery and wisdom, full of knowledge and wonder. Whenever you look in it, you will see revealed your true self." The princess accepted the gift. They bowed and left each other's company.

The princess received many gifts and kept them all together in her room. The weeks and months went by and she forgot all about the gift. But the day came when she was to go to one of the court functions and she dressed in all her finery. She planned on making a grand entrance so that all would notice her and her father the Lord would be pleased and amazed at her beauty and elegance. She was dressed but could not find her mirror. Then she remembered and hunted for the old woman's gift. She lifted it and what she saw made her stop dead in her tracks. What looked back at her with regal proud eyes was a peacock with tail unfurled, with deep luscious greens and purples spread out in a great train behind it, her head held high and disdaining to look at anyone else, sure of herself. She almost dropped the mirror. Instead she hid it away and tried to put the peacock image out of her mind. When she walked in moments later to the ahs and murmurs of appreciation all she could think of was the peacock strutting among the others. She knew it was true.

Afterward she was bothered. Was she just a vain bird? Was she only interested in gowns and jewels, having her hair coifed, and her appearance before others? Was she only interested in looking beautiful as befitted her privilege and status in the court? Days later she had to admit that the answer to all those reflections was certainly a disheartening "yes." How awful!

It took time but she decided to change her life, and before another year had passed she approached her father the Lord and told him that she was leaving the palace and was joining a monastery. She would become a Zen nun and search for and study the truth, seeking to learn compassion and wisdom. Her father was distraught but she was adamant. And so she was off. Years passed and she was diligent. Because of her gifts, her education, her obedience, her desire, and her past she quickly rose within the community, and within just a few years she was appointed by the other nuns to become their abbess.

The day of her installation dawned gray and overcast. She dressed in her robes and thought of the mirror, which was the only possession she had taken with her from the palace years before. She had been wondering how much she had changed and what she would see when she looked in the mirror now. Slowly and cautiously, with a bit of trepidation, she picked up the mirror and looked. She cried out when she saw a great eagle swooping and soaring high high up above the mountains, apart from all else, including all other birds. Was that what she had become? Was it any better than the peacock? Once again she hid the mirror away.

All during the ceremonies she wondered about the eagle. The years passed. She was elected again and again to her office. And she questioned herself ruthlessly. Did I just change one kind of outward reality for another? Do I really think of myself as above everyone else? Have I learned nothing of compassion, of enlightenment, or of the truth in all this time? The mirror was a shadow over all her days, though she did not pick it up again.

Finally her terms of abbess were over. She had pleaded not to be elected again because she wanted to leave the monastery and her position, her old ways, and try her hand at begging, at living with other people, living simply as most had no choice but to do. She finally set off, found herself a small hut, planted a vegetable garden, carried her water from a spring, and begged. She was hospitable to all who came. She meditated and prayed. She worked hard. She played with children and took care of the sick and those who were alone and elderly. And she forgot about the mirror. She learned to just live day to day and moment to moment. She learned compassion, friendship, and knowledge of people, understanding and kindness. She learned humility and a great sense of freedom and light-heartedness. She was happy. Oh, she was poor, often without, hungry sometimes, and lonely, but she knew this was living. And she knew that she was loved by many, many people who had come to know her. But she also knew that she had not yet known what enlightenment was.

The years passed by, and everyone in the palace and her old monastery forgot about her. She lived just here and now. And one night a storm broke in all its fury right over her little hut. It tore off the roof and she cowered wet and shivering under a few boards and branches until finally it passed. She went digging through the rubble and found very little that she could rescue and use. But she did find her mirror that she had lost and so forgotten about altogether. She smiled and picked it up, turning it so that she could see herself reflected in its glass. And she smiled again at what she saw. Before her was a single deep purple iris, wild and free, planted in the soil, the roots reaching down into the earth that touched the underground stream of water that ran down the mountain side to the great sea that rose in mist and moisture into the heavens and fell again as rain or was caught into the clouds that soaked up the sun and floated out into the stars and were lost in the universe's great song, flowing gently between the Buddha's fingers held in peaceful repose. She smiled and thought to herself, It is done, almost finished. I think I'll sleep now.[8]

Like Eve's and Mary's stories, it is a story of choices. None of the stories is a script to follow. Each of the stories of these women simply roughs out options, sets precedents, and warns us about knowledge and its consequences. Each of the stories is a mirror full of mystery and wisdom, knowledge and wonder, a mirror that helps reveal our true selves.

Lately, as I've been writing this book, I have a recurring image. Mary dies, and as she enters heaven, Eve is standing at a distance watching all the jubilation. But Mary has no interest in all the glory whatsoever. She's intent on looking for someone. She spies her, over on the side, in the shadows, and goes to her, ignoring everyone else. She reaches out, and they fall into each other's arms like old and dear and long-lost friends. Eve and Mary hold on to each other and weep. Each had wept at morning's light and with mourning's loss. Each had cried out in agony and anguish over what their children could do to each other. Each had been amazed at how life turned out. Each had

---

8. Richard McLean, *Zen Fables for Today* (New York: Avon Books, 1998), 106–7.

sought new words and images for what they experienced and came to know in life, in birth, in suffering, in joy, with others, alone and in death. Now together they have a song to sing, tears that flow freely, and laughter that spills out of their mouths. The Holy Ones listen and are well pleased. And to everyone's surprise, Mary and Eve walk off together away from the crowd. Oh, did they have stories to tell and worlds to share! They still do. Amazingly, it's up to us now. Our lives, our choices, and what we do with the universe and all our children, as well as our sufferings and deaths, make up their stories. Grandmothers. How they love to talk about their children to one another still. Once upon a time . . .

SELECT BIBLIOGRAPHY

Asedillo, Rebecca. *Women of Faith: Bible Studies for Women's Groups.* Manila: Institute of Religion and Culture, 1996.

Asia Partnership for Human Development, ed. *Awake: Asian Women and the Struggle for Justice.* Sydney, Australia: Asia Partnership for Human Development, 1985.

Bellis, Alice Ogden. *Helpmates, Harlots, Heroes: Women's Stories in the Hebrew Bible.* Louisville: Westminster/John Knox Press, 1994.

Bronner, Leila Leah. *From Eve to Esther: Rabbinic Reconstructions of Biblical Women.* Louisville: Westminster/John Knox Press, 1994.

Brown, Cheryl Anne. *No Longer Be Silent: First-Century Jewish Portraits of Biblical Women.* Louisville: Westminster/John Knox Press, 1992.

Buchmann, Christina, and Celina Spiegel, eds. *Out of the Garden: Women Writers on the Bible.* New York: Fawcett Columbine, 1994.

Byrne, Lavinia, ed. *The Hidden Tradition: Women's Spiritual Writings Rediscovered: An Anthology.* New York: Crossroad, 1991.

Chopp, Rebecca S. *The Power to Speak: Feminism, Language, God.* New York: Crossroad, 1991.

Darr, Kathryn. *Far More Precious Than Jewels: Perspectives on Biblical Women.* Louisville: Westminster/John Knox Press, 1991.

Frankel, Ellen. *The Five Books of Miriam: A Woman's Commentary on the Torah.* New York: G. P. Putnam's Son, 1996.

Frankiel, Tamar. *The Voice of Sarah: Feminine Spirituality and Traditional Judaism.* San Francisco: Harper San Francisco, 1990.

Gallares, Judette A. *Images of Faith: Spirituality of Women in the Old Testament.* Maryknoll, N.Y.: Orbis Books, 1992.

Grassi, Carolyn M., and Joseph A. Grassi. *Mary Magdalene: And the Women in Jesus' Life.* Kansas City: Sheed and Ward, 1986.

Grey, Mary. *Redeeming the Dream: Feminism, Redemption, and Christian Tradition.* London: SPCK, 1989.

———. *The Wisdom of Fools? Seeking Revelation for Today.* London: SPCK, 1993.

Hellwig, Monika K. *Christian Women in a Troubled World.* New York: Paulist Press, 1985.

Henderson, Michael. *All Her Paths Are Peace: Women Pioneers in Peacemaking.* West Hartford, Conn.: Kumarian Press, 1994.

Hillesum, Etty. *An Interrupted Life: The Diaries of Etty Hillesum 1941–43.* New York: Pantheon Book, 1983.

Hinsdale, Mary Ann, and Phyllis H. Kaminski, eds. *Women and Theology: The Annual Publication of the College Theology Society.* Vol. 40. Maryknoll, N.Y.: Orbis Books, 1995.

Hollyday, Joyce. *Clothed with the Sun: Biblical Women, Social Justice, and Us.* Louisville: Westminster/John Knox Press, 1994.

Huwiler, Elizabeth. *Biblical Women: Mirrors, Models, and Metaphors.* Cleveland: United Church Press, 1993.

Hyman, Naomi M. *Biblical Women in the Midrash: A Sourcebook.* North Vale, N.J.: Jason Aronson, 1997.

Isasi-Díaz, Ada María. *Mujerista Theology.* Maryknoll, N.Y.: Orbis Books, 1996.

Jeansonne, Sharon Pace. *The Women of Genesis: From Sarah to Potiphar's Wife.* Minneapolis: Fortress Press, 1990.

Johnson, Elizabeth A. *Women, Earth, and Creator Spirit.* New York: Paulist Press, 1993.

Kam, Rose Sallberg. *Their Stories, Our Stories: Women of the Bible.* New York: Continuum, 1995.

King, Ursula, ed. *Feminist Theology from the Third World: A Reader.* Maryknoll, N.Y.: Orbis Books, 1994.

Kinukama, Hisako. *Women and Jesus in Mark: A Japanese Feminist Perspective.* Maryknoll, N.Y.: Orbis Books, 1994.

Kluger, Rivkah Scharf. *Psyche in Scripture: The Idea of the Chosen People and Other Essays.* Toronto: Inner City Books, 1995.

Laffey, Alice L. *An Introduction to the Old Testament: A Feminist Perspective.* Philadelphia: Fortress Press, 1988.

Loades, Ann, ed. *Feminist Theology: A Reader.* Louisville: Westminster/John Knox Press, 1991.

Mananzan, Mary John, ed. *Women and Religion: A Collection of Essays, Personal Histories, and Contextualized Liturgies.* Manila: Institute of Women's Studies, St. Scholastica's College, Philippines, 1992.

Martini, Carlo M. *Women in the Gospels.* New York: Crossroad, 1990.

McFague, Sallie. *The Body of God: An Ecological Theology.* Minneapolis: Fortress Press, 1993.

Moltmann-Wendel, Elisabeth. *The Women around Jesus.* New York: Crossroad, 1982.

Moltmann-Wendel, Elisabeth, and Jürgen Moltmann. *Humanity in God.* New York: Pilgrim Press, 1983.

Moody, Linda A. *Women Encounter God: Theology across the Boundaries of Difference.* Maryknoll, N.Y.: Orbis Books, 1996.

Nowell, Irene. *Women in the Old Testament.* Collegeville, Minn.: Liturgical Press, 1997.

Oden, Amy, ed. *In Her Words: Women's Writings in the History of Christian Thought.* Nashville: Abingdon Press, 1994.

Ostricker, Alicia Suskin. *The Nakedness of the Fathers: Biblical Visions and Revisions.* New Brunswick, N.J.: Rutgers University Press, 1994.

Phillips, John A. *Eve: The History of an Idea.* San Francisco: Harper San Francisco, 1984.

Praeder, Susan M. *The Word in Women's Words: Four Parables.* Wilmington, Del.: Michael Glazier, 1988.

Pui-Lan, Kwok, and Elisabeth Schüssler Fiorenza, eds. *Women's Sacred Scriptures.* Vol. 3 of *Concilium* 1998.

Reid, Barbara E. *Choosing the Better Part: Women in the Gospel of Luke.* Collegeville, Minn.: Liturgical Press, 1996.

Ricci, Carla. *Mary Magdalene and Many Others: Women Who Followed Jesus.* Tunbridge Wells, England: Burns and Oates, 1994.

Rosen, Norma. *Biblical Women Unbound: Counter-Tales.* Philadelphia: Jewish Publication Society, 1996.

Schneiders, Sandra M. *The Revelatory Text: Interpreting the New Testament as Sacred Scripture.* San Francisco: Harper San Francisco, 1991.

Sölle, Dorothee. *Great Women of the Bible in Art and Literature.* Grand Rapids, Mich.: Eerdmans, 1993.

Steinsaltz, Adin. *Biblical Images: Men and Women of the Book.* New York: Basic Books, 1984.

Stendahl, Krister. *The Bible and the Role of Women.* Philadelphia: Fortress Press, 1966.

Tamez, Elsa, ed. *Through Her Eyes: Women's Theology from Latin America.* Maryknoll, N.Y.: Orbis Books, 1989.

Tavard, George H. *Women in Christian Tradition.* Notre Dame, Ind.: University of Notre Dame Press, 1973.

Trible, Phyllis. *Texts of Terror: Literary-Feminist Readings of Biblical Narratives.* Philadelphia: Fortress Press, 1984.

Wainwright, Elaine M. *Shall We Look for Another? A Feminist Rereading of the Matthean Jesus.* Maryknoll, N.Y.: Orbis Books, 1998.

Zones, Jane Sprague, ed. *Taking the Fruit: Modern Women's Tales of the Bible.* San Diego: Women's Institute for Continuing Jewish Education, 1989.